# Girls and Autism

Often thought of as a predominantly 'male' disorder, autism has long gone unidentified, unnoticed and unsupported in girls – sometimes with devastating consequences for their social and mental well-being. As current research reveals a much more balanced male-to-female ratio in autism, this book provides crucial insight into autistic girls' experiences, helping professionals to recognize, understand, support and teach them effectively.

Drawing on the latest research findings, chapters consider why girls have historically been overlooked by traditional diagnostic approaches, identifying behaviours that may be particular to girls, and exploring the 'camouflaging' that can make the diagnosis of autistic girls more difficult. Chapters emphasize both the challenges and advantages of autism and take a multidisciplinary approach to encompass contributions from autistic girls and women, their family members, teachers, psychologists and other professionals. The result is an invaluable source of first-hand insights, knowledge and strategies, which will enable those living or working with girls on the autism spectrum to provide more informed and effective support.

Giving voice to the experiences, concerns, needs and hopes of girls on the autism spectrum, this much-needed text will provide parents, teachers and other professionals with essential information to help them support and teach autistic girls more effectively.

**Barry Carpenter**, CBE, OBE is professor of mental health in education at Oxford Brookes University, UK.

**Francesca Happé**, FBA, FMedSci is professor of cognitive neuroscience at the Institute of Psychiatry, Psychology and Neuroscience, King's College London, UK.

**Jo Egerton** is a schools research consultant, running school-based research courses for teaching school alliances and academies.

# Girls and Autism

## Educational, Family and Personal Perspectives

Edited by
Barry Carpenter,
Francesca Happé and
Jo Egerton

Routledge
Taylor & Francis Group

LONDON AND NEW YORK

First published 2019
by Routledge
2 Park Square, Milton Park, Abingdon, Oxon OX14 4RN

and by Routledge
52 Vanderbilt Avenue, New York, NY 10017

*Routledge is an imprint of the Taylor & Francis Group, an informa business*

*British Library Cataloguing in Publication Data*
A catalogue record for this book is available from the British Library

*Library of Congress Cataloging-in-Publication Data*
Names: Carpenter, Barry, editor. | Happâe, Francesca, editor. | Egerton, Jo, editor.
Title: Girls and autism : educational, family and personal perspectives / Edited by Barry Carpenter, Francesca Happâe and Jo Egerton.
Description: Abingdon, Oxon ; New York, NY : Routledge, 2019. |
Includes bibliographical references.
Identifiers: LCCN 2018045593 (print) | LCCN 2018056106 (ebook) |
ISBN 9781351234429 (eb) | ISBN 9780815377252 (hbk) |
ISBN 9780815377269 (pbk) | ISBN 9781351234429 (ebk)
Subjects: LCSH: Autistic girls--Education. | Autistic girls--Family relationships. |
Autistic girls--Health and hygiene. | Autistic girls--Life skills guides.
Classification: LCC LC4717 (ebook) | LCC LC4717 .G57 2019 (print) |
DDC 371.94--dc23
LC record available at https://lccn.loc.gov/2018045593

ISBN: 978-0-8153-7725-2 (hbk)
ISBN: 978-0-8153-7726-9 (pbk)
ISBN: 978-1-351-23442-9 (ebk)

Typeset in Bembo
by Taylor & Francis Books

Printed and bound by CPI Group (UK) Ltd, Croydon, CR0 4YY

# Contents

# Acknowledgements

The editors and authors of this book would like to extend their heartfelt thanks:

To the National Association of Head Teachers for hosting the Autism and Girls Forum.
To Alison Foyle and Elsbeth Wright for nurturing us through the publication process,
and, along with Routledge generally, giving us a platform through the book, to advocate
for and with girls on the autism spectrum.
To the girls and their families who have shared their stories with passion and conviction.

We hope that this book is true to the 'many voices' we have tried to capture, all of
whom share a common commitment to improving the lives of girls with autism.

# Contributors

**Venessa Bobb** is the mother of three children, all with neurodevelopmental conditions. Due to her challenges with her son (diagnosed with ADHD and autism), she set up A2ndvoice as a voluntary group to meet the needs of the local autism community, hosting a range of activities and events supporting autistic children and their families. Over the past several years she has hosted events focusing on different perspectives of autism, including girls and women, faith communities, Black, Asian and Minority Ethnic communities and healthy relationship programmes in keeping safe for youth. Venessa is currently the branch officer for the National Autistic Society Lambeth Branch and a member of the All Party Parliamentary Group on Autism Advisory Group. She has partnered with other autism groups and also volunteers for the Cassandra Centre based in Norbury, a charity supporting adolescents who have experienced domestic abuse and violence.

**Katie Buckingham** is the founder and director of Altruist Enterprises; an experienced provider of resilience, stress management and mental health awareness training to organisations and schools nationally. Diagnosed with Asperger syndrome at the age of 16 years, Katie sees her autism as an advantage. After completing her A levels, Katie went on to attend the Peter Jones Enterprise Academy, where she set up Altruist Enterprises in 2013. Since then, she has won various awards, including Young Social Entrepreneur of the Year 2018, *Birmingham Mail*'s Young Achiever of the Year 2017 and the New Entrepreneurs Foundation 'Future Face of Business'. In 2014, Katie was invited to attend the prestigious 'Women of the Year Lunch' in honour of her work raising awareness of and reducing the stigma attached to mental health. She enjoys public speaking and recently delivered her first TEDx talk titled, 'I'm fine. Let's stop masking our mental health issues' which is available to watch on YouTube. Katie has been featured in both *The Guardian* and *Evening Standard* newspapers, and also regularly writes for the *Huffington Post* on the subject of mental health.

**Barry Carpenter**, CBE, OBE is professor of mental health in education at Oxford Brookes University, UK. He is also honorary professor at universities in the UK, Ireland, Germany and Australia. In a career spanning more than 30 years, Barry has held the leadership positions of head teacher, chief executive, principal, and director of the Centre for Special Education at Westminster College, Oxford. In 2009, he was appointed by the secretary of state for education as director of the Children with Complex Learning Difficulties and Disabilities Research Project. He is the author of over 150 articles and many texts on a range of learning disability/special needs topics.

Recently, he co-authored the book *Engaging Learners with Complex Learning Difficulties and Disabilities* (Routledge, 2015). Barry lectures nationally and internationally. In recent years this has included China, Japan, Abu Dhabi, Norway, Australia and New Zealand. He is co-founder of the National Forum for Neuroscience in Special Education. For the Mental Health Foundation, he chaired the National Inquiry into the Mental Health of Young People with Learning Disabilities, and is currently chairing, for the National Association of Head Teachers, a working group looking at the needs of girls on the autism spectrum.

**Sarah-Jane Critchley** is passionate about helping autistic people, their families, friends and supporters live happier lives of their own choosing. She is the internationally recognised author of *A Different Joy: The Parents' Guide to Living Better with Autism, Dyslexia, ADHD and More …* She has written an 'Introduction to Autism' to support adoptive and foster parents of autistic children. She is an international keynote speaker. For over 10 years (2008–2018), Sarah-Jane managed the Autism Education Trust working to improve educational provision for young people with autism. She was instrumental in the development, monitoring and management of the training programme that reached over 180,000 education-based staff in the UK and adapting the AET's highly successful training programme to meet the local context in Italy and Greece. She worked with stakeholders to produce guidance on exam accommodations and exclusions. Sarah-Jane holds a Masters of Business Administration (MBA) specialising in the management of change from London's City University. She is a mother to two autistic teenagers (a late-diagnosed girl and a boy) and an autistic husband.

**Jo Egerton** has been a schools research consultant since 2013 running one- and two-year school-based research courses for teaching school alliances and academies. She worked for Leeds Beckett University as Erasmus Plus research fellow on an international, three-year special education training project (2014–2017). She also supports and evaluates organization- and school-based practitioner research initiatives, most recently for Books Beyond Words' Department for Work and Pensions-funded wordless books initiative to support people with learning difficulties towards employment. Previously she worked as lead research coach on the Research Charter Mark Award for schools at SSAT (The Schools Network) Ltd (2010–2013), and as lead researcher on Department for Education and Teaching Agency 'Engaging Learners with Complex Learning Difficulties and Disabilities' (2009–2011) directed by Professor Barry Carpenter. She has co-authored and co-edited books, training materials and articles, most recently *Engaging Learners with Complex Learning Difficulties and Disabilities* (Routledge, 2015), two books on fetal alcohol spectrum disorders (Routledge, 2012, 2013), *Creating Meaningful Inquiry in Inclusive Classrooms* (Routledge, 2012) and the DfE's online *Training Materials for Teachers of Pupils with Severe, Profound and Complex Learning Difficulties* (2012). Jo worked in special education and residential care settings for 12 years as a researcher, teacher and key worker. She has a PGCE and a masters in learning disability studies.

**Helen Ellis** was diagnosed on the autism spectrum, aged 21 years, after struggling at university. She quickly became passionate about changing the way society views autistic people, and forcing the world to become more accessible to people with invisible disabilities and sensory needs. She has been involved in a variety of research and advocacy roles over the past 10 years, including the European Union's 'Autism in Pink' project. She is an active member of both the Westminster Autism Commission and the Advisory Group for the All Party Parliamentary Group on Autism (APPGA). Her current goals are focused on improving autistic people's experiences of work, celebrating and valuing the achievements of individuals and improving society's understanding of sensory needs.

**Ruth Fidler** is an experienced education consultant specializing in complex autism, pathological demand avoidance, interactive approaches and emotional well-being. She worked at an all age non-maintained special school for 94 pupils across the autism spectrum for 22 years until 2014, since when she has worked independently. She provides training and consultation across the UK to support families and professionals to work collaboratively in meeting the educational needs of children and young people with complex autism and PDA. She has contributed to publications in the *Good Autism Practice* (*GAP*) journal on the subject of promoting emotional well-being, and is co-author of three books published by Jessica Kingsley: *Understanding Pathological Demand Avoidance Syndrome in Children* (2012), *Can I Tell You about Pathological Demand Avoidance?* (2015) and *Collaborative Approaches to Learning for Pupils with PDA* (2019).

**Jane Friswell** is a national and international special educational needs and disabilities (SEND) advisor as well as a parent of a young man with Asperger syndrome and additional learning needs. She provides both a strategic and practitioner edge to challenge current policy for SEND, and aims to be an agent of change in the world of SEND, and to deliver tangible and sustainable difference to improve outcomes for children, young people and their families. She is director of SEND Consultancy, a newly formed, ambitious social enterprise established with young people with SEND providing tailored support solutions for those working to achieve and improve outcomes for children, young people and their families with SEND. She is co-founder and director of SENDRadicals (www.sendradicals.org.uk), an intensive SEND development programme designed by Dr Helen Sanderson and Jane Friswell together with family leaders and young people. She is also specialist SEND adviser to the Abu Dhabi Education Council (ADEC) in the United Arab Emirates. As chief executive of nasen, Jane convened the Girls and Autism Forum. She is author of a DfE-funded national programme of training for primary and secondary SENCOs – 'A whole-school approach to access, participation and achievement' – as well as various editions of *School Inspection Guidance for SENCos* (nasen, 2012, 2014, 2015), and *The SEND Handbook* (nasen, 2015).

**Carrie Grant** is a well-known broadcaster and president of the Unite Union for Health Visitors and Community Practitioners. In 2018, Carrie received an honorary doctorate of arts from the University of Bedfordshire for her services to charity. She is mother to four children, three birth children and one adopted, all with special needs. Two of her girls are diagnosed with autism spectrum conditions, and Carrie, her husband David and daughter Talia are ambassadors for the National Autistic Society. Carrie sits on the largest Transforming Care Partnership Panel in the UK for Learning Disability and Autism, and has given keynote addresses at many health and education conferences in the UK, Europe and America. Her work has seen her influencing government policy, contributing to government command papers and supporting the launch of the world's first All Parliamentary Group for ADHD.

**Francesca Happé** is professor of cognitive neuroscience and director of the MRC Social, Genetic and Developmental Psychiatry Centre at the Institute of Psychiatry, Psychology and Neuroscience, King's College London. She completed her undergraduate degree in experimental psychology at Oxford University and her PhD at University College London, supervised by Professor Uta Frith at the MRC Cognitive Development Unit. Her research focuses on autism spectrum conditions. She has explored the nature of social understanding in typical development and 'mind-reading' difficulties in autism. She is also actively engaged in studies of abilities and assets in people with autism, and their relation to detail-focused cognitive style. As well as cognitive methods, her research has involved functional imaging studies, exploration of acquired brain lesions, and behaviour genetic methods. She is the author of more than 200 research papers and a book on autism for general readers, and was recently ranked in the top 10 most productive and highly cited authors in autism research worldwide from a bibliometric analysis of autism research published in 2005–2014. She was president of the International Society for Autism Research (INSAR) from 2013 to 2015 and on the board from 2012 to 2017. She has received the British Psychological Society Spearman Medal, the Experimental Psychology Society Prize and the Royal Society Rosalind Franklin Award. She was made a fellow of the British Academy in 2014, and was elected fellow of the Academy of Medical Sciences in 2017.

**Grace Hershey** graduated from Oxford Brookes University with first-class honours in occupational therapy. Since qualifying Grace has specialized in child and adolescent mental health. She has spent time working with young people with eating disorders and a range of other mental health needs in an inpatient setting. Latterly she has been involved in the delivery of CAMHS community based services where she works as both an occupational therapist and a key worker/care co-ordinator. Grace has a particular interest in girls with autism spectrum and co-morbid mental health needs.

**Sheila, the Baroness Hollins** is the founder, editor and lead author of Books Beyond Words, an award-winning, independent, charitable publisher of wordless books that support people with communication and learning difficulties to understand and talk about adult concerns, experiences and feelings. She is emeritus professor of the psychiatry of disability at St George's, University of London, and sits in the House of Lords as a cross-bench peer. Sheila has advised the Government on the development of many initiatives and policies, such as the 2001 Valuing People white paper, the 2008 Healthcare for All independent report and the National Mortality Review. Until recently she chaired the Learning Disability Expert Reference Group for Health Education England on the health and social care workforce with respect to learning disability. She is a past president and honorary fellow of the Royal College of Psychiatrists, and past president of the British Medical Association. She chaired the board of science at the British Medical Association for three years, and is now president of the College of Occupational Therapists. She was a founder member of the Pontifical Commission for the Protection of Minors (including vulnerable adults) for four years.

**Sharonne Horlock** is a strategic leader of special educational needs and/or disability. She has worked in education for over 25 years as a class teacher, peripatetic teacher of travellers/gypsies, lead teacher within school for students with social, emotional difficulties, form tutor and special educational needs co-ordinator (SENCo). All her roles have involved challenge, difference, discrimination, practitioner research, significant minorities, demand, alternative provision and busyness. Within them, she has encouraged acceptance, questioned expectations and developed self-advocacy for individuals who struggle to find a voice that can be appropriately articulate, heard and proudly owned. Her areas of educational interest include differentiation that facilitates inclusion and participation for all, females with autistic spectrum conditions and effective leadership that enables inclusive educational environments. She has written on autism and presents at local and international conferences.

**Meng-Chuan Lai** is staff psychiatrist, clinician scientist and O'Brien Scholar in the Child and Youth Mental Health Collaborative between the Centre for Addiction and Mental Health and The Hospital for Sick Children, Toronto, and is assistant professor at the Department of Psychiatry, Institute of Medical Science, and Department of Psychology, University of Toronto. He is also honorary director of gender research in autism at the Autism Research Centre, University of Cambridge. He holds an adjunct attending psychiatrist position at the National Taiwan University Hospital, and is adjunct assistant professor at the National Taiwan University. Meng-Chuan's vision is to bridge and integrate multi-level (biological, cognitive, psychological, and social) research and clinical services. His clinical interests are in the risk and resilience processes in individuals with atypical social-affective development (e.g., autism spectrum, ADHD, anxiety and mood disorders), and how sex and gender modulate these processes.

**Wenn Lawson** is an autistic lecturer, researcher, psychologist, advocate, writer, poet and trans-guy whose knowledge and understanding of autism is internationally renowned and respected. Wenn's insights and professional knowledge, ranging from first class honours in social work to a doctorate in psychology, inform all he does. Wenn lived for 61 years as a woman, raising a family, traveling, writing and joining the dots! He published his first book on autism, *Life Behind Glass*, in 1998. Since then, he has written and/or contributed to a further 20 books, as well as many journal articles. Wenn is passionate about the rights of those who so often cannot speak for themselves and aims to promote justice and equality for all. His work explores the influence of neurological development in autism as well as focusing on autism across the life span, learning, social demand and bridging the gaps so AS individuals can truly be involved with an inclusive society. Living with his wife in Australia, Wenn has autistic and non-autistic adult children and grandchildren.

**Gillian Loomes** has a degree in English law and European law, a PGCert in special education (autism), a PGDipEd (Advanced PGCE) in lifelong learning, and an MA in social research. Her MA dissertation examined disability advocates' perspectives on their everyday practice in the context of recent legislative developments within the sector, drawing on her prior professional experience as a specialist autism advocate within a UK charity. Gill's current PhD research focuses on the Mental Capacity Act 2005, and how its implementation in practice engages with, and impacts upon, the voices of disabled people. Gill's research experience includes working with the International Disability Rights Monitor, where she acted as UK researcher on the *IDRM Regional Report of Europe* (2007), and on the international Essl Social Index for Disability Governance Pilot Study (report published in 2010). She has acted as a research consultant, including for the Autism Education Trust and the British Psychological Society, and holds a teaching fellowship with the Autism Centre for Education and Research (ACER) at the University of Birmingham. Gill has acted as guest-editor for the *York Policy Review*, producing a special edition of the journal on the subject of mental capacity. She is proud to be a convener of the Participatory Autism Research Collective (PARC), and is currently working for a West Yorkshire autism advocacy, information, and mentoring service as a peer development worker.

**Liz Pellicano** is professor in educational studies at Macquarie University, Sydney. As a developmental cognitive scientist and educational psychologist, she is committed to understanding the distinctive opportunities and challenges faced by autistic children, young people and adults, and tracing their impact on everyday life. She is dedicated both to ensuring that the outcomes of her research are as influential as possible in education policy-making and to enhancing public understanding of autism, its challenges and opportunities. Liz completed her PhD on the cognitive profile of children with autism in Perth, Australia before becoming a research fellow in psychiatry at the University of Oxford, UK. Prior to joining Macquarie University, Liz was director of the Centre for Research in Autism and Education (CRAE) at the UCL Institute of Education, University College London. She has won a number of awards for internationally recognized and outstanding research including the Philip Leverhulme Prize (2015), the Michael Young Prize (2007) and the Neil O'Connor Award (2006). She has been an editor for the international journal *Autism* since 2012.

**Carol Povey** has worked with autistic people and their families for over 35 years in the voluntary and local authority sectors. Carol joined the National Autistic Society in 2001, and in 2010 she was appointed as the director of the Centre for Autism. The aim of the centre is to promote innovation, excellence and understanding across the autism sector and to provide a hub for greater collaboration, both UK-wide and internationally. Carol is responsible for the NAS's diagnostic services, research, training and quality assurance. She is also the chair of the editorial board of the NAS's professional conference. She has contributed to a number of publications, and has trained and presented at conferences nationally and internationally. She is the UK representative of Autism Europe and chaired the scientific committee of the XI Autism-Europe International Congress.

**Tina Rae**, BA (hons) PGCE MA(Ed) Msc RSADipSpLD DipPsych ALCM Doc App Ch Ed Psy MBPS, HCPC registered child and educational psychologist, author and educational consultant, has over 30 years' experience working with children, adults and families in both clinical and educational contexts within local authorities and specialist educational services. She is currently working as a consultant educational and child psychologist in a range of SEBD/SEMH and mainstream contexts and for Compass Fostering as a consultant psychologist supporting foster carers, social workers and Looked after children. She was also an academic and professional tutor for the doctorate in educational and child psychology at the University of East London from

2010 to 2016. She is a registered member of the Health and Care Professions Council and a full member of the British Psychological Society. Tina is author of over 100 publications, and contributes to national and international conferences, most recently in Hong Kong. She can be contacted at tinarae@hotmail.co.uk.

**Felicity Sedgewick** is a post-doctoral researcher at King's College London, working on links between autism, mental health, and gender. Since 2017, she has worked with Kate Tchanturia on a project examining the links between autism and anorexia in young women. This research builds on issues that emerged from her PhD work (completed 2017) with autistic girls and women at the Centre for Research in Autism and Education (CRAE) at University College London's Institute of Education, supervised by Professor Liz Pellicano and Dr Vivian Hill. Her earlier research explored how girls on the autism spectrum interacted and socialized with their peers in mainstream educational settings, with a particular focus on how they experienced and managed conflict within those relationships, for which she received Economic and Social Research Council (ESRC) PhD Studentship funding. It built on her practice working with children on the autism spectrum in a mainstream secondary school. Felicity has published a number of articles around autism and anorexia nervosa, school exclusion and the nature of the friendships, social conflict and social motivation of autistic girls.

**Rachel Townson** has grown up learning about autism and trying her best to advocate for her older brother. After completing her studies she left university with an honours degree in psychology and a Master's in autism studies. Continuing her quest for knowledge, Rachel joined the National Autistic Society's training and consultancy team and has now worked for the NAS for over six years. She currently oversees the development of online training modules for professionals and ensures that all modules and face-to-face training from the NAS has the autistic voice represented throughout. Rachel has been very privileged to be able to attend many conferences and hear from so many inspiring people on the autism spectrum. This enabled Rachel to self-identify as being autistic, and led to a formal diagnosis of Asperger syndrome in 2014 by Dr Judith Gould. Rachel continues to work within the training and consultancy team and enjoys her continued work with others on the autism spectrum.

**Rona Tutt** OBE is a past president of the National Association of Head Teachers (NAHT). She has an MA in linguistics and a PhD in the education of children with autism. In the 1990s, she opened the first provision for pupils with autism in her county. She has received an OBE for her services to special needs education and an outstanding reviewer award for her work on the *International Journal of Educational Management*. Rona represents the NAHT on a number of specialist groups including the Expert Reference Group of the Autism Education Trust (AET). She is one of the founder members of the National Forum for Neuroscience and Special Education (NFNSE). During 2015/2016, she was the interim chair tasked with establishing Hertfordshire's All-Age Autism Partnership Board. Rona has written and co-authored a number of books including: the DfE-funded *Making it Personal: A guide to personalisation, Personal Budgets and EHC Plans – for educational establishments and local authorities* (2016); *The SEND Code of Practice: 0–25 years – policy, provision and practice* (2015) and *Rona Tutt's Guide to SEND and Inclusion* (2016), both published by Sage. Rona is much in demand as a speaker, writer, reviewer and judge. She remains actively involved in education through her books, articles and conference speeches, as well as being vice-chair of governors at two schools, one an all-age school for profoundly deaf pupils and the other a secondary school for pupils with autism, learning difficulties, and/or speech, language and communications needs. Rona is a Fellow of University College London's Centre for Inclusive Education (CIE).

**Sophie Walker** is leader of the Women's Equality Party (WE), being elected in March 2018 with 90 per cent of the vote after a period as interim party leader (2015–2018). Her early career was in journalism, as an international reporter and as an editor at Reuters news agency, covering finance, business, trade and politics. She has two daughters; her eldest is diagnosed on the autism spectrum. Sophie has written about their lives together in *Grace Under Pressure: Going the Distance as an Asperger's Mum* (Piatkus 2012).

**Sarah Wild and the students of Limpsfield Grange School**. Sarah Wild is head teacher of Limpsfield Grange School for girls with communication and interaction difficulties including autism. Sarah has worked in education for 20 years, in a range of settings. She has had experience of leadership in a mainstream secondary school in the East End of London, and in special schools in London and Brighton. Sarah is a qualified teacher of the deaf and an English teacher. Since her appointment as head teacher Sarah has dedicated time to raising awareness of female autism nationally. Limpsfield Grange School was the subject of the ITV documentary *Girls with Autism*, and students of the school have written two novels with author Vicky Martin, both published by Jessica Kingsley: *M is for Autism* (2015) and *M in the Middle* (2016). Sarah and students from Limpsfield Grange speak nationally about female autism, and have spoken at the Autism Show London, National Association of Head Teachers and the National Union of Teachers special education conferences and the National Autistic Society professionals' conference. Sarah is a member of the NAHT's Autism and Girls Forum, and has recently participated in a House of Lords roundtable discussion about female autism.

# Foreword

For people with autism, trying to understand the rest of us can feel like travelling to another country – learning another language and navigating a new landscape while brandishing a passport that allows you access, but not acceptance.

For women and girls with autism, it is more like sneaking into the same country under cover of darkness, wearing a disguise during the daytime and hoping every moment that no one blows your cover.

My daughter has autism. She was diagnosed when she was eight years old. It took five years to get the diagnosis. At the time I thought it was because our local systems were underfunded and overloaded, teachers and health professionals too busy, undertrained and defensive. Now I think that, while all that was the case, a good part of the delay was because my child was not a boy.

It is amazing that, thirty years after its release, the film *Rain Man* still sets the bar for what we understand as autism: boys and men who are extremely good at maths and do not understand other people. It is a picture based on the work of male scientists like Leo Kanner, who thought autism was mothers' fault for failing to love their children enough; of Hans Asperger, who thought no women and girls were affected by the syndrome he identified; and shored up by the work of Simon Baron-Cohen, who theorized that male and female brains are fundamentally different – men are better at systematizing, women at empathizing – and therefore autism is 'an extreme of the male brain'.

This template has not only trapped generations of men in cliché, but has also prevented thousands of women from getting the support and understanding they need because a male diagnostic gaze simply never sees them.

And while struggling to get by in a world that does not see them, many women and girls with autism will mimic the expected behaviour of 'neurotypical' women and girls, adopting social stereotypes to be quiet and biddable, which create an unbearable mental strain. Many are subsequently diagnosed with multiple mental illnesses while their autism remains unseen. Forty years ago it was believed that the ratio of men with autism to women with autism was 15 to 1. In 2015 data from the National Autistic Society suggested it could be 3 to 1.

As a woman who for years fought sexist attitudes and was dismissed as 'feisty' – who questioned lad culture and was called a prude – who objected to pink and diets and good behaviour, and was driven to distraction by being repeatedly shut down by aggressive condescension – it has been hard to watch my daughter experience a double discrimination: being female and autistic, defined and skewered twice over by patriarchal premise.

As Grace, now 16, puts it:

> When I was little I said I liked pink and princesses because girls around me said they did and I felt I had to because they did. But I felt uncomfortable on two counts – because I didn't like it and I didn't understand why I was supposed to.
>
> All girls are under immense pressure to fit in and be a certain way according to what they're told being a girl means. It's even worse for girls with autism because they're also trying to fit in with what being a human means.

Grace was lucky in one sense, in that, in the end, her frustration took the form of a 'typically male' reaction. She fought her way out of her predicament, literally swinging at the school bullies until her punches and kicks flagged a crisis to the authorities. I was also lucky that my employer agreed to my request to cut my hours at work, and I could take up a second job of cajoling my local education, healthcare and child support services to file reports on time and to the right people and agree a Statement of Special Educational Needs – now known as an Education Health Care Plan.

A diagnosis did not bring general acceptance from the outside world, nor did it bring sufficient support – but it brought just enough of each for Grace and me to function, while being aware daily of how thinly spun is the thread of our luck.

Grace still counters sexist ideas about autism every day:

> When a boy with autism has a bad reaction, he gets immediate support from loads of teachers. When I get overwhelmed, I get told off about my attitude.

And as her mother I counter discrimination that will be familiar to many carers – we are whingers, incapable of discipline; feckless, self-centred, hysterical … you name it. Because a society that does not value women does not value the care work that women do.

Female does not equal not-male. Autistic female does not equal not-autistic. The lived experiences of women and girls, wherever they are on the autism spectrum, are simply different. And while our society is terrible at understanding and embracing difference, it also relies on difference to progress. Every day Grace attempts to make her way in a world that does not understand her. Every day I work to build the kind of world that could.

This book sets out ways in which we can build bridges between our daughters, sisters, nieces, mothers, aunties and a world that does not see autism as female. It sets out the length of the journey ahead of us and the obstacles we must overcome. It questions assumptions, unpicks presumptions and answers questions to which we do not yet know the answer. And yet for all that, this is a work of huge optimism and encouragement. Because you cannot solve a problem until you identify that there is one. The biggest failing of our society has been to simply ignore the voices of women and girls. Thanks to this book, those voices can now be heard.

We should all embrace difference. We would all be better off.

Sophie Walker
Leader of the Women's Equality Party, UK
September 2018

# Preface

This book is born of the commitment of a group of professionals from a range of disciplines – academics, policy-makers, parents, and importantly including young women with autism – to advocate for a vulnerable and often unrecognized group in our society – girls with autism. The National Autism and Girls Forum, originally brought together as a short-life working group by nasen (the National Association for Special Educational Needs), has been hosted and supported by the National Association of Head Teachers (NAHT) for the last two years.

The Forum, chaired by Professor Barry Carpenter CBE, OBE, has campaigned around the unmet needs of girls with autism, evocatively described in the Forum's 2016 introductory booklet as 'flying under the radar' (available from www.nasen.org.uk).

This booklet is still widely used in schools and has helped to create much greater awareness of the needs of autistic girls, showing why so many still go unrecognized and misdiagnosed. The Forum's key messages resonate for me with some of my recent work as a psychiatrist on global issues concerning the protection of minors and vulnerable adults from both online and offline abuse (Child Dignity Alliance 2018).

The Forum's messages also add emphasis to the pictorial narratives created by Books Beyond Words for anyone who finds pictures easier to understand than words. I was delighted to be asked to host a debate for the Forum at the House of Lords, which brought together interested politicians from both Houses of Parliament, representatives from government departments, national organizations in the field of Autism, family members, professionals, and some girls with autism themselves. The girls spoke eloquently of their struggles to cope, particularly in school settings. They described how sensory overload affects them, the unfathomable dynamics of friendships, the feelings of isolation when peers did not understand and their anxiety in the fast-paced classroom.

The vulnerability of girls with autism was a recurring theme, and in this respect I am eager to explore the contribution the pictorial narratives created by Books Beyond Words might make to reducing the potential dangers for the girls. This series (www.booksbeyondwords.co.uk) includes stories about the relationship difficulties experienced by young people, including girls on the autism spectrum, who may have an intellectual disability (Hollins et al. 1994; Hollins et al. 2005; Hollins et al. 2016).

The National Autism and Girls Forum, having created a wide support base, worked through the NAHT to organize a national conference, 'The Big Shout', in January 2016. This sell-out conference brought together delegates from every sector of the field, unexpectedly including international delegates. Girls and women with autism shared their lived experiences; families talked of their struggles and triumphs in getting recognition of the needs of their daughters; members of the Forum shared their current research, evidence-based practice, training developments and critical insights. These presentations were the seeds of what you now see and read in this book, with its rich and diverse array of chapters.

A major output from the 2016 Conference was 'A Call to Action', co-constructed with delegates around key themes such as diagnosis, education and training, research, mental health, parents and carers, and post-school transition and employment.

The Big Shout became the 'call to action' that lived on beyond the conference and which enabled delegates to go back to their various settings, professional or personal, and share the conference's key messages. 'A Call to Action' has acted as a script for focused conversation with politicians, government departments, local authorities and many other groups. It has even been used internationally to highlight the unmet needs of girls with autism.

The Big Shout conference spawned many informed voices who have campaigned tirelessly to bring about change and a greater understanding. In this respect I congratulate members of the National Autism and Girls Forum for their vision and determination, which has contributed to the many conversations I now hear in many quarters, showing that with increased understanding comes deeper compassion and action.

'Many Voices' is the title of the conference to be hosted by NAHT on World Autism Day, 2 April 2019, where this book will be launched. I hope that its content will inspire you, and that your voice will be added to the many who are now advocating for the needs of girls with autism.

I commend this book to you.

Professor Sheila the Baroness Hollins
Independent Crossbench Peer
The House of Lords
September 2018

## References

Child Dignity Alliance (2018) 'The Declaration of Rome'. Retrieved from www.childdignity.com/blog/declaration-of-rome (accessed 13 September 2018).

Hollins, S., Roth, T. and Webb, B. (1994) *Hug Me, Touch Me*. London: Books Beyond Words. Retrieved from www.booksbeyondwords.co.uk (accessed 13 September 2018).

Hollins, S., Sinason, V. and Webb, B. (2005) *Jenny Speaks Out*. London: Books Beyond Words. Retrieved from www.booksbeyondwords.co.uk (accessed 13 September 2018).

Hollins, S., Egerton, J. and Carpenter, B. (2016) 'Book clubs for people with intellectual disabilities: the evidence and impact on wellbeing and community participation of reading wordless books'. *Advances in Mental Health and Intellectual Disability*, 10, 275–283.

# Part I

# Introduction

# Chapter 1

# Where are all the autistic girls?

## An introduction

*Barry Carpenter, Francesca Happé and Jo Egerton*

Where are all the autistic[1] girls? According to the UK's National Autistic Society (NAS), one child in every 100 has autism, and 70% of those are educated in mainstream schools (National Autistic Society 2013). A diagnosis of autism spectrum disorder (ASD) is based on core behaviours appearing in early development (usually before three years of age): impaired development in social interaction and communication, and restricted and repetitive interests and activities (American Psychiatric Association 2013; Wing and Gould 1979). Although behavioural-cognitive traits associated with autism are found in the general population, it is the quality, intensity and co-occurrence that lead to a diagnosis when, together, these traits are impairing in everyday life (Lai et al. 2013). Until recently, there was thought to be a large gender gap in autism, with the ratio of boys to girls widely accepted as at least 4:1 (Dworzynski et al. 2012).[2] However, researchers now propose a gender ratio in autism that is closer to 2:1 boys to girls (Zwaigenbaum et al. 2012).

Existing screening and diagnostic criteria have largely developed from Kanner's and Asperger's observations of autistic boys in the 1930s and 40s (Kanner 1943; Asperger 1991; Frith 1991; Silberman 2015; Wing 1981) and may lack validity when diagnosing girls (Cheslack-Potava and Jordan-Young 2012; Rivet and Matson 2011). There is some evidence of a gender-bias (Dworzynski et al. 2012; Gould and Ashton-Smith 2012); girls on the autism spectrum are typically diagnosed later and with more extreme behaviours than autistic boys, and those girls without additional intellectual or behavioural problems are likely to 'fly under the radar' (Dworzynski et al. 2012; Egerton et al. 2016).

In 2012, the NAS surveyed more than 8,000 people on the autism spectrum and their family members in the UK. They found that 41% of autistic females (compared with 30% of autistic males) had experienced misdiagnosis and were less likely to be given access to extra support. Only 8% of intellectually able autistic girls under six years (compared with 25% of boys) were diagnosed, rising to 20% and 50% respectively by the age of 11 years (Bancroft et al. 2012; Clark 2016). Nicola Clark, an autistic woman diagnosed in her forties, writes:

> Many women remain undiagnosed until their 20s or 30s … If a woman has had children, is in a relationship, is interested in makeup, music, fashion, or in my case doing stand-up comedy, this level of sophistication apparently makes diagnosis 'less clear-cut'. At worst, it apparently makes autism seem 'nonexistent'.
>
> (Clark 2016)

Almost every professional in the education, health and care sectors will work with children on the autism spectrum at some point during their career. While many will be aware of the behavioural profile traditionally associated with the male-oriented diagnostic criteria, psychologists and psychiatrists are now suggesting that many girls do not fit this profile (Happé et al. 2006). In mainstream schools, for example, girls on the autism spectrum are frequently misunderstood or overlooked for support, especially if they have intellectual functioning in the average range. As Baldwin and Costley (2016) observe, 'the absence of ID [intellectual disability] does not equate to an absence of learning support needs'.

Many autistic girls have a desire to fit in with their peers. It appears that, to a greater extent than most autistic boys, many girls use protective and compensatory factors to give the appearance of social conformity and integration with their peer group. They may use observational learning to interpret and imitate facial expressions, create scripts for social interaction and apply rules by rote to social-emotional situations and friendships (Tierney et al. 2016).

Girls' repetitive and restrictive interests, while having the classic autistic intensity and duration, tend to be gender-influenced – the 'little professor' approach but applied to pop stars, boys, pets and fashion, for example. As Sarah Wild, head teacher of Limpsfield Grange School for girls with communication and interaction difficulties, states:

> Just because the girls aren't obsessed with Thomas the Tank Engine and lining things up in neat rows doesn't mean they are not on the spectrum. Just because they can make eye contact, have a reciprocal conversation with someone for five minutes and exchange small pleasantries doesn't mean they are not autistic. It means they've learned to do it. We have to redefine what we think autism is.
>
> (Lee-Potter 2016)

Autistic girls' education is also at risk unless they receive appropriate support or reasonable adjustments for their autism (Baldwin and Costley 2016). Unable to cope with the unrealistic expectations and demands of the school environment, unsupported girls on the autism spectrum may become school refusers or exhibit behaviours that lead to school exclusion (Sproston et al. 2017). Others become the quiet, anxious girl at the back of the classroom, concealing their difficulties behind a socially acceptable mask (Tierney et al. 2016).

For many autistic boys, their autism is externally expressed (e.g. in conduct disorders); however, autistic girls seem more likely to conceal and internalize difficulties. Over time, this imposes a detrimental psychological burden, making autistic girls vulnerable to emotional difficulties and to mental health disorders such as anxiety, self-harm, depressive, personality, and eating disorders (Baldwin and Costley 2016; Hull et al. 2017; Rubenstein et al. 2015). There are growing indications that autism may be an underlying cause for a significant number of undiagnosed girls experiencing these difficulties.

Currently, many professionals do not have sufficient awareness or knowledge of autistic girls to consider or identify autism as a possible cause of mental health or behavioural issues. Girls with undiagnosed autism and their families may receive blame, censure and exclusion instead of support. The strategies adopted to address their issues may be inappropriate and, at worst, have catastrophic lifelong impacts.

Professionals need new information to better understand girls on the autism spectrum, enabling them to recognize, understand, refer, support and teach autistic girls effectively.

To avoid bleak outcomes, autistic girls need a timely diagnosis, followed by an in-depth needs assessment leading to relevant, personalized interventions in the areas of education, social skills and relationships. Without this scaffolding, these girls are in danger of growing up to be women who remain 'undiagnosed, without employment, hav[ing] no social contacts outside the family and ... almost wholly dependent on their parents to support them in everyday living' (Gould and Ashton-Smith 2012).

In the following chapters, autistic girls and women, their families, and professionals from a range of disciplines offer insights, knowledge and strategies from their lived experiences and professional perspectives to enable those living or working with girls on the autism spectrum in educational environments to provide more informed and effective support to these girls and their families.

## Overview of chapters in this book

*Girls and Autism* is presented in five parts, contextualized by Chapter 2, 'What does research tell us about girls on the autism spectrum?'. In that chapter, Francesca Happé, professor of cognitive neuroscience at King's College London, reviews what we do, do not and must know about girls on the autism spectrum based on the latest research findings. She considers male-to-female ratios in autism and contemplates a 'missing' population of autistic girls and women which has been overlooked by traditional diagnostic interpretations. She discusses the male-biased stereotypes and diagnostic overshadowing that can result in misdiagnosis, late diagnosis or lack of diagnosis for autistic girls and women, and the implications for girls' mental health and educational needs as they develop within a neurotypically oriented world.

Following Parts I and II, the part-title pages for, Parts III–V include insights from girls on the autism spectrum at Limpsfield Grange School, a residential secondary special school in the UK for girls with social communication and interaction needs, many of whom have an ASD diagnosis.

### Part II: Girls and autism: The lived experience

The chapters in Part II describe the experiences of autistic girls and their families from early life, through school to adulthood. Chapter 3 is written by Katie Buckingham, founder and director of the award-winning Altruist Enterprises. Diagnosed with Asperger syndrome at 16 years old, she describes her personal account of living with autism, mental health issues and her journey to discovering the advantages of the condition.

Chapter 4, by well-known broadcaster and Royal College of Medicine patient lead Carrie Grant, describes her family's experiences, focusing on two of her daughters, who have autism spectrum diagnoses. She writes about their developmental differences, school experiences and the fight to get help; she writes about strategies, looking after yourself as a parent, and the great hope she and her husband have for their children.

In Chapter 5, Sarah Wild, head teacher of Limpsfield Grange School in Surrey – the only maintained special school for girls with communication and interaction difficulties in the UK – introduces the reflections on autism by Limpsfield Grange girls that are interleaved throughout the book.

Venessa Bobb, founder of A2ndvoice, run by parents and carers of autistic children and adults, and a National Autistic Society branch officer, is mother to three children on the autism spectrum, two of whom are girls, and only one of whom is diagnosed. In Chapter 6, Venessa reflects on bringing up her autistic children within her own community, and considers autism from a Black and Minority Ethnic (BAME) perspective.

Sharonne Horlock, a secondary academy SENCO and parent of a young autistic woman, writes in Chapter 7 about the need for school communities to know more about, understand, and recognize autism within girls, and to acknowledge that supportive strategies, embedded in whole school practices, are a corporate responsibility. She introduces strategies identified by female autistic students within a mainstream setting that can shape an autism-welcoming environment.

## Part III: Girls, autism and education

In Part III, the chapters focus on education – from leadership perspectives and curriculum emphases to exclusion experiences. In Chapter 8, Rona Tutt, educational author, speaker and a former president of the National Association of Head Teachers (NAHT), situates autism in relation to recent SEND system reforms and considers the implications for education professionals supporting autistic girls. She focuses on how leaders in educational settings can use the reforms to improve the recognition of girls on the autism spectrum at all stages of education, and how schools can develop these girls' well-being and sense of self-worth.

Sarah Wild, in Chapter 9, explores teaching approaches and strategies that can be used when educating autistic girls, and considers the importance of building a curriculum that enables their academic progress, communication, independence, positive mental health/ emotional wellbeing and potential employment routes.

In Chapter 10, Jane Friswell, an international education consultant, author and director of SEND Consultancy, an enterprise established with young people with special educational needs and disabilities (SEND), discusses school exclusions and the emerging evidence of higher exclusion rates among autistic girls – both those with a diagnosis and those as yet unidentified – and how to ensure sympathetic and personalized inclusion of girls on the autism spectrum.

Ruth Fidler, an education consultant specializing in pathological demand avoidance (PDA), describes how PDA is increasingly becoming recognized as part of the autism spectrum. In Chapter 11, she explains the effective educational strategies which, while overlapping to a degree with those for other autistic students, require adaptations in style and a different dynamic in order to reduce anxiety around demand-associated loss of control, to achieve co-operation, to facilitate learning and to promote emotional wellbeing for girls with PDA.

## Part IV: Autism, adolescence and social networks

This section focuses upon adolescence and identity in relation to sex, gender, friendships and mental health. In Chapter 12, Dr Meng-Chuan Lai, assistant professor at the Department of Psychiatry, University of Toronto, discusses the importance of neuroscience when considering autism, sex and gender. He considers the insights that neuroscience provides into how and why autistic people process, experience and respond to social situations differently to their neurotypical peers, as well as the influence of gender on the brain.

In Chapter 13, Dr Tina Rae, a consultant educational and child psychologist, and Grace Hershey, an occupational therapist specializing in child and adolescent mental health, explore mental health difficulties in undiagnosed or misdiagnosed girls on the autism spectrum and their high risk for developing mental health problems such as self-harm, anxiety and eating disorders. The authors address the importance of mental health screening, therapeutic interventions, staff skills and sharing quality information to ensure that autistic girls receive essential and effective support.

In Chapter 14, 'Friendships on the autistic spectrum', Dr Felicity Sedgewick, a post-doctoral researcher at King's College London, and Professor Liz Pellicano, Macquarie University, Australia, report on research into autistic girls' experiences of friendship, what their friendships mean to them, what they look for in and expect from friends, and how their friendship models differ from those of neurotypical peers and autistic boys.

In Chapter 15, Gillian Loomes, teaching fellow in autism studies at the University of Birmingham, considers adolescence and sexuality among autistic girls and women, what they need to know in order to navigate and assimilate their own experiences, and how families and others can usefully support them. Her chapter situates first-hand auto-biographical accounts in the broader contexts of social and political identities, identity construction and social world impacts.

## Part V: Autistic girls: Looking to the future

Part V looks forward in development to adulthood, but also forward in time to when autistic girls and women will enjoy equity with their peers, taking their places as valued contributors within a neurodiverse society that endorses and accommodates their strengths and aspirations. In Chapter 16, 'Girls for the future: transitions and employment', Jo Egerton, schools research consultant, Helen Ellis, autistic advocate and member of the Westminster Autism Commission and the All Party Parliamentary Group on Autism (APPGA) advisory group, and Professor Barry Carpenter, Oxford Brookes University, draw upon literature and personal experiences to review post-secondary education and employment opportunities and their aspirational synergy for autistic girls and women. They explore how autistic girls, autistic women and neuro-typical colleagues can deepen their understanding of one another's needs to establish parity of esteem and progress collaboratively towards a mutually enabling working environment.

In Chapter 17, Sarah-Jane Critchley, international autism education consultant and author, discusses training, standards, competences and partnerships with respect to developing skills in the workforce. She focuses on building the effectiveness and con-fidence of professionals to work with girls on the autism spectrum and the knowledge to provide the girls with the tools they need within a competency-referenced, school-based training and support structure.

Rachel Townson, online training and development manager for the NAS and autistic self-advocate, and Carol Povey, director of the NAS Centre for Autism, ask in Chapter 18, 'What is essential to ensure autistic women are able to take their rightful place in society; what alterations does society need to make; and how can we create a society of acceptance rather than settling for awareness?' They consider the received roles and expectations presented to autistic girls as they make the transition from child- to adulthood, and discuss how they can maintain their sense of integrity while negotiating obstacles to societal inclusion.

Finally, Dr Wenn Lawson, psychologist, lecturer, author and trans-guy, in his epilogue, 'A call to action', highlights the need for a rallying call on behalf of all autistic females, stating 'Action needs to be relevant, and it needs to be now'. The epilogue focuses on areas of co-produced research ('Nothing about us without us'). He addresses the need to educate clinicians and professionals, the need to educate all teachers/trainers in girl and women specifics, the need to address the mental health needs of this population, and the needs for post school education, employment and ongoing relationships.

We hope that this volume gives voice to the experiences, concerns, needs and hopes of autism girls; this long-overlooked, vulnerable and too-often silent group have so much to teach us, if we can learn to listen and to recognize their vital role in and contribution to a fair and neurodiverse society.

## Notes

1  'Identity-first' language is currently preferred by many autistic adults, in contrast to the 'person-first' language that many professionals feel more comfortable with; the strong feeling that autism is not something that can be removed from a person, not something one 'has', is respected here. Because different views exist, however, even in the autism community, both forms of language will be found in this book.
2  Throughout the book, chapter authors have used different, but evidence-based, statistical sources so the figures quoted may vary slightly according to the sources used.

## References

American Psychiatric Association (2013) *Diagnostic and Statistical Manual of Mental Disorders* (5th edition). Washington, DC: APA.
Asperger, H. (1991). '"Autistic psychopathy" in childhood' (trans. U. Frith). In U. Frith (ed.), *Autism and Asperger Syndrome* (pp. 37–92). Cambridge: Cambridge University Press.
Baldwin, S. and Costley, D. (2016) 'The experiences and needs of female adults with high-functioning autism spectrum disorder'. *Autism* 20(4), 483–495.
Bancroft, K., Batten, A., LambertS. and Madders, T. (2012) *The Way We Are: Autism in 2012.* London: National Autistic Society.
Cheslack-Postava, K. and Jordan-Young, R. M. (2012) 'Autism spectrum disorders'. *Social Science and Medicine*, 74, 1667–1674.
Clark, N. (2016) 'I was diagnosed with autism in my 40s. It's not just a male condition'. *The Guardian*, 30 August. Retrieved from www.theguardian.com/commentisfree/2016/aug/30/diagnosed-autism-male-condition-women-misdiagnosed (accessed 23 August 2018).
Dworzynski, K., Ronald, A., Bolton, P. and Happé, F. (2012) 'How different are girls and boys above and below the diagnostic threshold for autism spectrum disorders?'. *Journal of the American Academy of Child and Adolescent Psychiatry*, 51(8), 788–797.
Egerton, J., Carpenter, B. and the Autism and Girls Forum (2016) *Girls and Autism – Flying Under the Radar: A Quick Guide to Supporting Girls with Autism Spectrum Conditions*. London: nasen.
Frith, U. (1991) *Autism and Asperger Syndrome*. Cambridge: Cambridge University Press.
Gould, J. and Ashton-Smith, J. (2012) 'Missed diagnosis or misdiagnosis?'. *Good Autism Practice*, 12(1), 34–41.

Happé, F., Ronald, A. and Plomin, R. (2006) 'Time to give up on a single explanation for autism'. *Nature Neuroscience*, 9, 1218–1220.

Hull, L., Petrides, K. V., Allison, C., Smith, P., Baron-Cohen, S., Lai, M.-C. and Mandy, W. (2017) '"Putting on my best normal": social camouflaging in adults with autism spectrum conditions'. *Journal of Autism and Developmental Disorders*, 47, 2519–2534.

Kanner, L. (1943) 'Autistic disturbances of affective contact'. *Nervous Child*, 2, 217–250.

Lai, M.-C., Lombardo, M. V., Chakrabarti, B. and Baron-Cohen, S. (2013) 'Subgrouping the autism "spectrum": reflections on DSM-5'. *PLoS Biology*, 11(4), e1001544. Retrieved from http://doi.org/10.1371/journal.pbio.1001544 (accessed 23 August 2018).

Lee-Potter, E. (2016) 'Supporting autistic girls', *SecEd*, 27 April. Retrieved from www.sec-ed.co.uk/best-practice/supporting-autistic-girls (accessed 27 August 2018).

National Autistic Society (2013) 'Myths, facts and statistics'. Retrieved from www.autism.org.uk/About/What-is/Myths-factsstats (accessed 7 March 2016).

Rivet, T. T. and Matson, J. L. (2011) 'Review of gender differences in core symptomatology in autism spectrum disorders'. *Research in Autism Spectrum Disorders*, 5, 957–976.

Rubenstein, E., Wiggins, L. D. and Lee, L.-C. (2015) 'A review of the differences in developmental, psychiatric, and medical endophenotypes between males and females with autism spectrum disorder'. *Journal of Developmental and Physical Disabilities*, 27(1), 119–139.

Silberman, S. (2015) *NeuroTribes: The Legacy of Autism and How to Think Smarter about People Who Think Differently.* London: Allen & Unwin.

Sproston, K., Sedgewick, F. and Crane, L. (2017) 'Autistic girls and school exclusion: perspectives of students and their parents'. *Autism and Developmental Language Impairments*, 2, 1–15.

Tierney, S., Burns, J. and Kilbey, E. (2016) 'Looking behind the mask: social coping strategies of girls on the autistic spectrum'. *Research in Autism Spectrum Disorders*, 23, 73–83.

Wing, L. (1981) 'Asperger's syndrome: a clinical account'. *Psychological Medicine*, 11(1),115–129.

Wing, L. and Gould, J. (1979) 'Severe impairments of social interaction and associated abnormalities in children'. *Journal of Autism and Developmental Disorders*, 9(1), 11–29.

Zwaigenbaum, L., Bryson, S. E., Szatmari, P., Brian, J., Smith, I. M., Roberts, W., Vaillancourt, T. and Roncadin, C. (2012) 'Sex differences in children with autism spectrum disorder identified within a high-risk infant cohort'. *Journal of Autism and Developmental Disorders*, 42(12), 2585–2596.

# Chapter 2

# What does research tell us about girls on the autism spectrum?

*Francesca Happé*

## Introduction

In this chapter I will highlight what is and is not currently known about girls and women on the autism spectrum from research, with a focus on psychological research. The aim is to give a succinct overview of key areas, and to complement and frame the multiple perspectives provided in the other chapters of this volume. As will become clear, females have traditionally been neglected in autism research, and many gaps exist in our knowledge. However, researchers are now waking up to this gender inequality, and focus is turning to women and girls on the autism spectrum. The chapter will end with some suggested future directions for research on this important topic.

### Autism and girls: what we thought we knew

Autism is a relatively recent diagnosis, although there is little doubt that there have always been autistic people (see Houston and Frith 2000 for a historical case study). The diagnosis is made on the basis of behaviour (difficulties in social interaction and communication, plus rigid and repetitive behaviour and interests), and over time the diagnosis has widened as clinicians and researchers have become more aware that, for example, autism can be seen in individuals with average or high intelligence, in those with good formal language skills, and in adults as well as children. It is probably the widening of diagnostic criteria (especially in the 1990s, when Asperger syndrome entered diagnostic manuals), as well as the increase in awareness, diagnostic services and provision, that largely explain the rise in numbers of diagnosed autistic people, rather than a real rise in the incidence of autism.

Boys predominated in the first descriptions of autism, by Leo Kanner and Hans Asperger in the 1940s, and until very recently researchers estimated that there were approximately five times as many males as females on the autism spectrum. Researchers also believed, until recently, that females, when autistic, were more severely affected (i.e. more likely than males to have additional intellectual disability, and to require substantial support). At the end of the autism spectrum previously described as Asperger syndrome, that is autism without additional intellectual or language impairment, the estimated male-to-female ratio was approximately 10 to 1 (Fombonne 2009).

The widely accepted conclusions that autism was far more common in boys than girls, and that it affected girls more severely when present, were taken as important clues to the biological basis of autism. For example, Simon Baron-Cohen's 'extreme male brain' theory suggested that autistic people of both sexes had brains that were (structurally and functionally) more masculine than expected (Baron-Cohen 2002). In related work, his research group also reported that high testosterone levels during pregnancy predicted more autistic traits in children in the general population (Knickmeyer and Baron-Cohen 2006), although this work is not without its critics.

In terms of the biology of autism, the so-called 'female protective effect' has received support from a range of studies. This refers to the idea that females are less susceptible to whatever factors cause autism, and so require a higher 'load' of those factors before they show the diagnostic signs of autism. This idea has received some support from genetic studies that have found more genetic changes (e.g. new gene mutations, and deleted or duplicated sections of DNA, known as copy number variants;) in females than males diagnosed autistic (e.g. Jacquemont et al. 2014). A clever test of the female protective effect is to look at the rates of autism (or high levels of autistic traits) in the siblings of autistic girls versus boys; if autistic girls have a larger genetic load for autism than boys, their siblings (regardless of the sibling's sex) should be more likely than the siblings of boys also to be autistic/have many autistic traits. This has been confirmed in several studies in different populations (e.g. Robinson et al. 2013).

## Revisiting and revising what we thought we knew about autism and girls

Recently, Loomes et al. (2017) re-examined all the published studies on gender ratio in autism, conducting a meta-analysis that considered the quality of the evidence from different study methods. For example, if you estimate how many girls have an autism diagnosis from clinical or school records, you will be likely to miss some people who 'fly under the radar'; especially important if more females than males are missed routinely. If, instead, you actively go out and try to screen every child in a specific area or population, you are more likely to get an accurate estimate of numbers and male-to-female ratio. Loomes et al. concluded that the best current estimate of male-to-female ratio from good epidemiological studies is not 10:1 or even 5:1, but 3:1. In addition, they did not find strong evidence that this ratio changed much according to where on the autism spectrum (in terms of degree of intellectual ability and need for support) you looked. So the idea that girls are far less often affected by autism, but are hit harder when they are autistic, was called into question.

A striking conclusion from Loomes et al.'s comparison of different studies, using different ways of finding autistic women and girls, was that currently many autistic females are undiagnosed or misdiagnosed. Since studies that actively screened populations found around 3:1 males to females, while studies that looked at numbers of females known to clinical or other services found approximately 4–5 males to 1 female, the difference between the ratios represents undiagnosed or misdiagnosed females on the autism spectrum.

## Why are we missing girls on the autism spectrum?

It is important to acknowledge that, in part because we have for so long thought that autistic males vastly outnumbered females, women and girls have been under-represented in research, the media and popular conceptions of autism. In research, many studies have systematically excluded females, because if you plan to recruit 30 autistic adults for your brain imaging study and expect to find only 3 women (based on the 10:1 ratio for those with good intellectual abilities), you will probably decide to include only males, because 3 are too few to study as a subgroup and sex/gender might introduce unintended effects. A recent estimate from published autism brain imaging studies suggested male participants outnumbered female participants 8 to 1. This means that what we think we know about autism from research is actually just what we know about male autism. And of course it is research, as well as clinical experience, that shape the diagnostic criteria and the diagnostic tools in general use, creating a vicious circle.

In the media, male portrayals of autism predominate; think of *Rain Man*, Christopher in *The Curious Incident of the Dog in the Night-Time*, Sheldon in *The Big Bang Theory*, etc. And because so many more males than females have traditionally been diagnosed, clinicians, teachers, educational psychologists, and other professionals have all seen many, many more autistic boys than girls; the pattern they have extracted, and are looking for, is a male one.

When you think about the process of getting an autism diagnosis, it is clear there are several stages or steps:

- First, you have to feel different and/or others around you have to notice that you are different from other children/adults.
- Next, someone (a teacher, parent, grandparent, maybe you yourself) has to think that maybe your difference might be something to do with autism.
- Then, you might go to see your family doctor or maybe an educational psychologist; this professional has to conclude, too, that autism might be a good explanation for your differences, and refer you to a specialist for diagnosis (e.g. a child psychiatrist, paediatrician, clinical psychologist).
- Probably after a long wait, when you get the diagnostic appointment, the clinician specialist needs to decide you fit the diagnostic criteria for ASD. S/he'll probably get a developmental history from your parent(s) and see how you interact using a standardized diagnostic interview like the Autism Diagnostic Observation Schedule (ADOS; Lord et al. 2012). You'll need to score past the cut-off on these instruments to get a diagnosis of ASD.

Now if you, or the child in question, is a girl rather than a boy, there is the risk that bias and barriers are introduced at every one of those stages (see also Kopp and Gillberg 1992). Your own conception of autism, from the media and from what you have read and seen, may not fit your sense of self because autism is portrayed as largely male. Similarly, your parents, teachers, family doctors and even specialist clinicians may not think 'autism' if they see a girl who is struggling socially, when this would be an immediate thought when seeing a boy. Instead, problems more associated with girls, such as social anxiety or eating disorders, might come to their minds. Even if, for example, an eating disorder is a part of what you are struggling with, the clinician may fail to see that this is anorexia in the context of autism. This problem is referred to as 'diagnostic overshadowing', and may account for under-diagnosis of autism in many cases, given that additional mental health difficulties are common in ASD. In one study of women where eating disorders were the presenting problem, 23% (14/60) of women hospitalized for anorexia actually passed the ASD cut-off on the ADOS (Westwood et al. 2017). While further research is needed to be sure these women's social and communication difficulties predated their eating disorder and were not due to starvation, it is very likely that autism is under-recognized in women receiving clinical help for other conditions.

## What do we know about girls and women on the autism spectrum?

Given the problems of recognition detailed above, it is likely that research on girls on the autism spectrum is not fully representative; most studies recruit diagnosed females, and we know little about those who may be on the spectrum but (for the reasons above) not yet diagnosed. With these provisos, what does recent research tell us about autistic girls? The evidence base is small but growing (Rubenstein et al. 2015). Some points that seem to emerge from research to date are as follows:

- Girls are, on average, diagnosed at a later age than boys (Begeer et al. 2013).
- Girls are less likely to be diagnosed than boys when they show the same level of behavioural symptoms (Russell et al. 2011).
- Girls, more than boys, need additional red flags (such as intellectual disability or behavioural problems) to get identified for autism diagnosis (Dworzynski et al. 2012).
- Some girls may show their autism differently from the classic male presentation:
  - lower levels of rigid and repetitive behaviour (van Wijngaarden-Cremers et al. 2014);
  - narrow special interests may appear more neurotypical (e.g. horses, boy bands versus electricity pylons; Sutherland et al. 2017);
  - social differences may be shown in a 'clingy' rather than 'aloof' style of interaction (Kopp and Gillberg 1992); and
  - in the playground, girls on the spectrum look less conspicuous and less different/isolated from their peers than boys on the spectrum.

- Many girls and women on the spectrum describe 'masking' or 'camouflaging' their autism (Dean et al. 2017):
  - gender role expectations may lead females on the autism spectrum to modify their behaviour (e.g. copying the behaviour, clothes and voice of a popular classmate); and
  - camouflaging or compensating to fit in with neurotypical expectations is described by many autistic girls as exhausting, and may have negative consequences for mental health (Livingston et al. 2018).

## Priorities for future research

It is clear that far more research including women and girls on the autism spectrum is needed, and that this must extend beyond recruiting only those who have managed to get a diagnosis (Lai et al. 2015). To avoid circularity, in studying only girls who meet our probably male-biased diagnostic criteria, we need population-based studies taking a wide view of how autism may be manifest in females. Qualitative research exploring the lived experiences of autistic girls is needed to complement quantitative research in order to develop better tools for recognition and better interventions to help girls on the spectrum live the lives they want, and achieve the goals that matter to them. There is little doubt that our current practices are letting down autistic girls; research is urgently needed to establish rates of autism and associated needs in disadvantaged and marginalized groups such as pupils excluded from school, young people in the criminal justice system, the trafficked and homeless. It is very likely that in these groups, there are raised proportions of girls on the autism spectrum, who are missed, misdiagnosed, misunderstood, and highly vulnerable.

## References

Baron-Cohen, S. (2002) 'The extreme male brain theory of autism'. *Trends in Cognitive Sciences*, 6(6), 248–254.

Begeer, S., Mandell, D., Wijnker-Holmes, B., Venderbosch, S., Rem, D., Stekelenburg, F. and Koot, H. M. (2013) 'Sex differences in the timing of identification among children and adults with autism spectrum disorders'. *Journal of Autism and Developmental Disorders*, 43(5), 1151–1156.

Dean, M., Harwood, R. and Kasari, C. (2017) 'The art of camouflage: Gender differences in the social behaviors of girls and boys with autism spectrum disorder'. *Autism*, 21(6), 678–689.

Dworzynski, K., Ronald, A., Bolton, P. and Happé, F. (2012) 'How different are girls and boys above and below the diagnostic threshold for autism spectrum disorders?'. *Journal of the American Academy of Child and Adolescent Psychiatry*, 51, 788–797.

Fombonne, E. (2009) 'Epidemiology of pervasive developmental disorders'. *Pediatric Research*, 65(6), 591.

Houston, R. A. and Frith, U. (2000) *Autism in History: The Case of Hugh Blair of Borgue*. Oxford: Blackwell.

Jacquemont, S., Coe, B. P., Hersch, M., Duyzend, M. H., Krumm, N., Bergmann, S., Beckmann, J. S., Rosenfeld, J. A. and Eichler, E. E. (2014) 'A higher mutational burden in females supports a "female protective model" in neurodevelopmental disorders'. *The American Journal of Human Genetics*, 94(3), 415–425.

Knickmeyer, R. C. and Baron-Cohen, S. (2006) 'Topical review: fetal testosterone and sex differences in typical social development and in autism'. *Journal of Child Neurology*, 21(10), 825–845.

Kopp, S. and Gillberg, C. (1992) 'Girls with social deficits and learning problems: autism, atypical Asperger syndrome or a variant of these conditions'. *European Child and Adolescent Psychiatry*, 1(2), 89–99.

Lai, M.-C, Lombardo, M. V. and Auyeung, B. (2015) 'Sex/gender differences and autism: setting the scene for future research'. *Journal of the American Academy of Child and Adolescent Psychiatry* 54(1), 11–24.

Livingston, L. A., Colvert, E., Social Relationships Study Team, Bolton, P. and Happé, F. (2018) 'Good social skills despite poor theory of mind: exploring compensation in autism spectrum disorder'. *Journal of Child Psychology and Psychiatry*.

Loomes, R., Hull, L. and Mandy, W. P. L. (2017) 'What is the male-to-female ratio in autism spectrum disorder?:a systematic review and meta-analysis'. *Journal of the American Academy of Child and Adolescent Psychiatry*, 56(6), 466–474.

Lord, C., Rutter, M., DeLavore, P. C. and Risi, S. (2012) *ADOSTM-2 Autism Diagnostic Observation Schedule* (2nd edn). Torrance, CA: Western Psychological Service.

Robinson, E. B., Lichtenstein, P., Anckarsäter, H., Happé, F. and Ronald, A. (2013) 'Examining and interpreting the female protective effect against autistic behavior'. *Proceedings of the National Academy of Sciences USA*, 110, 5258–5262.

Rubenstein, E., Wiggins, L. D. and Lee, L. C. (2015) 'A review of the differences in developmental, psychiatric, and medical endophenotypes between males and females with autism spectrum disorder'. *Journal of Developmental and Physical Disabilities*, 27(1), 119–139.

Russell, G., Steer, C. and Golding, J. (2011) 'Social and demographic factors that influence the diagnosis of autistic spectrum disorders'. *Social Psychiatry and Psychiatric Epidemiology*, 46(12), 1283–1293.

Sutherland, R., Hodge, A., Bruck, S., Costley, D. and Klieve, H. (2017) 'Parent-reported differences between school-aged girls and boys on the autism spectrum'. *Autism*, 21(6), 785–794.

Van Wijngaarden-Cremers, P. J., van Eeten, E., Groen, W. B., van Deurzen, P. A., Oosterling, I. J. and van der Gaag, R. J. (2014) 'Gender and age differences in the core triad of impairments in autism spectrum disorders: a systematic review and meta-analysis'. *Journal of Autism and Developmental Disorders*, 44(3), 627–635.

Westwood, H., Mandy, W. and Tchanturia, K. (2017) 'Clinical evaluation of autistic symptoms in women with anorexia nervosa'. *Molecular Autism*, 8(1), 12.

# Part II

# Girls and autism

## The lived experience

# Chapter 3

# The advantages of autism

## A personal journey

*Katie Buckingham*

I waited in silence for what felt like a lifetime. Anxious, on edge and unable to think, I stared at the intimidating grey door just in front of me. As the two psychologists re-entered the room, I looked over at my parents and was ready to receive my fate.

They sat down. The lead psychologist looked at me, my dad and then my mom and said, 'We believe Katie has autism.'

There was a sigh of relief from my parents, who had fought tirelessly for years to enable me to receive a diagnosis. I, on the other hand, was overcome with disbelief. Eighteen months on the waiting list still had not prepared me to hear those words. I had conflicting thoughts like, 'I didn't cover it up well enough', and 'They're wrong; I can't possibly be autistic.' You see, I had only ever seen documentaries and TV programmes about boys with autism. I was not like them. I could hold a conversation, I could make eye contact and I had had a group of friends. I was now aged 16; why had it taken so long to receive a diagnosis?

We left the room having been promised a follow-up appointment, and I got into the car, still unable to contemplate what had just happened. I am lucky that I have very supportive parents. I remember on the drive home, my dad said to me, 'You know, Kate, some cars are petrol and others are diesel but they all get to where they need to be. Do you understand?' I shrugged. My dad continued, 'Just because you are different, it doesn't make you any less of a person and you can still achieve whatever you want to in life.' I thanked him for his kindness but was unsure as to the validity of his input.

Hours later, my disbelief turned to anger. Despite my dad's previous comments, I believed that my life was over. I am autistic. I just about survived school; what am I going to do now? Is there hope for employment, relationships, a family? Will I even be able to live independently?

It was now increasingly difficult to think about my future. I was in the middle of GCSE revision and exams, and my anxiety had hit new levels. I found it difficult to cope and was subsequently referred back to Child and Adolescent Mental Health Services (CAMHS) just two months after I had been discharged.

I had been in touch with counsellors and psychologists for most of life. Now on to my 11th mental health professional, I began my second programme of cognitive behavioural therapy (CBT). However, this time was different. This time, I was able to access help that had my autism in mind – a psychologist who understood the difference between my autism and my mental illness. She showed empathy and involved my mom and my brother to incorporate strategies that, collectively, were able to support me in a way that worked.

Once the negative thoughts and feelings had somewhat subsided, along came some more comforting thoughts. For years, I had lived thinking that there was something wrong with me and not understanding why I saw things differently to other people. I now realized why I was the way I was, and had started the journey to understanding myself. I would think back to situations or events that at the time did not make sense and was now able to make sense of them.

One of my first memories was when I was two or three years old. My mom took me to nursery as she thought that this may help in getting me to socialize with other children. However, I did not seem to want to engage with anyone and tended to play on my own. I remember the teacher asking us to close our eyes and imagine we were in different places, such as on a beach holding a bucket and spade. This was quite difficult for me, and I did not really understand the purpose. We were sitting on the floor in a building not far from home, not on the beach. I did not take part, and instead just sat there until the end of the workshop, much to the dismay of the teachers.

There were many occasions like this growing up when I did not understand the situation or how to act, and felt like everyone else knew what was happening. As a result, I would become withdrawn and lost for words which often meant I spent time alone, trying to 'keep it together'.

I found it difficult to communicate, let alone articulate my feelings so was often described as naughty, ignorant and shy by teachers and school staff. My mom was asked on many occasions, 'Oh, how on earth do you cope with her?'

I remember, when I was eight years old, my school had come together to form a choir, and it was our first rehearsal. My class were allocated the middle row. Being surrounded by lots of children, coupled with the heat of the room and loud noises, made me feel very uncomfortable. I became occupied with my feelings and started forgetting the words to the songs. My peers began noticing that I was not singing and so, one by one, started looking over at me. Out of embarrassment, I smiled back at them to signal that I was okay in the hope that they would turn back around and stop drawing attention to me.

The teacher did not see it that way unfortunately. She thought that I was being difficult, refusing to sing and then smiling mischievously at my friends. The teacher shouted at me and told me that she did not want me to be part of the choir anymore. I was so shocked that I did not speak for the rest of the day until I got home when I told my mom what had happened.

My parents were desperate to help me and regularly had meetings with my class teacher, the head teacher, educational psychologist, special educational needs co-ordinator (SENCo) and attendance officer to discuss my behaviour. This time was no different. In the end, my mom visited the school so much that I had to tell my peers that she worked there!

It was not just my parents who helped; I have two supportive brothers too. I have an older brother with a keen interest in football, and he always looked for ways to get me involved. I too enjoyed football so my dad decided to take me to a local girl's football team. I have never looked back. Playing football was and still is a great passion of mine. It has helped me to interact with others and make friends, manage my emotions and vent my frustrations in a positive way.

I was in Year 5 when I made my first group of friends. I felt accepted for once and they actually enjoyed my company despite our differences. They even thought that I was funny. Individuals with autism are different but this should be seen as a positive. It is nice to be around someone with an alternative perspective; refreshing, perhaps.

I had experienced anxiety on a regular basis for as long as I could remember but it was at the age of 10 when I began experiencing symptoms of an anxiety disorder. I would feel on edge and unable to relax. I would have a sense of impending doom and found it difficult to breathe. I began experiencing panic attacks and, one day, ended up in hospital.

I had never really heard of mental health problems, anxiety or panic attacks; well, why would I? I was only 10 years old. It was because of this that I did not know how to explain my illness to the doctors or my parents, so I just said that I sometimes found it difficult to breathe and that it was causing me to have a stomach ache. Following consultations with various doctors, I was diagnosed with acid reflux disease. Really, it was anxiety.

I took two weeks off school and, during that time, only left the house once due to fear of having another panic attack. When I finally returned to school, my teacher approached me, enquired about how I was feeling, and asked what the doctor had suggested. I was glad that my teacher took the time to ask how I was feeling, but standing in the classroom on my way out to break was not the best time for me to open up. Perhaps my teacher or a member of the support staff could have sat down with me at the beginning of the day, asked how I was feeling and let me know that they were there for me if I needed to talk. Of course, no one was to know that my physical illness was really a manifestation of how I was feeling emotionally but I think it is important to be aware of different possibilities.

I did not understand my anxiety. It would come out of nowhere, attack my whole body and make me fearful of everyday things. When I had a good day, I would convince myself that I had got better and that I did not need to talk about it because I was fine now. So, I decided not to tell anyone how I was really feeling.

Instead, I started building up coping mechanisms to help me manage my emotions. Drinking cold water was one, getting some fresh air was another, and having some time out on my own was also helpful. I found that the last one could be quite difficult in school so often went and sat in a toilet cubicle for a break. I figured that no one would disturb me there. A quiet room would have helped me a great deal to cope at difficult times.

With the support of my family and friends and using the coping mechanisms that I had established, I transitioned to secondary school fairly well.

Throughout school, I copied facial expressions, gestures and behaviours from other students to become more socially accepted. One example was when people would say, 'Hi, are you all right?', and I would just reply 'Yes' and then walk off. What I noticed was that other students would reply 'Yes thanks, are you?', and this would get a better reaction. I started doing that instead.

I was navigating school okay at this point and, luckily, my older brother attended the same school so he was always on hand in case I needed anything.

My brother left school the next year and went on to sixth form. I entered Year 8, said to be the best year at school, due to lack of exams, coursework and decisions to be made on our future. This was not the case for me unfortunately.

I relapsed. Crippled by anxiety, I found it difficult to go to school or even leave the house without having a panic attack. I would experience around two panic attacks a day, and I was exhausted. My school work subsequently suffered. Again, my feelings manifested themselves in a physical way and so I took time off school. This time, it was lower back pain which the doctor was unable to prove or disprove was a kidney infection so I just accepted the diagnosis. I also started experiencing migraines which would interfere with my vision.

I carried on keeping my problems a secret and would create milestones to achieve in my recovery. The first one was to leave the house. Other milestones included going to school, getting the bus and going for a meal with my family; things that would seem easy to other people.

When I returned to school, I was on edge and closely managed my feelings to prevent meltdown. I started completing rituals to distract my mind and help me to manage my anxiety. I would count the number of lights, tap the table so many times or keep checking I had everything in my bag. It worked. I continued, not knowing what this would eventually lead to.

It was a few months later when I started realizing my entrepreneurial abilities. My dad's friend bought us a large tub of pear drops. I tried them and was not too keen and nor were the rest of the family. I decided to pack the pear drops into bags of five and sell them for 20p each, using the money made to buy sweets I actually did like. I believe that my autism allows me to think creatively and find new opportunities and feel that this is also true for many others with autism.

I have always been quite quiet, and did not tend to speak up in class, but I had a group of friends, which enabled me to just fade into the background. As I grew older, however, around the age of 14, group dynamics began to change. Girls my age were increasingly worried about the look of their hair. They started wearing make-up and were going out more. I was not really at this stage and did not understand why they cared so much about their appearance, nor why they would be so nice to someone and then talk about them behind their back. Again, I felt different, isolated and alone. The other girls decided that because I was different, and therefore 'weird', they did not want me to hang around with them anymore.

Although that was quite a difficult experience for me, I am proud that I did not give into peer pressure and was able to be myself. I would say that this is another advantage of having autism.

I started walking around on my own at break times, and my anxiety grew and grew. I continued playing sports including football to help me manage my feelings. I would go for bike rides with my family and I ate well but I was not healthy. I would fear going into certain classrooms where I had previously experienced panic attacks. I would look forward to the bell at the end of break and lunch times so I could escape the awkward social situations. I would look forward to the end of the day so I could feel a sense of achievement for surviving.

But it was not all bad. I would enjoy working alone on projects, planning and then executing them. I was often scared to ask the teacher for help so used my initiative to help solve problems. When I did ask for help, I would have a list of well thought out questions which would ensure that I did not need to get up to ask questions more than once. If I felt ill in a lesson and could not concentrate, I would take the information home and teach myself or ask my mom to help me. I was a grade A student, and focusing on my work helped to distract me from the sadness I was feeling.

In Year 9, we were given the opportunity to go to Disneyland with the school. I got my parents to sign the form as I had always wanted to go to Disneyland, like most children. It was then that I thought, 'I can't even go out on my own, what will happen if I go abroad where my family won't be there?'

And so, five years after my anxiety disorder had begun, I made the decision to tell my mom what I had been experiencing. I was not going to let my anxiety stop me from doing things I wanted to do anymore. It was difficult, and I was terrified but, in the end, I felt relieved once I had told her.

My parents took me to see our family doctor and I was referred to CAMHS. After my initial assessment on 19 November 2008, just under two months later, I was added to the 12-month waiting list for CBT through CAMHS and the 18-month waiting list for an autism diagnosis.

While slowly moving up the waiting lists, the school allocated me a bereavement counsellor whom I would meet with weekly. I had not experienced a bereavement, but I was grateful for someone to talk to and that I was able to have time out of the lessons that made me feel particularly anxious.

In the spring of 2009, after much trepidation, I decided at the last minute to go to Disneyland with my school. I remember getting onto the coach, wearing my white top, jeans, white pumps and my leather jacket. I remember sitting near the front of the coach on my own and waving my dad goodbye as the coach pulled off. There was some excitement buried underneath all of the anxiety and worry.

It was about an hour into the journey, when a teacher on his NQT year starting talking to me. His first question was 'Have you ever been on a ferry before?' To which I replied 'No'. He said, 'Nor me – we're in the same boat.' I smiled, but told him how bad the joke was and then turned away. He carried on talking to me. At first, it was annoying, but after a while, I quite enjoyed the chat. He began involving other students around me, and we discussed things like music, TV and what rides we were hoping to go on when we got to Disneyland.

I had an amazing time in Paris, and was more social than normal. I spent my time and explored the theme park with a new group of girls and was told by teachers that I could go and sit with them if I ever felt anxious.

I began CBT on 18 November 2009 and I attended CAMHS weekly and then fortnightly before being discharged a month or so before leaving secondary school. I remember the dates as 18 November is my birthday.

This brings me back to my diagnosis. It was something that made most of my previous experiences make sense, but there was still a long way to go in my journey to understanding myself, not least because my anxiety had returned quite badly during my GCSEs and I was subsequently diagnosed with obsessive–compulsive disorder. A once useful coping mechanism had now turned against me and was influencing my thoughts to painful effect.

I would experience intrusive thoughts, images and scenarios in my head that bad things were going to happen. To manage this agonizing anxiety, I would complete compulsions, which increased in frequency as fear of these unwelcome ideas grew.

I was referred back to CAMHS two months after I had been discharged. I began another programme of CBT, which this time was able to distinguish between what was me and what was my mental illness.

Alongside the great CBT that I received and, of course, the medication, I was encouraged by my parents and mental health services to attend a local youth group. This was not an average youth group but rather one for those experiencing mental health problems. It was there that I improved my communication skills and self-awareness through outward bound activities and the Duke of Edinburgh Award where you take part in volunteering, physical activities, life skills workshops and expeditions.

I started building up more coping mechanisms. I would think through possible situations such as being stuck in a shopping centre and then decide on a few possible next steps. I found it easier to make decisions beforehand rather than when I was in the situation.

As my self-awareness increased, I started realizing more of the advantages of autism. Through the youth group, I was invited to attend a consultation to inform changes to local mental health services. It was there that I realized my talent of thinking independently, 'outside the box' if you like. At the consultation, we were asked to write down what we thought of current mental health services for young people. The others began writing on a piece of flipchart paper; however, this seemed to me too obvious for the professionals to really engage with.

Then an idea came to me. They needed something physical, something that was going to intrigue them. I made a 'chatterbox' and the letters CAMH for 'Child and Adolescent Mental Health' fitted on each corner. Under each one of these, I wrote a problem with mental health services and then, underneath, a series of solutions. The facilitators really liked them and invited me along to the local authority conference. I started believing in myself, and it was the start of a passion to help improve mental health services for the better.

I was encouraged to make a positive change in my community and, with the help of a leadership development charity, was successful in gaining funding from my local authority.

At the age of 17 and with this new-found drive and determination, I set up my first mental health project and made it my mission to raise awareness of mental health and reduce the stigma so that other people could get the support that they needed earlier without fear of discrimination.

I started delivering mental health awareness workshops in schools and saw that there was a real gap in knowledge among both pupils and school staff. I recruited a group of young people as a steering group with support from the council, and we decided to create an educational resource for schools of which the content was later verified by the local NHS Trust. The pack includes activities on mental health, a video, case study cards, support contacts and two posters. We continue to provide this pack and our mental health awareness workshops to schools to this day.

For me to write this pack, I understood that I would need to undertake some extensive research. I had experienced anxiety personally so was able to write about that but had limited knowledge on other conditions such as psychosis, bipolar disorder and eating disorders. I sat in my room for two days and wrote the pack, all 70 pages of it. Thanks to my autism, I am highly focused, and mental health became a passion of mine or 'special interest' if you like. I was able to work on this project for hours with dedication.

The resource pack was very successful, and I was subsequently invited to St James's Palace to meet Princess Anne in honour of my work.

This project had given me a lot of confidence so, once it was completed, I applied for a job as a youth worker to occupy myself during the following summer. I enjoyed working directly with the young people but a few days into the role, things got a little difficult. I was working away from home on residentials and was required to be around people all day as well as in the evenings. I became tired, agitated and somewhat withdrawn, but I carried on. My productivity dropped and I would occasionally sit alone but still in view of my colleagues.

I had previously made my employer aware of my autism but, other than a quick chat, was offered nothing further. It was three weeks in when I was asked to a meeting. I was told that my behaviour was not acceptable and I looked as if I 'didn't want to be there'. I reminded them of my autism and what they said next was very worrying: 'Well, you shouldn't let your autism affect you', my then boss said, like I could leave it at home and not bring it with me! I was later 'let go' by the organization. I was disappointed, but it was a learning experience for me.

I completed my A levels and, rather than going to university, I applied to the Peter Jones Enterprise Academy. I had enjoyed starting my previous mental health awareness project and wanted to learn more about creating a sustainable business.

From the start of the course, my motivation was clear: I wanted to create a business that enriched people's lives. Many autistic individuals are self-motivated and, rather than being swayed by what others think, can stay true to their own purpose.

In 2013, at the age of 19, I set up Altruist Enterprises – a passionate and caring provider of Resilience, Stress Management and Mental Health Awareness Training to organizations and schools. Now 24, I have grown Altruist Enterprises to national scale and enjoy helping people every day. I believe that my autism has enabled me to do this.

Autistic people are different, but they have a set of unique qualities that others do not have, and need to be supported and encouraged to find their own way of doing things. We need to stop trying to force autistic children to 'fit in' and instead create a society that welcomes these distinct traits and capabilities.

Too often, we dismiss autistic individuals from achieving because they have a 'disability'. Yes, having autism can be tough but if we continue viewing it in a negative way then this can have a detrimental impact on a person's self-esteem, confidence and ambitions.

We need a shift in mindset from the idea of overcoming deficiency to helping realize potential.

Imagine you were a child being told that you have an incurable condition that meant you would have difficulties for the rest of your life, and that your potential flaws would be discussed in meeting after meeting, sometimes when you were not there. How would that make you feel?

Now imagine you were a child being told that you have a condition that enables you to think differently from other people, a condition that inspires specific interests, in which you will have an expert knowledge and passion; that you may have an eye for detail and a logical mind which also allows you to think creatively. Imagine being told that it will cause problems along the way but that it is okay because you will be supported in facing these challenges.

Just because you are autistic does not mean that you cannot succeed in life. A career involving public speaking and running my own business would have seemed out of the question for me when I was sitting alone in my room as a child. I would encourage people to follow their dreams. Be who you want to be, not what others think you should be.

Together, we can create this inclusive society. Remember, as my dad would say, some cars are petrol and others are diesel, but they can all get to where they want to be.

# Chapter 4

# Raising the voice of the lost girls

*Carrie Grant*

## Not what we expected?

When you start a family, for many it is your first full-time experience of children, so noticing differences is not even on your radar. It is not until your child starts school, and teachers begin to take you to one side, that you realize perhaps your child is not quite the same as other children.

This immediately raises the questions of relationship between school and home and also the level of expertise and experience of the school in understanding difference in children. When we as parents begin our journey into the world of special educational needs (SEN) most of us know nothing, and we rely heavily on those who are 'in the know'. It's only later we realize, to our horror, we are the experts.

The SEN door opens, and we are led into the world of the acronym: 'Go and see the SENCo about SEN possibly ASD, ADHD, PDA and certainly SPD. CAMHS, OT and S&L may help, and you need to apply for an EHCP with the LA. Get some advice from IPSEA or the NAS and definitely apply for DLA.'

Oh my, those early days are confusing!

My firstborn Olivia (born 1994) was diagnosed with dyspraxia at 11 years and attention-deficit/hyperactivity disorder (ADHD) at 18 years. Talia was born seven years after Olivia (2001). She was different: very quiet, avoided affection and liked to play alone. I would find her in her bedroom in the morning lining up her toys in perfect height order. She would climb into our bed some mornings but not want to be held. I did not think this was odd, but instinctively I knew she wanted to communicate something, just not cuddly affection.

## The strategies begin

I started to tell her that my hand was Mr Hand, and he needed someone to look after him. I would feign sleep and leave my hand on the pillow. Talia would lavish love and affection on my hand and chat to it. In return, my hand would nod yes or no to her many questions or I would plaster her face suddenly with my palm, and she would laugh hysterically. After a while she began to rest her body spoon-style into mine while chatting away to my hand. She felt secure and comforted just like any other child, but in a slightly different way. One of the keys to understanding our girls is to try to hear what they are saying beyond the words. All actions, all behaviour, good and bad, are communication. 'What are you trying to tell me?' is always my first thought.

In those early years, other than a couple of quirks, Talia displayed no traits that most people would have at the time considered autistic, but the onset of school prompted some very different behaviours at home. She could only sit at a certain place around the table, with a certain knife and fork and plate; foods were limited and must never touch. At bedtime, certain routines had to be followed to ensure sleep. Suddenly, we were parenting a different child.

Talia was quiet in school but longed for friendship and was definitely sociable. These relationships were always fraught, complex and complicated. Every day she would come out of school with her head down. Asking how her day had gone led to meltdowns, shouting and frustration on her part and complete bewilderment on ours.

Question: Were these changes as a result of brain development or as a result of social and school anxiety?

Imogen came along some five years after Talia (2006), and she was adorably cute, chatty funny, quirky and highly sociable. At two years old she suddenly began to put her hands over her ears whenever there was a loud noise. Taking her into public toilets became a nightmare. If people used the hand dryers she would run. Then she began to put her hands over her ears when the kettle boiled or even if she was sitting too close to the fridge. She would wear all her clothes off one shoulder and had an obsession with buttons, doing them up and undoing them ... whoever they belonged to! When communicating directly with others she would keep her words to a minimum and talk about herself in the third person.

For a while we thought Imogen may have hearing problems as she would not answer when being called, but when she began putting her hands over her ears we realized she was hearing too much. We had never heard of sensory processing disorder (SPD) so I did what all good parents do – I went on Google. Autism came up straight away, but there also seemed to be a lot more extreme behaviours associated with it that Imogen did not have. My early perceptions of autism were like most people's including, sadly, a lot of the professionals. Imogen did not look autistic ... She spoke ... She made eye contact ... I had an impression of what autism looked like, and it was nothing like my girls.

I mentioned my concerns on my next visit to the health visitor. She advised us to have Imogen assessed for autism. After deeper conversation, alarm bells started ringing in my head for Talia. I knew we needed to get help, but no professional would assess Talia as her behaviours did not register as 'autistic enough'.

In August 2009, with Imogen aged three years and Talia aged eight years, we had both girls privately assessed. We were given immediate diagnoses: Talia with Asperger syndrome and dyscalculia, and Imogen with high-functioning autism. The diagnosis of Asperger syndrome has since been taken out as a separate category in the DSM-5 diagnostic manual (American Psychiatric Association 2013), and I think this is unhelpful as our two girls are totally different.

I am also concerned for parents and carers who cannot afford to have a private assessment. Some wait years for their local health service to agree to assess; what state are those children in by the time they get a diagnosis? If we agree that early intervention makes things better, then there has been and continues to be a serious failure to act.

## Early days

Autism spectrum disorder (ASD): the word 'disorder' is very unhelpful, and I am not sure the word 'spectrum' is right either. Many autistic people will tell you, 'On Mondays I'm "high functioning"; by Wednesday I may have slipped further down the spectrum.'

What we definitely have are varying degrees of ability to communicate, varying degrees of anxiety and ability to mask that anxiety, possible mental health challenges, learning disability sometimes but not always, possible other complex needs, like epilepsy, ADHD, oppositional defiant disorder (ODD), SPD, pathological demand avoidance (PDA), etc. It is also worth noting that being autistic does not mean there is nothing about you that is neurotypical; in the same way many neurotypical people have autistic traits without being classified as autistic. It is important we understand this if we are to break down the 'them and us' divide.

So how did we respond to hearing two of our children were autistic? Actually we were totally fine with it. We were still living with the same fabulous children. They were now fabulously autistic! In fact we went on to adopt our son Nathan in 2011 (at age two years) so we must have been up for the challenge, especially as he has been diagnosed with dyspraxia, ADHD and attachment disorder. Many parents struggle with grief when they realize the child they have is not going to be the person they had hoped for. This was never the case for us, perhaps because the world of the Arts where we work is full of people who are celebrated and valued for their uniqueness.

Some parents have asked us why we have pushed to have our children diagnosed or questioned why we have labelled our children. We have always believed that a label is only a problem if you have a problem with the label. In most cases, no diagnosis sadly equals no help. In speaking anecdotally to autistic people who have been diagnosed as adults, their biggest question has always been, 'Why weren't we diagnosed earlier?' It would have been really helpful in explaining who and how they are to themselves.

Walking on eggshells became our new style of parenting. We would veer between absolute passivity and strict assertion. Neither worked. The middle ground seemed impossible to hold. The challenge to shape ourselves into a new-style parent for each child began. It is a journey we are still on as we walk through each day learning about each child and their needs, preferences and challenges. We have attended conferences, learned therapies and strategies and sharpened our skillset to meet the needs of all our children. Like all SEN parents, we have had to become super-parents.

In 2014 we started a monthly support group in our home for parents of high functioning autistic girls. This group has grown to over 80 families, and we now even have a separate group for the girls themselves. Sometimes I wonder what we would do without these other parents around us. Together we share strategies, give advice about getting assessments, diagnoses, school issues, accessing services, medication, etc. Having a place where you can truthfully share what is going on is a lifeline especially if those closest to you are struggling to understand. Our partners' responses, our children's sibling relationships, our own parents' and extended family's views and the general judgment of others, can all be areas of challenge. Finding support in a group who 'get it' can be really meaningful. We have also been able to create space for an autism-specific version of a course on 'non-violent resistance' and a sub-group for parents of suicidal female teens on the autism spectrum. Non-violent resistance was started by Haim Omer in Israel to help any two parties in conflict. It has since been used as a form of parenting with a whole host of strategies to help both the parent and the child. We learned about it when trying to find help for our adopted son, but then realized it could be tweaked to possibly help our ASD girls.

## School

As our own girls have grown, the challenges have changed and, in many ways, grown – especially with the onset of puberty.

Throughout primary school, staff refused to acknowledge Talia's problems. They refused to see the autism and were simply happy for her to hit her academic targets. Her behaviour at school was not extreme so therefore demanded no help or adjustment. I use the word 'refuse' as opposed to 'failed' as I was in the school on a regular basis trying to help them to understand. It was Year 5 before things began to shift.

Talia hated school so much that she became depressed and began talking of suicide, I was heartbroken and fearful, and I began to negotiate much harder in order to make the school implement change. I finally became the parent–leader I needed to be. Walking on to someone else's territory with all your own school memories is never easy, but until we take authority as parents and begin to lead we will never get the necessary care for our children.

New school strategies included keeping an eye on her during playtimes and helping her with her friendships, but more than anything staff began to look at the classroom, the environment and their own style of teaching through Talia's eyes and understand where difficulties may arise. There are four things every teacher should consider if they have an autistic girl in their classroom:

1   *The room:* What is the sensory environment like? Is every wall cluttered with paper and artwork? Is it too hot/cold? Is it noisy or smelly? Are the children/young people squashed together?
2   *The teacher:* How is your relationship with the child/young person? If a child or young person feels there is a problem in the relationship, if you are angry or do not 'get them' they will become anxious, unable to concentrate on what you are saying and blocked from learning. Being liked, believed in and understood is important for any child and even more so for the child on the autism spectrum.
3   *The subject:* How does the child/young person feel about the subject? Do they hate it? Are they struggling? Have they missed handing in homework?
4   *The friends:* What are the relationships like with the child's/young person's peers? Have they fallen out with a friend? Did they have a hard time on social media the previous night? Are they being bullied?

At best our girls can sometimes manage one or even two areas being challenged, but when things are tough even one thing can throw them into a blind panic and lead to days of school refusal.

## Applying for an Education, Health and Care Plan

Late in 2012, I started the uphill battle to get an Education, Health and Care Plan (EHCP) (or Statement of Special Educational Needs as it was called back then) for Talia. Imogen had been given one in her reception year and was receiving great help in the classroom. With Talia floundering, getting help was essential. The local authority rejected the application the first time, and a date was set for a tribunal. The primary school said it would be difficult as Talia was hitting her academic targets; the new secondary school told me I would never get it. Crestfallen, I gathered more information, read the law, wrote down everything I could think of to argue her case and submitted the paperwork for the hearing. Just before the date of the hearing, the local authority came back with a positive response. By then Talia was in her first term at secondary school.

It felt like we had won the lottery. These moments of victory are to be treasured. Little did I know that having a Statement makes no difference if the school has no commitment to SEN, no flexibility and cannot think outside of the box. The 2014 SEN reforms with the new EHCPs came in and the language of 'co-production' began: team around the child, parental involvement, expert parents, the voice of the child – entered into the vocabulary. Our experience on the ground showed it made very little difference; we were still banging our heads against the neurotypical wall.

By definition a school is an institution. The problem with institutions is that often they have no room for movement. An institution holds enormous pride in its tradition. An institution is a beautifully constructed box that has worked throughout its history, and this proven history can unfortunately create an inflexible pride. As a parent, whether you have limited knowledge, are a read-up, keen learner or a revered expert, you are still just one parent facing a historic, authoritarian giant, and the weight of the scales is not in your favour.

A school where the leadership is forward thinking and has a head teacher who does not desire to be identified as an old fashioned charismatic hero leader, but as a team player, a catalyst and coach, is essential for the success of those with SEN. A good leader understands leadership happens with people, not to people. As a voice coach, I have learned that one of the key components to growth is learning how to listen, to truly hear. When people are prepared to lay down their status and become part of a passionate team that will get round the table and listen to one another, they can create a curriculum and environment that works for the child. Only then can the young person fully interact and thrive within the system.

Is it not ironic that our autistic children are often met with a lack of empathy and inflexibility of thinking (just the characteristics sometimes ascribed to autism)?

When school does not get it right our children suffer terribly. Adjustments can take months, sometimes years, to fight for or wait for, and in the meantime our children experience a decline in their well-being.

## Living in crisis

Talia loved secondary school to begin with. She would rush home to do homework and thrived with the encouragement. Unfortunately, the school (like many others) gave the kids a few weeks to bed in before introducing detention, and this fear/threat-based control upturned Talia's world. The fear of failing and getting a detention left her unable to complete homework or engage. A teacher shouting at a class made her feel like she could not get things right. Those early heady days of having loads of new friends changed as girls began to pair off or gather into friendship groups. Talia became immobilized by fear and began to refuse to go to school. Every morning became a battleground, trying to convince her to get up, get dressed and get to school.

At the same time Imogen would require a sensory start to the day – massage and gentle waking for about 20 minutes – and would then need us to dress her under the covers … another 20 minutes. Olivia required help to get through university, and

Nathan was in an incredibly violent phase. By the time we walked though those school gates in the morning, we were frazzled.

Talia began to be bullied at school, and the school did very little to address the problem. Her mental health really began to decline, and at the age of 13 we had our first hospital stay with Talia on suicide watch. Having your child want to end their life changes you as a parent. Our world was rocked to its very foundations, and now we really began to grieve.

Question: Is it inevitable that all girls on the autism spectrum develop mental health problems or is it that school is so difficult that mental health problems occur?

Conversations at the school gate became hard to engage with. Talking about SATS (statutory assessments) and dance club became irrelevant. All we could think about was the relentless pressure of keeping our child alive. Every day the first thing other parents do is make breakfast for their child; the first thing I do is check my child is breathing.

And when it comes to accessing services and school provision, if the warrior parent in you has not already risen it is sure to come crashing in now.

As suicide watch became a regular experience (six times over the next two years) playing Mrs Nice-but-Firm Parent went out the window. If the school was not prepared to make adjustments and work with us, then we would hold it to account. We would quote the law, get others to support us, rally an army of experts and demand change.

At home, we stretched and adapted our parenting even further. We learned to sit with our child's mental pain without trying to shift or change it. We learned to listen at a deep level. Conversations became reflections.

Dialogue had previously been:

> Child: 'I hate school, the teacher hates me, and I don't want to go.'
> Parent: 'It'll be fine when you get there.'

This became:

> Child: 'I hate school, the teacher hates me, and I don't want to go.'
> Parent: 'I hear what you are telling me – you hate school, the teacher hates you, and you don't want to go.'

Being heard is so vital to every human being, especially those struggling to process their inner thoughts.

## Fighting all the way

A new EHCP was written and fabulous provision put in place. I am so happy that together with the school, health services and local authority we have finally managed to get it close to right. The only problem is that it finally got approved and actioned in Year 11, Talia's GCSE year. How will she ever catch up in time? This issue is the same for many parents and children. Even if parents do manage to get the services required for their children, often it is too little too late.

It appears that mainstream secondary schools do not really want SEN students in their schools, and after GCSEs I am certain Talia's school will drop her, leaving us to begin another journey with a new school/college. I really hope the next one is easier.

Despite the challenges she faces, Talia is lovely to live with. She is funny, deep, empathetic, creative, caring, loving and truthful. She is great at art, dance, singing and song writing and has a big vision for her life. She attends a Saturday stage school, has deep faith and goes to church. She is obsessed with social media, brilliant at make-up and great at being a girlfriend. In many ways she is a typical teen, and in the past year has begun to realize that being autistic is a gift as well as a challenge.

During the holidays, away from the pressure of school, Talia is a different young woman. She is stronger, more resilient and can take other life pressures more easily.

Question: What would need to change in school to make her able to be the person she is during these out-of-school times?

## Next up – Imogen

I would like to be able to say Imogen's educational experience has been easier, having had a Statement throughout her school life. Like many autistic people, Imogen does not have a learning disability; she is bright and academically strong. The difference between Talia and Imogen can be summed up in the following description of blending and masking:

- *Blending:* an attempt to blend in with neurotypical people.
- *Masking:* the ability to hide or hold in your anxiety so you appear calm.

Both girls blend, but Imogen cannot mask. She will let you know exactly how she feels, how you are matching up to her expectations and give you a running commentary. Basically, she is a blurter. This has proven to be a huge challenge at school.

At the beginning of October 2016 Imogen, aged 10, was given a two-day exclusion for bad behaviour. She was then allowed back into school for mornings only. Afternoons would be added once she could manage five particular behaviours for three mornings in a row. Needless to say, she spent every afternoon in October at home.

Imogen can try to change, but she cannot stop being autistic. She was eventually allowed back in for the afternoons when Talia went back into hospital on suicide watch, and we physically could not pick her up at midday.

Trying to find an appropriate school setting for Imogen is proving impossible, and we have had one secondary school failure already. Imogen was diagnosed with ADHD in 2016, and this more complex presentation is proving to be a real challenge. Not least to her own self-esteem. And while she waits at home for a school to appear, her mental health is crashing.

## A new educational view

The big question is: Where are the schools for these and the many other children with various differences? Schools that are not mainstream or traditional special schools? Places for children who are neurodiverse but bright, with little or no learning or intellectual disability? Schools with a high ratio of staff to young people? Schools where the Arts are appreciated and encouraged as much as the academic subjects? Settings where social, emotional and mental health needs are put first, but where young people can still achieve their academic or vocational goals?

The answer is always 'nowhere' due to lack of funding.

We have to realize these young people are going to grow up into adults, and if they are unable to work they are going to cost the system a lot more for a lot longer. If they are pushed from pillar to post and end up with mental health problems, they are going to be even more costly.

It is not solely about funding either; it is also about mindset and policy. It will take a massive shift at root level, a change in Department for Education policy: a policy that reflects the true role and value of teachers.

Early investment in our children is essential if we are going to have a fruitful and dynamic society with all the benefits of the autistic community fully flowing through it. We need to raise the autistic voice because when we do we will all benefit.

## Reference

American Psychiatric Association (2013) *Diagnostic and Statistical Manual of Mental Disorders* (5th edn). Washington, DC: American Psychiatric Association.

# Chapter 5

# Introducing 'What we want the world to know'

*Girls of Limpsfield Grange School and Sarah Wild, head teacher*

Limpsfield Grange is a school in Surrey for girls aged 11–16 years with communication and interaction needs. The majority of girls who attend Limpsfield Grange have been identified as autistic, and all of the students who attend the school have high and persistent levels of anxiety that affect their day-to-day life.

The girls of Limpsfield Grange are encouraged to be proud of and speak out about autism. Limpsfield Grange was the subject of the ITV documentary *Girls with Autism* screened in 2015, and the girls have written two novels, *M is for Autism* and *M in the Middle*, both published by Jessica Kingsley. They are currently working, together with writer Vicky Martin, on their third publication.

We asked some of the girls at Limpsfield Grange to tell us what they would like the world to know about their autism. The quotes you will read from the girls, interleaved at intervals throughout this book, are just that: their words, their stories; their points of view. They are grouped under specific headings but go beyond them – 'being unique', 'anxiety …', '… anxiety', 'respect', 'think outside the label', 'confusion and masking', 'friends', 'autism and gifts', 'things need to change'.

On the following pages, you will find the first part of 'What we want the world to know' from the girls at Limpsfield Grange School. It is vitally important that we listen to these girls, alongside #actuallyautistic women and girls of all ages, so that we can build better understanding, practice and a better future, together.

## Being unique

Having autism is normal for me. I've never known what it's like to be 'normal' … Every person, autistic or not, is unique, like a snowflake.

(Lauren, Year 9)

For me, autism isn't something that I really think about. I don't relate myself or my actions to autism, I'm just me.

(Lauren, Year 9)

Some people don't like being labelled with autism, but I don't mind people knowing. I do mind when people take it the wrong way. I really dislike it when people see autism and not the person.

(Lauren, Year 9)

## Think outside the label

'Autism: a mental disorder that can cause difficulty with speech and language.' To be honest, I don't feel like that at all. Sure, there are some things that I can relate to, like noticing small details that have a big impact in me, but most of the symptoms don't apply to me.

(Phoebe, Year 10)

I hate this label, this thing we are meant to be. It's like we barely know ourselves. We want to be normal.

(Hannah, Year 9)

I guess being someone with autism, all of your senses are heightened. You can hear the quietest sound, you can spot the smallest details and some subtle tastes are really strong.

(Rhiannon, Year 9)

## Respect

No matter how much research you do or books you read about autism, you will never know enough about it. Every single person on the spectrum is different to each other. We have a right to be treated the same as everyone else and we will not be quiet when we are told to be silent; we will fight until our requirements are met. No matter how many barriers are put in our way we will never give up because we are resilient.

(Hannah, Year 9)

People who do not have autism need to treat autistic girls with respect.

(Abbie and Lowri, Year 10)

The world needs to know that people with autism act differently, but despite this we can do anything we put our hearts to.

(Daisy, Year 10)

# Chapter 6

# Black girls and autism

*Venessa Bobb*

When meeting other Black families raising an autistic girl, I see how much society is failing autistic girls, and especially Black autistic girls. In this chapter, as a Black mother raising a young adult and pre-teen girls with 'hidden' conditions, I will share my family's journey and experiences over the last ten years. In the context of my own experiences of autism and as an advocate, I will reflect on issues around autistic girls growing up in my community in particular. However, many of the issues I raise are also those of other Black, Asian and Minority Ethnic (BAME) communities so, when appropriate, I will widen my discussion to include them.

Although I was asked to write this chapter from a 'BAME communities' perspective, readers whose communities find themselves grouped together under the 'BAME' acronym will know this is an impossible undertaking. We talk about BAME communities, but BAME is hugely diverse. Whereas the Irish, Scottish, Welsh and English have cultural commonalities, 'BAME' unites massively different countries and cultures. In the Black community alone, you have the different communities from African countries, the Caribbean islands, and many more. And when you break that down, you have the different mother tongues, different cultures, different dress styles, different body languages as well. It can be easy to misinterpret people. For example, in one stereotype, particular Black communities such as Africans and Jamaicans are described as speaking very loudly, using big hand gestures. It may seem to an outsider whose 'norm' is to be very composed as though they are being aggressive when they are just expressing themselves with a different cultural body language. Generalization has caused many of the disagreements and divisions among communities.

## Introducing my family

I have three children. At the time of writing, my oldest daughter is 17 years old, my son is 15, and my youngest daughter is 12. All three of my children have neurodevelopmental conditions.

My children are Black. Yes, Black people can be autistic too! However, in our community, as with other BAME communities, there is a problem of under-diagnosis. One of the impacts of under-diagnosis, for BAME autistic communities, is that we lack strong voices to bring about lasting change. Our experiences are not widely reported, and our voices are largely missing from research literature, conferences and awareness-raising materials about autism.

The struggle to get my children's needs met has been a hard one. There have been times when I wanted to give up and quit! Times when I have had enough of meetings, of appointments. All I needed was one person who had the relevant autism training to get it – that my youngest child's behaviour stemmed from her autism. It took 10 years for my youngest daughter to get her diagnosis – a late diagnosis – at 11 years old. Every minute that her diagnosis was delayed, her mental well-being deteriorated. During that time, I saw her regress from a bubbly and confident girl to a child who was described in reports as overbearing, challenging and attention seeking.

Late diagnosis is a typical experience for autistic girls from all cultures. Both my daughters have waited longer for their diagnoses than my son. For years, it was denied that they may be on the autism spectrum. As is common with autistic girls, my oldest daughter's and my youngest daughter's behaviours were not a clear match with the classic male-oriented diagnostic criteria. My son was diagnosed at five years old, while my oldest daughter, despite the presence of autistic behaviours, had to wait until age 16 before she was diagnosed with moderate learning difficulties in April 2017. My youngest daughter was diagnosed with attention-deficit/hyperactivity disorder (ADHD) in January 2017, with Asperger syndrome in December 2017, and with benign Rolandic epilepsy in March 2018.

Professionals and people from my community have struggled with accepting my children's diagnoses. Both my daughters' behavioural difficulties were initially labelled as attachment disorder or attributed to low self-esteem. I have been blamed for bad parenting, for neglect and for not showing love towards my children. I have been accused of being mentally ill and suicidal. I have suffered personal character assassinations on when and how I was supposed to have failed my children. However, these responses to my children's difficulties came not only from professionals, but from family and friends also.

To give you an insight into my cultural background, my family are not Jamaican, and they are not African, but my mum's roots are in Guyana, South America, while my dad was born in Aruba, a tiny Dutch Caribbean island off the coast of Venezuela. Growing up, autism was not recognized; in the eyes of my parents' generation and among Black communities autism was probably overlooked as being 'slow' or 'sick'. I grew up in a community where children should be seen and not heard. My community believed a child 'like that' (today some would understand their autism) was rude; if the child did not listen, they needed to be disciplined – this was done in the spirit of tough love, firm boundaries.

Today, there is still that same ethos in many BAME communities. In a Black household, children should be well behaved; adults expect eye contact and that children should speak only when they are spoken to. This caused stress and strain for my son. He had limited speech up to the age of five or six years old. He was described as 'aggressive and uncontrollable' and would attack his siblings or me at home. He was misunderstood at school and professionals and peers did not understand him or his needs – he had no other way to express himself. Yet, according to others, there was nothing wrong with him – he was 'just a typical Black boy; you know, boisterous and very hyperactive'.

When my son, was diagnosed in April 2008 with Autism and ADHD, it was like a swear word. No one wanted to accept his diagnosis. They overlooked his behaviour and questioned my parenting skills; when he had obvious, classic autistic behaviours, what chance was there that they would recognize my daughters' more subtle conditions? With my youngest girl, the community had a different interpretation. All the same behaviour traits that my son had were there, but this time, I was told that I was not being firm enough with her and that 'she was getting away with too much'.

My community believes that my daughter has been misdiagnosed and is no different to any other child. Despite her official diagnosis, in Year 8 there has been no change in people's attitudes; they now treat her as if she is using her diagnosis to excuse her behaviour. They expect me to deal with her exactly the same as I would a neurotypical child, ignoring the fact that she has struggled to fit into mainstream settings from her early years.

When you speak to my youngest daughter now, she is a very angry child from those years of being misunderstood. Professionals tell me she's a very bright child, which she is. However, throughout her early years to date, she has struggled to sustain friendships. Even now, she finds it easier being around familiar friends (mainly from her previous school) who are more accepting of her diagnosis than new friends. She seems much happier when she is on her own or among those who understand her.

When I meet other families, who have an autistic child the first thing they always say on finding out that my children have autism, is, 'Oh but they look normal.' and then question the diagnosis. As their mother, my journey has been a traumatic and lonely one at times. I have learnt to walk my own path. I have come to understand what autism is. I have learnt to go to events for professionals and ask questions; and from these events, to build my understanding from multiple perspectives.

## BAME communities and under-diagnosis

Collective data on autism in BAME communities is poor. Despite many children from BAME communities being diagnosed with autism, there are few reliable prevalence statistics for BAME communities, although the Government and local authorities are slowly rectifying this.

There are fewer able Black young people being diagnosed on the autism spectrum. There may be at least two reasons for this. First, we may never find out the number of autistic children from BAME communities because many families within our communities are not part of the data collection process. They do not get involved. The Black community tend to reject labels of illness or disability as shameful and a sign of weakness. (There is even low take up for screening for life threatening medical conditions, such as prostate cancer, so what hope is there for anyone on the autism spectrum?)

Families stay away partly from embarrassment, partly from shame, and partly because they believe they are on their own, that there is no support. There is however some high-profile representation, from Black, male, autistic role models:

- artist Stephen Wiltshire MBE;
- micro-sculptor Willard Wigan MBE;
- Joshua Beckford – 13 years old at the time of writing, and one of the top 10 brainiest young boys in the UK; and
- John Paul Horsley (a.k.a. rapper J-Rock, front-man of the MOBO award-winning group, Big Brovaz), whose son was diagnosed with autism.

As John Paul Horsley said, reaching out to the Black community about autism is very, very difficult and the more TV programmes there are that show the positives and the highs and lows of autism, the better.

The second reason is diagnostic circularity. Many autistic Black children are apparently successfully integrated within their communities and, while as severely affected by autism as their White peers, they seem to have fewer externalized autistic behaviours; therefore, some who are autistic may not be meeting the diagnostic thresholds for autism. Those who do receive a diagnosis may be misdiagnosed with speech, language and communication disorders (SCLN; Slade, 2014). This difference is not straightforward. Black families ensure their autistic young people have greater self-reliance, autonomy and social conformity within their community to keep them safe – a point I pick up later.

As fewer intellectually able autistic Black youngsters are diagnosed, professionals come to believe that mainstream Black communities are less affected by autism. As those responsible for referring children for diagnosis expect to find fewer Black children demonstrating autistic behaviours, that is exactly what they do find through the lenses of alternative stereotypes. It is a self-fulfilling expectation leading to under-diagnosis. Black autistic girls therefore may experience four levels of discrimination – ability, race, culture and gender.

However much autism event organizers think they have tried to include BAME communities, there is low representation. Inclusion never means what it says. I have attended quite a few All Party Parliamentary Group on Autism (APPGA), NAS and autism events. When I first started going to them, it was 'spot the Black person', 'spot the BAME people'. Often, I was the only person of colour there. Now more autistic people and families from BAME communities come to events – most travelling into London from Cambridge, Birmingham and beyond; and I see the same small proportion of Black individuals and families from London attending.

Within a White culture, the gatherings of families with autistic children tend to be around conferences and formal meetings or events – a style that only a small group within the wider autism community may feel comfortable with. There are often very low numbers of participants from BAME communities attending, and, because they do not attend, it is very hard to challenge BAME community assumptions about autism, encourage their participation, and build bridges for families.

## Cultural mismatches

How many professionals are trained in understanding the dynamics of working with BAME communities as well as recognizing autism spectrum conditions? Autism affects all individuals the same, yet in BAME communities the impacts are different. For an outsider professional, the recognition of autism is often overshadowed by media perpetrated cultural stereotypes, while on the flip side, autism is largely unacknowledged and taboo within BAME communities, who view autistic behaviours through the lens of traditional, cultural and religious expectations. Denial and concealment of autism cause more distress and more broken families than there would be if autism was acknowledged and faced head on; autistic children and their families need early diagnosis and informed professional support.

Support for families with autism is usually presented from a White cultural perspective. Cultural differences, language barriers and family traditions affect how BAME communities respond to autism. Service take up depends on whether local authority supports can be accepted without individuals from that community compromising their cultural and religious integrity. Lack of representation from BAME communities in developing support services, and shaping how that support is offered, means that there is often a mismatch with BAME communities' cultural and family structures.

Autism community events too, in the way they are set up, can unwittingly create barriers to inclusion for families from BAME communities. All these mismatches lead to delays and loss of essential support for autistic BAME children and their families, causing significant damage in the long run.

However, misunderstandings do not occur only with community-outsider professionals. You would expect insider professionals to be able to support families from their own communities more effectively than others could, but this is not always the case. I have experienced entrenched wrong assumptions and a lack of understanding from professionals within my own community when cultural expectations have conflicted with autism-related behaviours; diagnosis was mostly the loser.

Upbringing and respect is important within Black households. Influenced by cultural expectations and interpretations, some Black professionals struggle to accept autism as the explanation of a child's behaviour. Instead of remaining professionally open-minded about the cause of behaviours and giving the Black parent respect for their knowledge of their child, they may label the child's behaviour as unruly and conclude that there is a lack of discipline in the home.

Among non-community professionals, cultural stereotypes play a significant part in the delays in diagnosing autistic Black youth. The media have often presented a negative picture of Black boys and girls. Where Black boys are portrayed as boisterous, unruly and out of control, Black girls will be seen as loud, abrupt and feisty. Autistic behaviours are often overshadowed by these stereotypes, with the result that parents and children are punished and sanctioned instead of supported.

If we talk about socioeconomic difficulties, drugs, addictions, gangs, crime, teen mothers, mental health and childhood sexual abuse, whether victim or perpetrator, Black and Asian communities are more heavily linked to these issues than others. Once again, the outcomes of an undiagnosed child's social difficulties, vulnerabilities and misunderstandings may be misinterpreted through these stereotypes rather than their autism; the concerns of their family in relation to autism may be ignored and discounted with disastrous consequences.

Until we can respect people's differences then maybe it would help when assessing a child for autism to acknowledge how cultural influences can affect one's assessment of children from BAME communities.

## Black autistic children and school

To get my son the education he needed, I attended four tribunal appeals for him from 2009–2011. All found in favour of my son. The first was fighting for his Statement of Special Educational Needs (now Education Health and Care Plan); then it was getting him to the right school. I remember the judge saying that, with my son's IQ, he would have been further forward in his education if his needs had been met in the early years.

Many of my son's teachers were Black. However, instead of understanding my son, building his self-esteem, and taking account of his autism, they undermined him ('This is boring. Why are you repeating yourself?' – a comment penned on a story painstakingly written in Year 3) and refused to put 'Reasonable Adjustments' (Equality Act 2010) in place. To my request that he sit at the front or side of the class to avoid repetitively annoying another boy, the response which I later read on his file was, 'Parents can't tell teachers where children should sit'.

My youngest daughter's primary school could not cope with her behaviour issues either. She was excluded numerous times and placed at a pupil referral unit in Year 6 – four half days part time. I knew she should not be at the referral unit, but I had no other choice; she would constantly tell me she should not be there, but this was her only alternative to permanent exclusion. However, she liked being in small classes and seemed happier.

Everyone has an opinion about a child with a behaviour problem. Rather than my youngest daughter's autism being recognized and addressed, both Black and White professionals considered every reason for her behaviours but the correct one. The school's explanation of her behaviours? – attachment disorder; their assumption? – that due to my involvement with autistic children she was copying their behaviours to gain my attention.

These professionals had interpreted my daughter's behaviours through the cultural stereotypes of 'feisty Black girl', 'socioeconomic status' and 'single parent family' ('missing her dad'). They did not want to think about autism or ADHD as possible explanations because in their opinion I was diverting attention away from my youngest daughter's behaviour. That is how I was labelled; according to them, my children's behaviours were down to my parenting skills. My home has been broken and become dysfunctional because professionals did not acknowledge my children's autism and their needs and put appropriate support in place.

For my youngest daughter's and our family's sake, they should have taken the time to assess for autism early. Too many children like my daughter experience serious secondary problems caused by late diagnosis. If a professional does not understand autism or other related conditions it is important that they admit it and signpost that family to someone who can help. You cannot 'have a go' at helping a family with an autistic child, even an autistic parent, because once you have got it wrong you are left with the tragic result – a broken home.

On the flip side, there are excellent professionals – those who recognize autistic behaviours and do something constructive. Sometimes it is parents who are in denial. Many Black parents tend to ignore their able autistic children's social difficulties and well-being, and celebrate their intellectual skills. This can have a serious impact on their autistic child's future social relationships and chances of successful employment.

For many BAME communities, acceptance of autism is easier if the autistic person is either at the higher end of the spectrum (super extraordinary) or they are at the classic end of the spectrum needing 24/7 care. If they are profoundly autistic with severe learning difficulties, their behaviours are classic and clearly recognisable as autistic – the rocking, the touching, the snapping fingers or the flapping hands, the lack of eye contact and the non-verbal communication – and the community may seem to be more accepting of the diagnosis. However, the higher the autistic child's academic ability, the more insistent the detractors become.

Entrepreneurial families from Black communities would be seen to highlight an exceptionally bright child at community events with little or no mention of their condition. However, if that child is on the autism spectrum, while academically they are doing well, their social skills may be deteriorating; if unrecognized and unsupported, the child's struggles to conform socially may overwhelm them and lead to mental health issues. Even if an autistic child is doing well academically, there need to be resources to accommodate the child's autism; for example, a room where they can go when they become overloaded with the sensory stimuli, social tensions and social demands of the classroom. If not, school can become too much. Even if these children manage to hold their behaviour together at school, once home they may lash out at their families or withdraw into themselves completely. Parents may not recognise this.

## Sex, stereotyping, social media and special educational needs

In 2015 my oldest daughter left home without my consent. She was 14 years old. When she did come home in 2017 for her school graduation, I realized that, as she had been when she left, she was still very childish, still very innocent, still very naïve but then I saw a side of her I did not recognize – someone who was very needy, very tearful. To my shock, I found out she was seven months pregnant. I believed I had failed my daughter, but after speaking with her, she disclosed things that made me realize her school and those around her had failed her.

These situations happen across all cultures and communities. However, when they occur within a BAME community, many professionals interpret it unquestioningly through cultural stereotypes. In the case of the Black community, many immediately assume 'gang culture', and then the racist stereotype of Black people having highly sexualized behaviours comes into play. The lack of respect, the lack of understanding, and the stigma that I, as my daughter's mother, experienced from health professionals was as if they thought I condoned my oldest daughter's situation.

In my oldest daughter's case, professionals had jumped to those conclusions without seeking to know her history. Cultural bias had blinded them to evidence-based interpretations; in my daughter's case, her autism-associated traits – her lack of social awareness, literal thinking, and inability to interpret social situations.

As parents, we need to be very vigilant around social media for people with special needs. They can get easily caught up in abuse and exploitation – wanting to be friends with people, but not understanding social cues. Like my youngest daughter, my oldest daughter has struggled with friends.

While my daughter was living away from me, she was able to have open access to the internet. I raised concerns, but I was told that all safeguarding precautions were in place. She started to meet with new people whom I did not have a clue about. If she had been living with me, I would have made sure I kept her close to me; I know that young people, autism, and social media do not really go hand in hand. Although she did not have an autism spectrum diagnosis, I could clearly see she had social communication difficulties.

This is not a specifically Black issue. Appropriate sex education for autistic girls must be addressed across all communities. We need to approach sex education in a neurodiverse way. We need to find the middle ground between enough information and too much detail. At a House of Commons Women's Equality Party event in 2016, my youngest daughter stood in front of a packed room and announced to everyone that sex education should not be taught in primary school, because she said it was too much information (no sense of time and place!). She went on to share what she had been taught – stroking, kissing, making love: 'Mummy I can remember the images in my head …' Now imagine that for a child at the age of 10, 11 or 12 years! If I had known she had Asperger syndrome, I would have declined her attending the lessons.

When I look back over the years, my oldest daughter was very needy. She was quiet, very polite; her reports said that she lacked self-esteem. When people found out that she was pregnant, the first thing somebody said was 'How did that happen?' She was the one under people's radar; she got lost in the system, and she was taken advantage of. People say she knew what she was doing, but knowing what you are doing and being as vulnerable as she is are two different things.

I fear for autistic girls in mainstream schools. Parents need to be more socially aware, street aware, about their needs than they would be for their neurotypical daughters. Many parents believe their autistic children can live *ordinary* lives. However, this is not the case for many autistic girls who appear to 'fit in'; they need a lot of guidance and support. Do not assume that when your autistic daughter is out with her friends that she is safe; there is going to be a risk factor. If your child seems to be behaving differently from her peers, take notice of the warning signs and look into it.

My daughter's literal thinking continues to emerge as her baby son develops. Before my grandson was born, she used to say that she did not want him, as though she could change the future by thinking it would go away. She had no idea about the invasive process such a decision would mean, but, when speaking with her, I could see that friends and other people can be unkind.

More awareness and support for expectant autistic women and teens are needed. I delivered my grandson at home as my daughter was not aware that she was having contractions.

After the baby was born, she struggled to understand why she could not put off feeding the baby until she felt like it – she would say, 'But I'm too tired, Mum.'

She interpreted her baby's development by 'the book'. Her literal thinking can cause barriers. She is precise in her planning and follows the estimated developmental milestones in the handbook given to her by the midwife to the day.

If I say something to her that is a bit off track from the book, she challenges me, and will not back down. She says, 'Mum, the book says …'. I say, 'I don't care about what the book says.' People overlook that she has special needs. My grandson is one year old at the time of writing, and my daughter has had to learn how to look after and care for him fast.

There is significant and worrying research highlighting that women on the autism spectrum are at higher risk of becoming sexually victimized. A study by the Association for Child and Adolescent Mental Health (Gotby et al. 2018) found that there is almost a three-fold increased risk of coercive sexual victimization compared to women not on the spectrum.

A small-scale study (Bargiela 2016) found that 9 of 14 autistic females had been sexually abused by their partners. The first common theme was that the abuser used the 'typically unassuming and trusting nature of autistic individuals to gain control over them, and slowly and subtly, use this control for the abuser's own ends'. How many of these young women would be from BAME communities? To find this out would be difficult as BAME communities do not like to air their dirty linen in public or put shame on their family.

We have to be more vigilant. This is a major issue that needs to be addressed across all communities, but, sad to say, when tackling it within the BAME communities there is a lack of response, participation and contribution.

Talking with BAME communities about abuse and trauma remains a big challenge; then when you add in autism it becomes a greater issue. One way of targeting communities is by running groups and events hosted by professionals, representative of that community, who are trained and understand the facts of cultural diversity and difference.

'Staying Safe' programmes address these issues and engage vulnerable young girls and women including for those on the autism spectrum. They aim to build the recovery, resilience and independence of young women.

## Cultural stereotypes and vulnerability

Standing out from the crowd sets young autistic people apart, and makes them more vulnerable. From an insider perspective, I know my daughter and my son in particular do not fit in. Every community, and groups within it, have a style – of dressing, of talking, of walking – that people who 'belong' conform to. If young people are autistic and Black, others from the Black community mostly do not see the autism; they see somebody who is socially awkward without an identity. They see someone who does not fit the 'norm' expected of a young Black person, someone who does not 'dress Black' – I do not even know what that means! At times, I have had to question my children's dress sense as they do not follow the fashion trends, but my youngest daughter would try and mimic her friends' style of clothing or that on social media, which I will not allow.

Yet autistic Black young people also stand out from an outsider perspective, drawn without understanding from media perpetuated images. For example, there is a young Black boy walking down the road with a hood on his head. He looks like an average young Black boy in the road, and now he is running. Responding to the stereotype, passers-by look up and around, alert and alarmed. This could be my son, who has ADHD and autism. He would use his hood, or a baseball hat, to block out the sun, or his tinted glasses (even indoors) but, in everybody else's eyes, he has got his hood on his head, and he is someone to be wary of, a potential gang member.

If the police stop and search a young person with autism, that young person experiences immediate sensory overload. One young man on the spectrum told me of his experiences. He was angry: 'They just come up to you, grab you, encircle you, push you against the wall, and by then all your sensory overload happens, you may fight out.' When the police stopped him, they came into his personal space; they demanded eye contact ('Son, look in my eyes'), which is overwhelming for an autistic person. The young man reacted, and the police thought he was going to attack them. As the young man said, 'I don't mind getting stopped by the police but what I'd prefer is if they said, "We're going to stop you because there's been a call and you look similar to the person that's been described."'

If this had been my son, I do not know how he would have acted. The mother of this young man was a social worker, and went to the police station to talk to the sergeant in charge. This mother got it right as her son was traumatized and she wanted to know exactly what happened. The sergeant whom she spoke to had a son with autism, and he understood the young man's issues. We need people in the police station who can be parent champions, who, if somebody comes in with a diagnosis of autism or seems not to understand social cues, can signpost them to the right people. There should be police autism champions in every prison and every police station. This would minimize a lot of the misunderstanding about autism. The National Police Autism Association is an online independent support group for those affected by ASC and other related conditions. Every law firm should be aware of this organization.

More understanding of the needs and issues of autistic offenders and ex-offenders, including post-prison aftercare, is essential. When one young, autistic person I know came out of prison (he had been charged as 'guilty by association' due to his 'friends' taking advantage of his vulnerability) and returned to live with his mother, he was not the same person he had been before. He refused to leave the home, and was terrified that what happened before would happen again.

## Cultural taboos and autism

Every community needs to identify the potential clashes between an autistic individual and their own taboos, so these can be addressed, and the solutions accepted by all within that community. Families and their autistic children need to receive support, strength and understanding from their communities, not judgement, criticism and blame.

Beyond disability and autism, every community has got different taboos. If the people working in that community are not aware or sensitive to these taboos, and they give information and guidance that conflict with those taboos, the families of autistic children in that community cannot use their advice because it does not fit into their lifestyle. Autism professionals rarely have the authority to mediate with the community or advocate on behalf of a family; what is needed is an independent advocate from within that community.

Some young autistic people's sensory difficulties can clash with other, highly politicized issues. A young Muslim girl, for example, may not be able to tolerate her hijab due to the texture of the material. Although the family may understand about autism, they may need a Muslim professional or representative within their community who also understands autism and who has the authority to be heard to advocate for them. Such an advocate could explain to the community why that autistic girl may reject wearing a hijab; that she is not being difficult or Westernized or disrespecting her family and culture.

Christian church taboos around autism and disability is another issue. Some congregations also refuse to accept a child's autism and its impact. There can be misunderstanding and breakdown in communication to the point where other church members will challenge the parents about the child's behaviour and blame it on demonic spirits or question the parents' faith. When this happens, the family may decline returning to church, keeping the child at home: This rejection leads to further isolation of families and their autistic child. Thankfully, other congregations are more accepting.

## Conclusion

In my opinion the issues for people with autism in BAME communities are no different to those in other communities. In each of our communities, people with autism and their families have to fight stigma and stereotypes. What is different is how cultural and religious perspectives shape each community's response to autism. One way of overcoming culture-driven perspectives is for families to go to professional and autism organization events (e.g. local autism groups, the National Autistic Society, Autistica, Royal Society of Medicine, university events) where they can ask the questions they need to and deepen their understanding of autism. It is through these events that I learned about autism and met autistic adults.

Families of autistic children from BAME communities can easily become isolated in their community bubble. Therefore, the topics that are discussed and decisions that are made within the wider autistic community are culturally one sided. Organizations need to outreach to BAME communities, but if this is done as a consultation, a forum, a sit-down meeting, many families are not interested; it is not their 'norm' and they do not feel included and accepted at these kinds of gathering. However, if gatherings were more like a festival with entertainment, music, food, with BAME autism community representation in the event organization and community outreach, autism organizations would find that the BAME autistic communities would be more likely to attend. At least, that is what I have learned, and I run a lot of ASC events.

On occasions, I have been asked if I would run some groups for Black mothers of autistic children. However, I have already mentioned the difficulties at the beginning of the chapter – for which community? Each culture has different needs and perspectives. Then there are families with dual racial heritage. Depending on the strength of ties to different sides of the family, their culture may be different. A family situation may be atypical; for example, a single father bringing up an autistic girl child. They all need differently orientated support.

It can be very different when dealing with the other communities because of the language barriers. There may be shared culture, the faith, the beliefs, but if you do not have that language connection, that community is being lost because they have no insider representation. We need somebody in all these communities with personal links to autism who is willing to speak out in their community. I share only because of what I have been through with my children, so when people ask, 'How do you know that?' I say, 'It's because I've gone through it personally.'

Identifying the needs of and outreaching to BAME autistic individuals and their families is ongoing in its complexity, and the lack of resources available for the county and borough councils to provide for them is a massive challenge. Each council has different resources. However, if all councils in one area or one region came together, I think that they could bridge all the gaps. But would they dare to do this? I do not think so.

People should not be scared to say 'I'm autistic and Black' because, when people say autistic, Black and White, is the same, it is not. This is the same for all BAME communities. I have not 'lived White', but I've grown up in a White society. However, for somebody who has never understood this lifestyle, it is very hard to live in this world. It is the same with relating to an autistic person and their family in their own culture, we cannot imagine how somebody lives in their world, if we do not understand it. Similarly, we may understand the autism to an extent, but when professionals and advocates go into that family home, we can only ask what may work for that family. It does not mean it is going to work, because the cultural dynamic is something they have got to look at – that is the difference. We have to make sure we are outreaching with the right package for them, not what we think as professionals or service providers. That's what it is.

## References

'Living with autism – Nathaniel's Story' (video), available at www.youtube.com/watch?v=nHfBxfh-mGo

'Autism awareness call', *The Voice* (article in which Kirsty Osei-Bempong talks to Venessa Bobb), available at www.voice-online.co.uk/article/autism-awareness-call

# References and selected further reading

Association for Child and Adolescent Mental Health ( 2018)

Bargiela, S., Steward, R. and Mandy, W. (2016) 'The experiences of late-diagnosed women with autism spectrum conditions: an investigation of the female autism phenotype', *Journal of Autism and Developmental Disorders*, 46(10), 3281–3294 (doi: doi:10.1007/s10803-016-2872-8).

Burkett, K., Morris, E., Manning-Courtney, P., Anthony, J. and Shambley-Ebron, D. (2015) 'African American families on autism diagnosis and treatment: the influence of culture', *Journal of Autism and Developmental Disorders*, 45, 3244–3254.

Corbett, C. and Perepa, P. (2007) *Missing Out: Autism, Education and Ethnicity – the Reality for Families Today*. London: National Autistic Society.

Gotby, V. O., Lichtenstein, P., Långström, N. and Pettersen, E. (2018) 'Childhood neurodevelopmental disorders and risk of coercive sexual victimization in childhood and adolescence: a population-based prospective twin study', *Journal of Child Psychology and Psychiatry*, 59(9), 957–965.

Hannon, M. D. (2017) 'Acknowledging intersectionality: an autoethnography of a Black school counselor, educator and father of a student with autism', *Journal of Negro Education*, 86(2), 154–162.

Jamison, J. M., Fourie, E., Siper, P. M., Trelles, M. P., George-Jones, J., Grice, A. B., et al. (2017), 'Examining the efficacy of a family peer advocate model for Black and Hispanic caregivers of children with autism spectrum disorder', *Journal of Autism and Developmental Disorders*, 47, 1314–1322.

Mair, S. (2015) *A Study of the Experiences and Perceptions of Parents of Black and Minority Ethnic Pupils Statemented with Autism in Relation to the Educational Support Provided for their Children and for Themselves*. Thesis. Cardiff: Cardiff Metropolitan University.

Slade, G. (2014) *Diverse Perspectives: The Challenges for Families Affected by Autism from Black, Asian and Minority Ethnic Communities*. London: National Autistic Society.

# Chapter 7

# Girls Group

## Respecting the female identity of girls with autism in a school setting

*Sharonne Horlock*

---

I am a riddle – I heard them discussing it. I am puzzled. I am a problem. I try so hard to watch, to listen, to work it out, get it right. I get it wrong every single day – my detentions prove it. I am ignored or, worse, laughed at. I think I am bullied but they say it's banter. I like routine but the routine keeps changing and they don't tell me why. I find not knowing frightening. I find the loudness of the dripping noises reassuring but then get told off for daydreaming. I find the sunlight reflecting on my desk pricks my eyes but the teacher won't move me. I find rocking soothing but they call me weird so I try not to. I lash out instead but then get into more trouble. I am bewildered most of the time. I know I am the problem.

These comments made by girls with autism in 'Girls Group' (a school-based support group for autistic girls that I facilitate) clearly demonstrate the need for teachers, senior leaders and school communities to know more, understand and appreciate autism within girls.

Girls are missing out on much-needed support, and formal diagnosis is frequently essential to access support. Frequently there is no support beyond diagnosis. Too frequently girls with autism are missed.

I am not autistic. I think that is an important statement to make. This contribution is written from a personal teaching perspective. I am a special educational needs co-ordinator (SENCo). I am proud of being a SENCo.

Actually I have a fancy new title – 'strategic leader of special educational needs and/or disability' – and work for a multi-academy trust. I have qualifications deemed appropriate to do my job. I have contributed to a successful bid to build and open a 'free school'[1] specifically for children with autism. I have presented at conferences. I am a friend, and some of my friends are autistic. I am a parent. One of my amazing children is a beautiful talented daughter who has a diagnosis of Asperger syndrome. Diagnosis came late, at 18 years. Sometimes this has helped me professionally; sometimes this has not helped at all. But, what I am very aware of, and what I do know, is that autism and gender do not detract from each individual's breath-taking uniqueness. Autism is not a box to shut tight but a portfolio of strengths and weaknesses to be discovered, held and accepted.

## Girls are different

Increasing questions about the true numbers of girls with autism are being raised but within the setting I work although numbers are increasing, girls with a formal diagnosis are still vastly outnumbered by boys. This has very real consequences, as girls are different. Girls are a whole different gender after all.

Hence, Girls Group happened because the girls necessitated it. They wanted a gender specific group; they did not want boys. They needed a space to share, collaborate, and learn from one another in confronting their difference. They needed acceptance by people who 'got it'. They wanted a non-judgemental space.

Meeting weekly, the girls, between 11 and 17 years old, each have a diagnosis of autism. The group was initially supported by a teaching assistant and the SENCo. Both have completed additional autism specific training, and both are motivated to hear, to share, to guide, to try various strategies and tactics and to learn.

Participation in the group is through invitation and therefore voluntary; no invitation has yet been declined. Commitment and attendance is unwavering. Time spent together is largely unstructured although common aspects include a reciprocal welcome, drink and biscuit and lots of talk. This is not a place where challenge does not happen. The girls challenge themselves and one another regularly.

It is essential that we understand and accept that girls have autism too.

## Welcome

Difference is a single word. A plethora of difference.

'I am different; I don't fit in' is a common assertion by the girls.

'She was always different to the others [siblings]', recollect several parents.

'She was unwilling to make friends and struggled to fit in, then blamed the others for teasing her', commented a previous teacher.

The girls came to Girls Group understanding difference as idiosyncrasy, peculiarity and a lack of conformity. Over time, gradually, and meandering together, the girls explore difference as distinction, exception and delicious diversity.

And yet … experience of difference impacts on every aspect of their lives and the lives of those who care for them, who live with them, who want the very best for them. Difference leads to individual (collective) experiences of being laughed at: the hidden comments behind hands must be sniggering, unkind; quick darting looks intended to belittle; getting into trouble where no offence was intended; isolation, discrimination and mistreatment. It is true that the girls may not easily recognize the intention of others but bullying does happen. It is not an imaginary foe or friendly banter. It hurts. It stings. It is there.

Girls Group encourages a frank exchange of experiences, helps minimize feelings of isolation, builds confidence and self-esteem as the girls' successes are celebrated.

## The wrong path

Several of the girls had undergone educational and/or medical assessments that identified specific difficulties and challenges. One has previously been diagnosed with dyspraxia, hearing delay, developmental language disorder and dyslexia. Another has been described as having attention-deficit disorder, auditory processing disorder, speech, language and communication needs, dyslexia (which was later refuted by another specialist teacher) and severe depression. There appears to be a comprehensive lack of communication between medical and educational professionals that may contribute to a 'missed diagnosis'. Autism is frequently not mentioned and therefore presumably not given consideration.

It is not uncommon to learn that families and girls with autism were not heard for whatever reason, even when parents raised autism as a possible diagnosis or described similar behaviours in relatives with autism. Meetings with education professionals were often a result of their daughter's aberrant behaviour and the effect on the learning and progress of others. Wisdoms shared by some professionals with these families determined that their daughter was the problem.

A first step therefore is to listen, hear, and if accessible reflect on all relevant information before providing a comprehensive précis for colleagues.

## On the edge

The girls and their families demanded a diagnosis that 'fitted' or 'described our daughter', and in some cases they spent several years relentlessly seeking.

Formal diagnosis is not a must to participate in the group. Achieving a diagnosis post-primary stage is burdened with challenge, pervasive misunderstanding, extremely limited funding and contrasting agendas of different services. Access to effective provision appears to be a long, tedious, uphill path if it exists at all. Persistently damaging anxiety or severe mental illness (suicide risk) can open a door but why should girls and young women need to spiral downwards before help is given?

Education often sends families to the family doctor who often then refers them back to education. School may not have the expertise to recognize that a referral is essential and assert 'It's a home issue' or, worse, ignore parents'/carers' concerns: 'She doesn't behave like that at school.'

Autism is a medical diagnosis. It is preposterous that often it is the responsibility of the SENCo (who may have limited experience) to complete the referral paperwork, which in turn germinates more forms requiring families to present their narrative yet again. It is not uncommon for parents/carers to arrive at a meeting with several box files of information. Parental/carer comments reflect and determine lifelong patterns of behavioural characteristics: 'She has always been like this,' 'Her way or no way ever since she was tiny,' 'Has never appeared to understand or been able to follow simple rules,' 'Meltdowns are not temper tantrums; she can wreck the house now she is bigger,' 'Friendships have always been difficult.'

Why then is a diagnosis not made earlier? Were the girls' autistic traits less evident when they were younger? Were they simply not recognized? Are primary schools better equipped at supporting girls with autism? The girls and their families (often including grandparents) suggest 'not necessarily'.

Secondary school is not primary school. The route to school is often longer and may require a bus journey. The buildings are invariably bigger. Senses may become overwhelming. There are more teachers and more students. Social interactions become increasingly difficult. Endless scrutiny and imitation of behaviour is laborious and exhausting, precipitating more opportunities to 'get it wrong'. Humiliation. Anxiety heightens. Eccentricity is no longer deemed 'cute' or 'acceptable'. There is less tolerance for unusual behaviours. Relationship dynamics change, and previous friends may move on and away. Puberty and hormonal changes, with an increasing focus on mood, hygiene, bodily changes and sexual feelings can be difficult to appreciate and manage. The lack of apposite skills, confidence and intuition can lead to frequent skirmishes with inflexible behaviour policies. Adolescence and growing feelings of 'not fitting in' can become an acropolis dividing girls with autism (diagnosed or not) from peers.

Post-primary school transition should be flexible, carefully planned, begin as early as possible and include the student, family and current setting. Meeting key staff at local schools, sharing and promoting key characteristics of girls with autism, attending annual reviews as early as Year 5, being accessible to potential families and discussing honestly potential provision is helpful to enable effective collaborative relationships. Endeavour to provide an educational journey based on effective communication; understand that behaviour is symptomatic of underlying difficulties; and establish strategies that help.

## Diagnosis: a perspective

Early diagnosis is essential and can be linked with better outcomes. Yet diagnosis labels, and for some this is hugely negative and finite. Again and again some carers, families and professionals ask, 'Why label?' Diagnosis is not a quandary, a predicament and is most definitely not a 'no win situation'. Labels should not limit the potential of an individual or the ability to achieve that potential. Not understanding who you are, not knowing why you sense a difference about yourself, not being able to effectively interact, not being able to self-advocate, not liking yourself, not being easily able to develop and own a personal portfolio of strengths and weaknesses is an unacceptable reality for far too many. Diagnosis as a label informs and describes.

Each individual member of the Girls Group own and welcome their label. These include 'high functioning autism', 'Asperger syndrome', 'autistic', and 'autistic characteristics'. Each continues to live with autism. They always will. All are maturing into increasingly caring, intelligent, wonderful young women who connect; and experience stimulating and thought-provoking friendships. Together they are awe-inspiring.

Autism is not something the girls talk about endlessly each week but it is frequently discussed. Each have firmly expressed that diagnosis has been invaluable to better know themselves and helps them to develop an effective strategy toolkit to navigate the confusing world around them. They accept one another. Each girl has their own interests, strengths, family backgrounds. Anna is a computer geek, spending hours and hours on the computer, game playing and creating programs. Meg is a scientist, constantly asking questions beginning with 'why'. She is interested and wishes to learn about her condition, enjoying exploring from a neuroscientific perspective. Jenny is a musician.

Understanding and recognizing the female characteristics of Autism is essential. nasen's booklet *Girls and Autism: Flying under the Radar* (available at www.nasen.org.uk/resources/resources.girls-and-autism-flying-under-the-radar.html) provides an excellent starting point. Training for teachers and whole school staff is crucial but not enough. Effective flexible support is a corporate responsibility, should be proactively used, reviewed, personalized and embedded in whole school practices.

## *Jenny*

Since receiving a diagnosis of autism Jenny appears more content and more able to ask for help to manage when feeling unsure or overwhelmed. Jenny asked that possible potential changes in daily routine are discussed in advance. A perfectionist, Jenny asked to be given a half-termly overview of topics to be studied in some subjects that she finds more difficult. This allows more time for processing information and identifying potentially difficult areas of study. It also provides improved opportunities to be prepared and supported at home and by her form tutor.

Jenny's mother comments that Jenny is happier, and school morning routines are easier, now Jenny feels more in control of her daily routine. Jenny is increasingly willing to interact with siblings and spend time away from her computer. Jenny says, 'I know who I am now. Autism is part of me and it's okay.'

## Anxiety

The girls are emotionally vulnerable. Most have described episodes of meltdown, extreme anxiety, self-harming behaviours, a lack of self-worth and little confidence. Triggers are varied and include raised voices, sarcasm (perceived or otherwise), comments made about physical appearance or characteristics, untrue comments, conversational topics that change too quickly, being mimicked, not being listened to, being asked a question in class, being directed to try out new activities, and change.

The girls regularly discuss, explore, and practise strategies for recognizing and managing anxiety. There are ways to reduce the anxiety; except, in the moment, anxiety can spiral, can demarcate every step, seep into every body part and debilitate. 'The perfect dress may not be perfect. It may not fit. I will stand out. The dress is not perfect. It does not fit. People are staring. They are staring because I look stupid.' Why are these the first thoughts that come? The biggest thoughts? The only thoughts? Once again, one of the girls is trapped on a speeding roundabout, dizzy with despair.

### Evie

It is difficult to determine how Evie is feeling; her facial expressions are frequently inscrutable, and she rarely using gestures. Her body language can seem immature, inappropriate for her age but it rarely presents as anxiety. Rather she behaves impulsively, engages in repetitive behaviours such as constant tapping or calling out and so distracts others. Controlling the rate, pitch and volume of speech is difficult for her. Working collaboratively is rarely productive.

Evie was frequently in detention. All her teachers and support staff were invited to a meeting (sandwiches, cakes and tea/coffee provided) to discuss how anxiety affected her and showed itself in unusual ways. Her student profile (A4 information sheet) was shared and the included strategies discussed. Teachers were reminded to prepare Evie for change to the lesson routine, seating plan and classroom environment; to use a lesson planning sheet so that Evie understood explicitly each activity and whether there was choice available. Evie was able to use an exit card to stand outside the classroom for a few minutes to self-calm if she needed. Evie's detentions became increasingly fewer as teachers made flexible reasonable adjustments.

### Dani

Dani attended the Prom following much soul searching, argument at home, discussion, planning and finding the perfect dress. It was a primary source of conversation and debate at Girls Group for weeks, and began almost a year before the event.

On the night Dani looked gorgeous, but the evening began with a spat over the taking of a photograph. As any proud parent is adamant in the recording of this special moment, Dani was equally adamant there would be no photograph. The evening began in a maelstrom of emotion.

A three-course, sit-down meal delivered by smartly dressed waiters and waitresses was followed by short speeches and dances. Dani had experience and knew what to expect but still did not know how to behave. Noise, a persistent beat and the bright flashing lights did not bother her but the social aspect, not knowing how to behave and not easily 'fitting in' did.

However, when not fully understanding social norms or feeling ill at ease, Dani regularly employed the strategy of fulfilling a self-chosen role. At prom, this role was 'associate teaching assistant' helping other students with additional needs who found the reverberating noise, flashing lights and alien atmosphere too much.

'Everyone should attend their prom.' This had been a current conversational theme in the staffroom. I am not convinced. Everyone should, however, have the opportunity of attending their prom, or any other extra-curricular social event they wish to.

Preparation is clearly useful. Perusing previous years' photographs, clarifying the dress code (usually but not exclusively, long dresses) is essential. Who does not feel anxious about what to wear? But the girls' description of anxiety is so confining that it does not go away and often prevents them from participating in an activity they had previously looked forward to.

Once again, family relationships and dynamics can be tested. It is not unusual for an adolescent to have words with their parent in a shop when trying on clothes; a meltdown is a palpable possibility. Again, preparation can be useful in finding a smaller, autism-friendly shop and/or looking online to narrow down the choice. One student spent literally hundreds of pounds of her parents' money ordering 17 dresses to try on at home, missing the return date for a full monetary refund. More anxiety.

Mindful preparation for the prom itself again can be useful. Arranging to meet a friend and being seated on the edge of the room can help. People are not really staring. A discreet prompt from an adult may help. People are thinking, 'My dress looks good.' I will respond with a smile and say, 'Hello. Your dress is lovely.'

## Only connect

Friendships are difficult. Friendship implies association, connection, closeness, a relationship. And yet the girls frequently describe distance, separation, isolation and lonely difference. The theme of friendships is endless, persistently confusing. Friendship unescapably involves social interactions that are complex, unpredictable and anxiety-provoking. Similarly the girls prefer to interact with one or two friends at a time rather than a crowd. All the girls in the group experience difficulty maintaining equitable friendships. All find friendship a challenging concept.

A typical consideration for the girls is as follows:

'I wish I had some friends; a friend.'
'I heard you were going to a birthday party this weekend?'
'Yes.'
'Whose party?'
'Sabine's.'

'Is she a friend?'

'No, I've known her since primary but she goes to a different school now though.'

'I think she is a friend. Why would she invite you if she did not count you a friend? She didn't need to invite you.'

'Really? Is she? How do I know?'

Certainty is yearned for, but relationships are not always clear. They flow and ebb; they change and develop; they can involve dispute. Debate often signals an ending. 'I am never going to speak to you again,' honest and resolute. The disagreement is explored in detail. The argument is re-visited over and over again. It is taken into lesson. It is carried through lunch. It is taken home. It becomes self-deprecating anxiety.

Strategies to make, maintain and recognize friendship are talked about, dissected, practised in the safe space of the Girls Group. Successes are shared. Jenny telephoned another member of the group, and they went shopping. Together they planned the journey, decided in advance which shops to visit and when to come home.

Another accepted an invitation to a party that involved watching a film at the cinema, something she had never done before. Before the party, the girls who had been to the cinema shared their experiences including potential issues such as needing the toilet in the middle of the film.

Social skill workshops are helpful but need to specifically address and answer the questions, the worries and individual experiences as they arise. Delivering a prescribed set of lessons lacks the flexibility to be responsive and may miss opportunities.

### Anna

Anna had been (again) extremely distracted in an English class. She had barely engaged with any of the classroom activities, swung back and forth on her chair, and had subsequently failed to complete her written work. Issued with an 'invitation' to return at lunchtime to 'catch up' had left her feeling aggrieved and angry. These feelings were carried into Science where distraction quickly became loud agitation. Again, she got into trouble with her teacher for her 'lack of focus' and 'unwillingness to pay attention'.

Arriving at Girls Group she eloquently enunciated her intense frustration at teachers who 'hated her'. The majority of the girls had their own stories to share of teachers, peers and others who 'hated' them and regularly dispensed unjust detentions. The choice of vocabulary was compelling. The strength of frustration was debilitating. Talk, breathe, calm, find a solution.

English always seemed to trigger anomalous behaviours in Anna. Except it did not; sitting by the window in sunlight underneath the bright electric light did. Anna described the shooting pain in her eyes causing her head to scream. Charlotte suggested Anna ask for some glasses with coloured lenses, explaining that she had some at home and they worked really well. When asked why she did not wear them at school Charlotte replied that not only had she been told off for wearing sunglasses in school but that some of her peers had made unkind comments.

Listening to, and hearing the girls enabled Anna to work out for herself why English was a difficult lesson. It enabled better communication with staff. It allowed for a whole-school discussion around sensory sensitivities providing for a better understanding among all students and a growing acceptance of, for example, the wearing of earphones and ear defenders in class. Advise, action, actualize.

## Educational journey

Raising awareness of autism in girls is crucial. It is not a single assembly or a stand-alone training session. Consciously plan, consciously challenge, consciously promote dialogue and debate. Unpack stereotypical thinking about autism. Begin at the top, with senior leadership and with governors. Pronounce loudly the inclusive ethos. Expect everyone to hear: accept difference; welcome; quality education is inclusion, participation and excellence.

Excellence is innovative, perceptive, and celebrates individuality. Each child becomes the best possible version of themselves, and the best version of themselves changes and develops as they grow. This is success. This is outstanding.

## A message

The bracing honesty of Girls Group resonates. Their advice is simple yet powerful:

- Create a Girls Group.
- Listen, hear and believe us.
- Train teachers better to understand.
- Get to know me.
- Include me.
- Simple strategies work best.

There is much work to be done to ensure the professional development of colleagues is good enough, to ensure that characteristics are recognized and responded to robustly and sensitively. The journey continues.

## Note

1  In England, a free school is one that is set up by an organization or a group of individuals and is funded by the government but is not controlled by a local authority.

# Part III

# Girls, autism and education

## What we want the world to know

Girls of Limpsfield Grange School

### *Anxiety...*

'I get anxious and I feel like my brain is going to explode. People say "Stop being anxious! Don't be so autistic!" It's like telling me not to breathe.'

(Scarlett, Year 9)

'When I have a bad day and I feel worried, I take it home and then I have a bad time at home.'

(Poppy, Year 7)

'A big part of autism is anxiety. People need to understand that anxiety can affect you in different ways. Some people want to let their anxiety out and about and scream until they feel better; others want to curl up in a ball and cry. Some of us are unable to talk about how we feel, and just need people to tell that that everything is going to be OK.'

(Daisy, Year 10)

'When I am really anxious I get a terrible tummy ache and I feel really tensed up inside.'

(Molly, Year 10)

### *...Anxiety*

'When I get anxious I get very upset, and think negative thoughts. I can't concentrate and I have meltdowns where I physically shut down and I can't focus.'

(Abbey, Year 10)

'When I'm scared or anxious I feel like it is not me; I can't think. My head goes empty and I just lose control. I can't explain my feelings to anyone, I bottle them up and they all come out at home, because I am safe there.'

(Erin, Year 7)

'Whenever I have an anxiety attack I break down in floods of tears; I feel like I am no longer myself.'

(Isha, Year 9)

Part II

Girls, autism and education

# Chapter 8

# Leadership issues in the current educational climate

*Rona Tutt*

## Defining the current climate

The last few years have been an interesting time for children and young people who have special educational needs and/or disabilities (SEND), their families and those who support them. It has been a time when a spotlight has been shone on this group of young learners due to the implementation and embedding of the SEND reforms. By far the largest group whose needs are significant enough to require an Education, Health and Care Plan (EHCP) are pupils who have a diagnosis of autism. In a relatively short space of time, autism has gone from being described as a low incidence need to one of the most common. Until recently, it has been accepted that boys with autism far outnumber girls, but evidence is growing that the number of girls may have been significantly underestimated (Hendrickx 2015; Happé 2016).

Central to the SEND reforms (Department for Education 2010; Department for Education 2011) which form part three of the Children and Families Act (Her Majesty's Government 2014) and are enshrined in the SEND Code of Practice (Department for Education/Department of Health 2015), is the principle that the wishes, views and aspirations of young learners and their families should lie at the heart of making the decisions that affect their lives. At one time, people were content to let professionals decide what was in their best interests. Today, there is an expectation of a much more personalized approach. In terms of the SEND reforms, this means the professionals involved working alongside young people and their parents rather than telling them what decisions they have made on their behalf.

Unfortunately, the aim of personalising the experience of young learners has been made harder to achieve by successive governments' focus on what they see as the way to raise standards in schools. Far from being able to personalize the curriculum to some degree, this has resulted in a narrowing of the curriculum and a testing regime that treats schools, and the pupils within them, with little regard for their individual situations. Instead, all mainstream schools are judged as if they had similar populations and their pupils are expected to achieve similar standards by set ages. Special schools are also expected to keep detailed records of individual progress, but there is greater flexibility in how this is recorded.

The emphasis on a narrow range of academic achievements, as the yardstick by which schools and their pupils are judged, has placed school leaders in the invidious position of trying to deliver what is right for their pupils while achieving the results the government expects, and, without which, a school's future may be put at risk. Although children with SEND cover the whole of the ability range, those who are cognitively able are likely to have other factors that impede their progress. This is very evident in the case of those on the autism spectrum who range from those who have profound and multiple learning difficulties (PMLD) to those who will be among the most academically able, yet may still struggle to learn within the social setting of a school.

In 2010, when changes to the SEN system were first mooted, the context looked very different. Since then, the dual effect of austerity and more schools becoming academies, which removes them from local authority (LA) control, has contributed to a shortage of SEN support teams, specialist advisory teachers and educational psychologists, who, along with speech and language therapists, physiotherapists, occupational therapists and other health professionals can make so much difference to the lives of pupils who have SEND, including those who have autism.

## The relevance of the SEND reforms

At the heart of the SEND reforms is the principle that the outcomes the family wants should guide the arrangements that are put in place for the child. Schools are well aware that the most effective way of influencing the child's development and progress is made by home and school working together. This is particularly significant when a girl who is on the autism spectrum is involved, as behaviour at home and at school may be very different, for reasons that will be discussed later.

### SEN support, EHCPs and personal budgets

The reforms divide children with SEND into the majority who are placed on SEN support (currently around 11.6%) and those who receive an EHCP, the process which has replaced a Statement of SEN (Department for Education/Department of Health 2015; Tutt and Williams 2015). These more complex young people represent 2.8% of the school population. EHCPs should be co-produced with the family and reflect the desired outcomes. To emphasize the importance of the family's role, the government has brought in the option of personal budgets, which although known in social care, for instance through short breaks for carers of children with SEND (Sibthorp and Nicoll 2014), and in some aspects of health, have not previously featured in education (Tutt 2016a). Although personal budgets are not available for those on SEN support, the approach of person-centred planning and the importance of co-production are similar.

### The local offer and SEN information report

Under the reforms, every LA has to produce a web-based resource known as a local offer, detailing the provision it makes for children and young people aged 0–25 years with SEND, while schools have to publish an SEN information report explaining the support they give to pupils with special needs. Both of these should include what is available to children and young adults on the autism spectrum.

### Local area SEND reviews

To check that every local area is embedding the SEND reforms, the Care Quality Commission (CQC) and Ofsted have been inspecting every one of the 152 local authorities. At the time of writing, over 50 inspections have been carried out and well over a third of these have been required to produce a written statement of action because of significant concerns about their practice. It is striking how many of these mention autism as one of the area's weaknesses. Typical comments from the inspectors have been:

- 'There is a high level of parental dissatisfaction around how the needs of children and young people with autism are met.'
- 'The autistic spectrum disorder (ASD) strategy has taken far too long to be developed.'
- 'There are significant weaknesses in the local area's arrangements for completing specialist diagnostic assessments of ASD.'
- 'Assessments for autism and attention-deficit/hyperactivity disorder (ADHD) are taking too long and delays are increasing.'
- '[The local area] has a much higher proportion of pupils identified as having moderate learning difficulties than the English average and the recorded proportion of pupils with autistic spectrum disorder is smaller than the national average.'
- 'Professionals from the local area acknowledge that the accuracy of assessment and the recording of need must improve.'
- 'Children and young people who have ADHD and ASD are not identified quickly enough because their presentation is assumed to be a behavioural issue rather than a presentation of need.'

In these inspections, special schools have been seen as being effective in meeting the needs of pupils on the autism spectrum, while mainstream schools are sometimes said to lack the knowledge to provide for these pupils. This goes back to the point mentioned earlier about mainstream schools having less flexibility than their colleagues in special schools to gear the curriculum and its assessment to the needs of their pupils.

## The negative effect of the assessment and accountability system

From the time the UK National Curriculum was invented in 1988, it has undergone a series of changes, first of all to make it more manageable and, more recently, to make it more 'stretching' as the government would say. As well as piling pressure on both teachers and taught, this has opened up a wider gap between those who can cope and pupils who struggle to keep up with the pace. As the curriculum becomes tougher, so do the tests, yet schools are supposed to demonstrate that their results are continually improving.

Although governments have paid lip service to the dangers of too much testing, and some tests have been removed, others have crept in. An example of this has been the phonics screening check which children take at the end of Year 1 (at 6 years old). This assumes that everyone learns to read in the same way. Yet those on the autism spectrum are generally thought of as visual learners who have very good memories and so may learn to recognize whole words much more easily than learning the 44 sounds of the English language in isolation and then being able to blend them to make words. In any case, as English is said to be the one of the most irregular languages in Europe, an over-reliance on phonics is not necessarily very helpful. As half the test is composed of non-words (such as glig, strock, quend, etc.), more able readers have been known to fail the test, as they realize reading is about getting meaning from the printed page (or screen) and so they try to turn the nonsense words into ones that make sense, for which they are marked down.

While this kind of pressure is not good for any pupil, it is particularly tough on pupils with SEND and, perhaps, even tougher on those with autism, who may already have high levels of anxiety simply by being in the social setting of a school. Girls who are on the spectrum may be harder hit than boys because they are more likely to be concerned about keeping up with their peers and conforming to expectations.

## What school leaders can do to further the cause of girls with autism

As greater awareness is developing that girls with autism have been under-diagnosed, it is important that school leaders ensure their staff are aware of the need to look out for girls who may be on the autism spectrum. Under the SEND reforms, special educational needs co-ordinators (SENCos) are given a more strategic role, while all teachers, whether class or subject-based, have responsibility for the progress of all the pupils they teach, including those who have special needs. Depending on the age range of the pupils and the size of the school, the head teacher and senior leadership team (SLT) may or may not be directly involved with the identification of those who have SEND, but the responsibility for making sure this happens comes from the top.

## Helping to spot girls who may have autism

Unless they also have significant learning difficulties or some other co-existing condition, girls are likely to be identified later than boys. So, teachers throughout the age range need to be aware of the subtler signs of autism that girls may display, as they are inclined to mask their symptoms in an effort to be like the girls around them. Looking back on their school days, several women on the spectrum have remarked that they did not feel able to be themselves, which was a source of considerable and unrelenting strain on them.

### Signs and symptoms

Autistic girls may go out of their way to keep a low profile and to achieve this by watching carefully what their peers are doing and then following their lead. They may not resist making eye contact – although some will prefer using peripheral vision as less overwhelming. They may appear to be sociable. Yet, closer observation may reveal that they are more likely to be on the edge of friendship groups, moving from one to another without really joining in. Alternatively, they may have one very close friend whom they are unwilling to share.

The language they use may seem quite advanced and not stand out as different. Yet, observing a girl with autism more closely may reveal that she seldom answers questions because of her concern about giving a wrong answer. Her way of speaking may seem stilted and unnatural. She may be slow to respond if spoken to directly as she needs time to process language and to think of the right reply. Unlike the rather bizarre interests of some autistic boys, her interests may be similar to those of other girls, but they will absorb more of her time than those of her peers and change less often.

Of course, every autistic girl, in common with every non-autistic girl, will have her own personality which will influence how she behaves. Whether or not she also has significant learning difficulties or some other co-existing condition will again make a difference. Having said that, there does seem to be a pattern emerging that indicates the under-diagnosis of girls has been partly due to a pattern of presentation that is often different from boys on the autism spectrum and is less easy to recognize.

## Reducing anxiety and increasing enjoyment

It has often been said that the more complex a child's needs, the more society should be prepared to adapt the environment for them rather than expecting them to fit in with what is provided for the majority. School is not a natural environment for many on the autism spectrum. It is a place full of noise, lots of people and an abundance of change: different lessons, different classrooms, different staff, plus unexpected events.

### Sensory issues

It was mentioned earlier that autism is sometimes missed because it is seen as a behavioural issue rather than a presentation of need. One way of looking behind, beneath and beyond the behaviour of a girl who has autism, or is suspected of needing a diagnosis, is the use of sensory profiles. As is well known, many of those on the spectrum, as well as reacting negatively to sensory overload, can be hyposensitive (under sensitive) or hypersensitive in one or more ways. Being aware of what a pupil finds distressing and seeing what can be done about it can make an enormous difference to reducing anxiety, which is known to inhibit learning.

Sara hated loud noises. Even seeing a balloon would have her rushing from the room in case it burst. Over time staff worked with her, first of all to get her to accept that not every balloon will go pop and then to stay in the same room as one. Later, she could cope with a balloon popping if warned in advance that it was going to do so. For others, various kinds of music can be calming.

At first, Maryam's teachers at her Junior School did not understand why she would leave her seat and wander to the side of the room, giving the impression of not following what was going on. When they realized that, despite appearances, she was more able to pay attention and respond to questions when using peripheral vision, rather than feeling overwhelmed and distracted by being expected to make eye contact, they were happy for her to behave in this way.

### Understanding emotions

It is accepted that those on the autism spectrum find it hard to read emotional states in others or to understand their own feelings (Critchley 2016; Steward 2014). When she was at infant school, Paula coped quite well with the curriculum, but had great difficulty in sharing. She decided that the school's doll's pram should be hers and tried to grab it every time she went out for play. If someone got there first, she was inconsolable. As she progressed to the Junior School, time was spent on helping her to understand emotions. The breakthrough came when she had the vocabulary to explain how she was feeling and was able to say, 'I'm cross,' rather than having an outburst. Older girls may develop a better sense of how they are feeling and find their own ways of coping. For instance, Evie was clear that, while she could not talk about how she was feeling, she felt able to cope if she wrote down how she felt, while Thea would get rid of her anger by pummelling a pillow or cushion.

The approach these girls need, whether in helping them to come to terms with sensory issues or understanding emotions, is one of flexibility. Insisting on conformity to the point where it causes anxiety should be avoided unless it is incompatible with their learning or that of their peers. Maya would not leave the playground unless she was allowed to put all the outside vehicles in a neat line before returning to class. Confrontation was avoided by letting her have her way until there came a time when she herself was happy to abandon this routine. For others, flexibility may entail having frequent short breaks during the day when they can gain some relief from being constantly on the alert. Being allowed to listen to nursery rhymes, sitting alone with a favourite book, or having short bursts of physical activity, will increase the enjoyment of school and lessen anxiety.

School leaders and SENCos (who may or may not be part of the senior leadership team depending on the organization within the school), may have to work hard to help staff appreciate that minor adjustments can make a very real difference. Of course there are limits to how flexible teachers can be, but with a greater awareness of the advantages of taking a more personalized approach, combined with getting to know each autistic girl by observing her behaviour, school can be made a less overwhelming and more enjoyable experience.

## Creating a welcoming ethos and an inclusive environment

While school leaders are the ones to set the tone in making sure their school or setting is as welcoming as possible to pupils who have SEND, it is unrealistic to expect that every educational establishment will be able to meet the needs of every pupil who may be put forward to attend. In the case of pupils on the autism spectrum, it is not just a question of whether the school has the capacity to cope with the child, but whether the child feels able to cope with the environment of that school. Having said that, the majority of pupils on the autism spectrum, along with those who have other kinds of SEND, will be supported in mainstream classes (All Party Parliamentary Group on Autism 2017; Department for Education 2017).

Although there are people who still believe that inclusion is about *every* child being educated in a mainstream school, the divisive debates that took place around this topic in the 1980s and 1990s have largely subsided (Ofsted 2010; Tutt 2016b; Warnock 2005). 'Inclusion' should be seen as a process rather than a place and the test should be: 'Where can this pupil be most fully included in the life of this school community?'

### A continuum of autism provision

As pupils who have autism cover the whole of the ability range and also range from those who have classic autism (which is usually combined with moderate or severe learning difficulties), at one end, to those who have high functioning autism or Asperger syndrome at the other, it is particularly important to have a continuum of provision. This includes:

- Support in mainstream classrooms.
- Mainstream schools with specialist provision for autism in the form of a unit or base.

- Special schools where pupils on the spectrum make up part of the pupil population.
- Special schools with specialist provision for autistic pupils, perhaps in the form of dedicated classes.
- Special schools designed solely for pupils who have autism – an increasing number of 'free schools'[1] come into this category.

In addition, there are:

- Pupil referral units (PRUs) and other forms of alternative provision (AP) for any pupil who has been excluded or is at risk of exclusion. This can be a way of providing a more personalized curriculum within a smaller environment, and can be effective provided staff are experienced and knowledgeable about autistic pupils; however, this is usually a temporary solution rather than a permanent one.
- Specialist autism teachers and specialist autism support teams who work alongside schools to help them deliver appropriate support.
- Outreach services from special schools or mainstream schools with specialist provision.

Apart from providing a range of options for educating autistic pupils, these different environments often serve as a source of information, advice and training for those who wish to know more about helping their own autistic pupils to make the most of their education.

## Partnership working with providers and parents

Nowadays, it is common for schools to work together in a variety of ways and in different types of partnerships rather than in isolation. Some of these will be tied in with being an academy which is part of a multi-academy trust (MAT), or a teaching school where other schools will be part of the teaching school alliance. Other partnerships may be less formal. Trying to meet the needs of pupils with autism, and particularly girls where less is known about the best ways of recognising and supporting them, these links can be extremely valuable. Although successive governments have done much to pit schools against each other by creating an atmosphere of competition, happily this has not deterred them from recognising the value of working in partnership. And this is often a two-way process. Almost every school will have something to offer, whether or not they are a teaching school or run an outreach service, so it is both a question of receiving and providing expertise.

And, of course, working in partnership with parents is a central tenet of the SEND reforms and the value of this approach is very evident with regard to girls who are autistic. It is not possible to build up a holistic picture of these pupils unless it is known how they behave at home as well as at school and this knowledge can yield important information. Sometimes an accurate picture may not emerge straight away, as parents may be reluctant to admit how difficult their child is at home in case they are seen as having poor parenting skills. It is some time since parents suffered from the 'refrigerator mother' idea expounded in the 1940s by Bettelheim and others, who thought that the cause of autism was a lack of parental, and particularly maternal, love. While this has long been put to bed as a theory, there are still cases where a child's poor behaviour at home may be put down to bad parenting, rather than being the result of an autistic girl working so hard to appear to be like other girls, that all her pent up frustration and effort to conform is released when she returns home from school and feels able to 'let go'.

Turning to the physical environment of the school, visual timetables and prompts are now common in schools and suit children who have difficulty with organising and sequencing, as well as those who need to be reassured about the order of events. These can take many forms, from pictures placed in order of the sequence of a single activity to a pictorial representation of the timetable for the day or for the week. Some will find it helpful to have words and pictures, while others need just the words. Corridors with muted colours, such as mauve or grey; doors with clear signage; and orderly, uncluttered, clearly labelled classrooms also play a part in making the environment less stressful.

### Strengthening self-worth and self-belief

Young learners who are on the autism spectrum are often seen as having a weaker sense of self and a poorer autobiographical memory (despite a memory for facts being a strong point), finding it harder to develop a sense of self-worth and self-belief. Fatima, aged seven years, walked into her classroom when a video clip was running of a trip the class had been on the day before. She stood and watched as she appeared on the screen and commented to no one in particular: 'Girl looks like Fatima.' From then on, staff made a point of talking through with her what she would be doing on the class outing, speaking to her while she was on the trip about her part in the proceedings and sitting down with her afterwards to go over it again.

Mention has already been made of helping autistic girls to become aware of the sensory issues they have and of their own emotions, which is all part of gaining self-awareness, leading to a greater understanding of others as well. This is the kind of specific teaching needed to compensate for an inability to benefit from the incidental learning which is normally how children and young people learn so much about themselves and about other people. Ros Blackburn, who is one of a number of autistic women who have furthered an understanding of these differences, sums it up by including in her talks the phrase: 'I can only know what I am taught or told or shown.'

## Identifying and supporting mental health needs

Statistically, it is accepted that children who have SEND are more likely to have mental health needs and those who are on the autism spectrum are certainly no exception. In fact, the tendency for autistic girls not being identified as soon as boys, places them at even greater risk because they may worry about being different and not fitting in without understanding why and thinking it must be their fault. With the impeccable logic of the teenage girl, in trying to make sense of the world around her, Aisha was heard to remark: 'What is normal when everyone's different – which makes us all the same!' As they hit the teenage years, with all the other changes and growing pressures on them, these girls may start self-harming, develop an eating disorder or some other condition, and then the danger is that the underlying cause of their mental health difficulties goes unrecognized.

## The Mental Health Green Paper

In December 2017, *Transforming Children and Young People's Mental Health Provision: a Green Paper*, was published for consultation by the Department of Health and the Department for Education and is expected to lead to an Act of Parliament. A joint ministerial foreword by the two secretaries of state at the time, Justine Greening and Jeremy Hunt, says:

> This green paper therefore sets out an ambition for earlier intervention and prevention, a boost in support for the role played by schools and colleges, and better, faster access to NHS services …
>
> (Department of Health/Department for Education 2017: 2)

It goes on to explain that:

- one in ten young people has a diagnosable mental health condition; and
- half of all mental health conditions appear before the age of 14 years.

There is a requirement that, in the same way that a SENCo post is statutory in schools, the plan is for there to be a Designated Senior Lead for mental health. A training programme for all schools started in June 2017 with secondary schools being the first to receive it. Mental wellbeing also forms part of the work currently being considered on the most effective way of delivering personal, social, health and economic education (PSHE), and relationships and sex education (RSE), all of which push forward the need for building resilience as well as addressing mental health issues when they arise.

While school leaders and staff have been wary of being expected to take on too much responsibility for pupils' mental health issues, it makes sense for them to be better informed about the signs to look out for and when to refer to services such as Child and Adolescent Mental Health Services (CAMHS). This focus may help to ensure that it is not only the pupils who are disruptive and aggressive who come to staff's attention, but also the unusually quiet ones who suffer in silence, yet need just as much support and understanding. Some autistic girls will derive great benefit from having at least one member of staff who they feel understands them and whom they can turn to when worries threaten to overwhelm them.

## Building resilience through feeling valued and included

It should be part of the school leader's role to ensure that their staff make every pupil feel valued. For pupils with SEND, this is particularly important because they may see themselves as failures. Some girls and boys who have a diagnosis of autism may feel able, and indeed welcome the opportunity, to explain what it means to them to be autistic. It is important that other pupils realize this is not a condition that affects only boys. Speaking to their class, their year group or in an assembly can be very powerful in aiding fellow pupils' understanding. Other autistic pupils who are not as confident may be able at least to be included in some way. They may be happier talking about their interests or displaying their knowledge of a subject rather than talking about themselves.

Peers are often astonished when they realize these pupils have abilities they had not expected. While some may be tempted to bully those they see as weak or different, others will be anxious to help, particularly if it is explained to them the kind of help, support or friendship that is needed. For instance, many schools have a system of Buddies or Playground Peers, to be on the lookout for those who find it hard to make friends. Others have taken this further and developed systems such as having 'Autism Champions' (Beaney 2017). These young people may or may not be autistic themselves.

## Recognising and utilising strengths and interests

With pupils who have SEND, it is all too easy to concentrate on the difficulties they have and not think about their strengths. Yet, making the most of their strengths and building on their interests can do much to raise the autistic girl's self-worth and feelings of acceptance. One primary school has a system of 'senior monitors', which is seen as a prestigious role for those who exemplify the behaviour expected as well as a commitment to learning. Hayley, who is on the autism spectrum, was appointed because she was an avid learner and, with her keenness to stick to the rules, was always well behaved. There was some concern about how she would carry out the role, which included being in charge of the registers for all the classes and running errands as needed because she was used to having someone with her when she left her classroom. However, being given this responsibility enabled her to become far more independent as she rose to the challenge.

As girls with autism sometimes find it easier to make friends with younger children than their own age group, in one secondary school, an older girl on the spectrum called Sofia, was given the role of being a buddy to Lexi, an autistic girl who had just joined Year 7. As well as helping Lexi to make the transition to the larger environment of the secondary school, Sophia herself blossomed under these new responsibilities. Other autistic girls may have a subject where they can shine if given the chance, whether in sport, maths and sciences, the arts, or English, where their detailed knowledge of an aspect of the subject or their creativity in producing a painting or designing an object may help to raise their self-esteem.

Millie's passion was for acting and, as she progressed through secondary school, staff had many discussions about whether or not to allow her to take a major role in the school's musical production. There was no doubt about the quality and power of her singing voice, but she had a pronounced stammer, which was all too apparent when speaking her lines, although it disappeared when she was singing. In the end, Millie herself decided that she wanted to do it, despite being very nervous about getting her words out. On the night, the audience started by feeling quite uncomfortable about seeing her standing on the stage trying so hard to say her lines, but when she opened her mouth to sing, their attitude changed from one of apprehension to warm-hearted applause (for further examples see Chapter 7 of this book).

## An inclusive ethos comes from the top

While the role of a head teacher or principal is very different depending on the type of school, its size and its pupil population; whether they are more hands-on and know every child, or they are leading a team of a hundred staff, the ethos of the school comes from the attitude and behaviour of the person at the top. That key figure will be instrumental in collecting around them a team who show respect for each other, to the pupils they teach and to their families. A school that is welcoming of all comers, and not just the ones who are likely to improve their academic results, will be apparent to discerning visitors as soon as they step through the entrance doors. It can be seen in the way they are greeted, in how the pupils behave to each other and in the environment that has been created for them. At one secondary school which has a number of autistic girls, the head teacher makes a point of saying to them when they visit before starting: 'This is a place where you can be yourself and we will value you for who you are.'

Effective school leaders are creative people who will seek out ways to provide appropriate learning opportunities for all their pupils and make school an interesting and exciting place to be. They will put a premium on the well-being of staff and of pupils, caring passionately about pupils' achievements and not just their academic attainments. Their staff will feel free to be flexible in meeting their pupils' needs and find ways of motivating each and every one, while shielding them from undue pressure.

While it may not be possible to 'cure' autism – and many who are autistic would say they do not want to be cured; they just want people to understand them better – there is plenty of evidence that the earlier a child is diagnosed and receives support, the better their outcomes are likely to be. This is one reason why school leaders and their staff need to be vigilant in watching out for girls who may not have been identified, as well as becoming familiar with the kind of support and opportunities that help girls on the spectrum to thrive.

The SEND reforms are a reminder of the importance of working together, within and across schools and with pupils, families and the local community. The challenge for school leaders now is to take the best of the reforms and make them work in a climate of competition.

## Note

1 In England, a free school is one that is set up by an organization or a group of individuals and is funded by the government but is not controlled by a local authority.

## References

All Party Parliamentary Group on Autism (2017) *Autism and Education in England 2017: A Report by the All Party Parliamentary Group on Autism on How the Education System Works for Children and Young People on the Autism Spectrum*. London: National Autistic Society.

Beaney, J. (2017) *Creating Autism Champions*. London: Jessica Kingsley.

Critchley, S.-J. (2016) *A Different Joy: The Parents' Guide to Living Better with Autism, Dyslexia, ADHD and More*. London: WritingScorpInk.

Department for Education (2010) *Green Paper: Children and Young People with Special Educational Needs and Disabilities – Call for Views*. London: Department for Education.

Department for Education (2011) *Support and Aspiration: A New Approach to Special Needs and Disability – a Consultation*. Norwich: The Stationery Office.

Department for Education (2017) *Special Educational Needs in England: January 2017. National Tables* (SFR37/2017). London: Department for Education. Retrieved from www.gov.uk/government/statistics/special-educational-needs-in-england-january-2017 (accessed 9 September 2018).

Department for Education/Department of Health (2015) *Special Educational Needs and Disability Code of Practice: 0–25 Years*. London: Department for Education. Retrieved from www.gov.uk/government/publications/send-code-of-practice-0-to-25 (accessed 12 September 2018).

Department of Health/Department for Education (2017) *Transforming Children and Young People's Mental Health Provision: a Green Paper.* London: Department of Health.

Happé, F. (2016) Quotation in J. Egerton, B. Carpenter and the Autism and Girls Forum, *Girls and Autism: Flying Under the Radar.* Tamworth: nasen.

Hendrickx, S. (2015) *Women and Girls with Autism Spectrum Disorder: Understanding Life Experiences from Early Childhood to Old Age.* London: Jessica Kingsley.

Her Majesty's Government (2014) *Children and Families Act.* London: HMSO. Retrieved from www.legislation.gov.uk/ukpga/2014/6/contents/enacted (accessed 12 September 2018).

Ofsted (2010) *The Special Educational Needs and Disability Review: A Statement is Not Enough.* Retrieved from http://dera.ioe.ac.uk/1145/1/Special%20education%20needs%20and%20disability%20review.pdf (accessed 12 September 2018).

Sibthorp, K. and Nicoll, T. (2014) *Making it Personal: A family guide to personalisation, Personal Budgets and Education, Health and Care Plans.* Retrieved from https://councilfordisabledchildren.org.uk/sites/default/files/field/attachemnt/making_it_personal_family_guidance-1.pdf (accessed 12 September 2018).

Steward, R. (2014) *The Independent Woman's Handbook for Super Safe Living on the Autistic Spectrum.* London: Jessica Kingsley.

Tutt, R. (2016a) *Making it Personal: A Guide to Personalisation, Personal Budgets and Education, Health and Care Plans – for Educational Establishments and Local Authorities.* Retrieved from www.sendgateway.org.uk/download.making-it-personal-3-mip3.html (accessed 12 September 2018).

Tutt, R. (2016b) *Rona Tutt's Guide to SEND & Inclusion.* London: Sage.

Tutt, R. and Williams, P. (2015) *The SEND Code of Practice 0–25 Years: Policy, Provision and Practice.* London: Sage.

Warnock, M. (2005) *Special Educational Needs: A New Look* (Paper 11). London: Philosophy of Education Society of Great Britain.

# Chapter 9

# Building a specialist curriculum for autistic girls

*Sarah Wild*

> Alone we can do so little. Together we can do so much.
>
> (Helen Keller, quoted in Lash 1980)

At Limpsfield Grange we work with girls who astound us every day; who push our already sky high expectations of them; who deftly dispose of social stereotypes. Limpsfield Grange is a special school for girls with communication and interaction difficulties, most of whom have autism; which for women and girls is still sadly a very misunderstood condition.

The girls at Limpsfield Grange would be classified as vulnerable learners in any setting, and many will become vulnerable adults. Being female and having special needs adds an additional layer of vulnerability. The United Nations reports that being female and disabled or having special needs is a double disadvantage (United Nations Population Fund 2018). Women and girls around the globe are often treated as helpless objects of pity or subjected to hostility, and are excluded from enjoying their fundamental human rights and freedoms. Women with disabilities are reported to be at increased risk of physical, psychological or sexual violence, and face multiple levels of discrimination. Often they have no social value, and are either invisible or ridiculed.

Most of the girls at Limpsfield Grange have a myriad of complex needs, which often overlap with mental health difficulties. Many of the girls live in families that are economically disadvantaged; families that have experienced poverty for generations. High numbers of our girls have been adopted from social care or have experienced family breakdown and are 'looked-after children'. All of the girls have difficulties with managing their anxiety; and often their anxiety prevents them from living their lives as they would wish.

A few months ago an ex-student returned to Limpsfield Grange for a visit. On paper she had been very successful, gaining lots of great GCSEs and A levels, and holding down a job, but she was struggling to function. Her anxiety levels were crippling; she was unable to sleep and was finding communicating with others increasingly difficult. The expectations of the neurotypical world were causing her to burn out. It made me question what is really important for our girls, and what we should be doing to help them thrive not just survive in the wider world.

At Limpsfield Grange we work on the broad areas of well-being, achievement, communication and independence to equip our girls to take their place in society. We work with our girls and their families to help them identify gaps in each area, and design a tailored package to meet their needs. This includes asking questions such as can this young person function independently? Can they live safely? Can they communicate effectively with others? Can they manage change or uncertainty? Can they regulate their emotions effectively? Can they identify what keeps them emotionally, mentally and physically well? If the answer to any of these questions is 'no' then we have to do something about it. In short we are asking what we can do to help improve their quality of life now and in the future.

How we address the gaps is dependent on the young person, their needs and circumstances. However, there are some guiding principles and common approaches that we use, which might be helpful in your setting.

## Creating a positive whole-school culture

The bedrock of a whole-school culture that celebrates autistic girls is awareness and understanding. All stakeholders, staff, students, governors, parents and community members need to understand how female autism presents. Stakeholders need to understand that autism in girls often looks very different to autism in boys. Stakeholders will need to know that all autistic people are different from each other, and that being an autistic schoolgirl is exhausting, anxiety-provoking, confusing and relentless.

To create a female-autism-friendly school, there needs to be a whole-school ethos that enables:

- difference to be accepted and celebrated;
- the voice of each girl to be heard so that together we are working towards their desired future;
- the voice of each family to be heard so that we understand the place of each young person in their family context including the impact of their autism;
- a culture of support and challenge for students and staff;
- clear and concise communication across the organization;
- commitment to minimizing and managing all changes (from big changes like staffing restructures or changes in the curriculum to little changes like how to communicate room changes and staff absences to students each day);
- a clear shared understanding of anxiety and how it impacts on individuals;
- flexibility to treat all members of the community as individuals (this means that people will be treated differently according to their needs and circumstances, and that everyone acknowledges, understands and promotes this flexibility); and
- an understanding that behaviour is communication.

The idea that all students are different and equal needs to permeate through the school, and all stakeholders need to understand that it is their responsibility to be a champion of autistic girls.

## Understanding the impact of masking

In the last five years there has been an increased awareness in the medical profession that autistic girls present very differently to boys, with anxiety being an over-riding emotion. Gaining a diagnosis and support can be hard, as there are still family doctors who say, 'Your daughter can't be on the spectrum because she can make conversation and eye contact.'

But lots of girls on the spectrum can do exactly that. Many of them do not understand what is going on socially but want to make conversation, while not understanding the subtext. The stereotype of someone with autism being locked into themselves and obsessive does not necessarily apply with girls, who are reaching out and trying to engage socially with other people.

> Secretly, I just want to be normal.
>
> (Students of Limpsfield Grange School and Martin 2017: 10)

Some girls on the spectrum mask their difficulties. Masking is hiding or camouflaging social difficulties. This can be done through mimicking or copying the behaviours of other people, so that the difficulties with social interaction are hidden (Hurley 2014). This can lead to serious problems. It is mentally exhausting to continually supress your natural social reactions.

In places like school or college or work autistic girls and women are often surrounded by people who really do not get them. They have to mask their difficulties all day, and in effect try to be someone else. Masking can lead to autistic females feeling very socially isolated and anxious – anxious that they do not really know what is happening around them; anxious to please others; anxious that they are getting it all wrong.

This is why managing anxiety is absolutely crucial to autistic girls' physical, emotional and mental well-being in adult life. It is the difference between being a contained, emotionally functioning adult and an adult stranded at home by anxiety.

## Managing anxiety

Explosive behaviour is seen as a typical autistic response to anxiety but, where boys may tend to explode, in our experience at Limpsfield Grange girls are more likely to implode, internalizing their anxiety. Many girls on the spectrum suffer from extremely high levels of anxiety all day, every day. For the girls at Limpsfield Grange anxiety is a defining feature, and will in all probability always be with them.

Anxiety can be caused by a range of different factors, including:

- sensory needs, and the fact that sensory information can overwhelm them;
- trying to imitate social behaviour all day, without really understanding what it means;
- constantly vetting and editing personal responses to social situations without understanding what the right social response is;
- change or the possibility of change; and
- difficulties with understanding time and what is going to happen next.

In our novel *M is for Autism* the girls describe anxiety as 'an uncontrollable wild, savage beast that prowls beside me at its will' (Students of Limpsfield Grange School and Martin 2015: 18). The effects of anxiety can be debilitating – from being unable to leave your bedroom for weeks at a time, to being in a constant anxious state. Anxiety can totally preoccupy thoughts and feelings, and leaves no head space for learning. Living with such high and unrelenting levels of anxiety is exhausting, frustrating and demoralizing, and can have a significant impact on the young person's mental health and on their family.

Puberty and body changes can also be an incredible source of anxiety. Often girls will not fully understand that puberty lasts for a few years and is irreversible; or that you have more than one period in your lifetime; or that they will not grow up to be male. Puberty can cause real spikes in the levels of anxiety that a young person experiences, can lead to an array of controlling behaviours intended to stop or contain puberty such as dramatically reducing eating or excessive exercising to delay periods and physical development. Unfortunately puberty often coincides with secondary school, increased demands and pressures and an increasing complexity in social dynamics. This perfect storm of body changes, hormones and anxiety can make life really hard for an autistic teenage girl.

Indications that anxiety is building can include:

- An increased demand for routines to be kept the same, and the need for the autistic girl to exert a higher than usual level of control over a situation.
- Perfectionism and related frustration and anger when things are not perfect.
- Increased difficulties with getting to sleep; sometimes this is linked to an increase in ritualized behaviours around bedtime routines.
- Meltdowns becoming more frequent and/or prolonged, violent and/or intense.
- An increased avoidance of social situations or social spaces in school.
- An increase in stimming behaviours such as flapping, spinning, pacing or rocking.
- Poor attendance at school. This can be because being ill allows the young person to experience a lower demand situation, and they can control social interactions through becoming a patient. It is important to look at patterns of attendance – are there particular days where attendance is noticeably lower? What lesson happens on those days when a young person tends to be absent? Are they experiencing particular problems in areas of the curriculum, with particular peers or staff, or experiencing difficulties with physical areas of the school.
- Increased episodes of self-harming can often be linked to heightened anxiety. Self-harming can take many forms including cutting, head banging, hand biting, ingesting dangerous items, pulling out hair, restricted eating. Often the young person will try to conceal self-harming from adults. If you know an autistic girl is self-harming, contact your local CAMHS team or SelfharmUK (www.selfharm.co.uk) for advice and support.

Strategies for working with high levels of anxiety can include:

- Identifying situations that lead to anxiety.
- Talking through any planned changes in advance. It is also helpful if changes for the day can be physically recorded for the student to refer to over the day – in a school diary, for example.
- Talking about how their body feels when they are anxious, as it is possible that they will not have connected the physical sensation (e.g. feeling nauseous) with feeling anxious.
- Teaching calming strategies. This can be anything from concentrating on breathing; using some calming hand lotion; going for a walk or listening to music from a relaxation app; whatever makes the individual feel better.
- If something has gone wrong, talking about how it could be different next time, and making a plan for it to be different.

- Asking 'what is the worst thing that can happen?' and then discussing their fears, putting them into perspective and context.
- Try using cards with 'big deal' on one side and 'not a big deal' on the other. Ask the young person to categorize what the issue would be, and then talk through reasons why it might be less of a big deal than they think.
- The anxiety bucket. Get a selection of different-sized balls. Write what causes anxiety on each ball and add to the bucket. Talk about how the bucket fills up if you keep adding anxieties to it. Discuss what makes the young person feel calm. For each calm activity or calm item identified cut a hole in the bucket. Talk about the fact that you need to build in things that will keep you calm throughout the day or your anxiety bucket will overflow and spill out, leading to feelings of being overwhelmed.
- Celebrating difference. Everyone has things that they find difficult and things that they find easier. Build the young person's confidence and self-esteem, so that they believe in themselves, and develop their resilience.

## Staying safe

The girls at Limpsfield Grange want to be like everyone else; to be 'normal'. They want people to like them, they want friends, they want to have a relationship, and they want to be popular. For our community of students this can also mean that they are vulnerable and at risk of exploitation. Many girls have very low self-esteem, and are black and white thinkers who take a lot of what people tell them at face value. The girls are reaching out and trying to connect with people, without understanding any of the associated risks. They believe that people are who they say they are, and they can be easy to manipulate because they want people to like them.

The girls have often learnt how to 'mask' their difficulties through mimicking social behaviours from other people without understanding what those behaviours mean or where they can lead. At times this can mean that they behave in a provocative or risky way without understanding the consequences of their behaviour. They can behave in risky or provocative ways because they have seen other people behave like this.

Their autism often limits their capacity to transfer learning from one situation to another. The girls can find themselves in risky situations repeatedly without seemingly ever being able to learn how to avoid danger or risk. This can cause some professionals to make judgements about them, and believe wrongly that risky behaviour is something that they like or is something that they choose. A frightening number of autistic women have been sexually assaulted more than once, or have ended up in destructive relationships with people that control them. Many autistic women have shared their experiences of being manipulated by others socially or sexually, and the physical emotion and psychological pain that has caused (Holliday Willey 2012).

Safeguarding starts with teaching the girls how to be safe in and out of school. We do this through:

- Listening without judgment to what the girls tell us, and providing a safe reflective space to help them process the world.
- Setting clear, firm, consistent boundaries that make the girls feel safe.

- Establishing, through questioning, what the girls already know; in our experience there are lots of gaps and misconceptions.
- Building effective respectful relationships.
- Having an ongoing bespoke approach to delivering sex and relationships education. We have a weekly Well-being Wednesday tutor slot for all year groups where we talk about a sex and relationships topic or online safety. We have to drip feed sex and relationships education constantly through the student curriculum diet, and present the same information in a number of different ways to enable the girls to access and retain pointers for staying safe. Quite often we set a scenario activity, where girls need to talk about how safe a situation is.
- Implementing a relationships and sex curriculum which is led by student questions and uses unambiguous real life terminology. This is crucial for young people with social communication and interaction difficulties – without the right language they do not know what they are agreeing to.
- Explicitly teaching privacy awareness and rules around personal space and touching other people.
- Developing a curriculum and approach that builds self-esteem and self-advocacy. It is very important that the girls understand that they can say 'no' at any point during an intimate act. It is also really important to talk to them about the fact that the other person will not know what is in their heads, and if they are uncomfortable with a situation they must make this clear.
- Providing regular training and advice for all members of staff around relationships and sex topics and online safety.
- Working with external agencies widely and often.

Through taking a real-life approach to teaching the girls about the world that they live in, we hope to help them develop the skills, knowledge and understanding they need to keep themselves safe. Nichols et al. (2009) cover this area in depth in *Girls Growing up on the Autism Spectrum*.

## Clarifying communication

In a recent communication homework for our Year 10 students they had to make a phone call to a member of staff. All week members of staff received phone calls where no one spoke, which was little unnerving. It was only after the fourth call that the penny dropped, it was the Year 10 students completing their homework. We clearly had not explained the task well enough; we had assumed that the students knew that ringing someone was not enough, and that you had to talk to them too. I am hopeful that we will not make that mistake again!

Building a curriculum for autistic girls that enables them to thrive should include constant opportunities to communicate and to deconstruct the communication of others. Many autistic girls are articulate and able to reflect on their thoughts and feelings well but this takes lots of time and practice. However many of them do not really understand what other people's communication means or where it comes from. Interpreting people's behaviour when you do not understand what they are saying and what they mean is mysterious, challenging and disempowering.

Autistic girls are constantly trying to work out what other people mean. Not understanding what other people mean is confusing and can lead to high levels of anxiety, isolation and exhaustion. To help with this, we use a technique called 'wondering out loud'. We wonder if a person is behaving in a certain way or is saying something because of how they feel or something they have experienced. We talk through the process a person went through to arrive at a conclusion – making the invisible thought processes visible. This approach can be used in real life or when watching TV or a film, it helps to explain another person's behaviour, and ultimately helps to reduce anxiety.

Encouraging the girls to identify their emotions is an important part of developing their self-awareness. Autistic females may be more open to talking about their feelings and may be more expressive than autistic males (Simone 2010). Sometimes when we work with autistic girls at Limpsfield Grange they tell us that they do not know if they have any feelings, or they can only describe an emotional range of happy or sad. We work alongside the girls to develop a wider emotional vocabulary. We use tools including emotions keyrings, individual emotions thermometers, language suitcases, social scripts and role plays. We use the language of emotions all of the time. Staff are clear in signposting their emotional state with the girls; and will say things like 'I am not cross or angry with you; however you do need to follow my instructions or there will be a consequence.' As a team we also script some of our responses to the girls using agreed language, so the girls hear the same message from everyone, and often we will develop this script with parents, carers and families to ensure consistency across home and school settings. This helps the girls to transfer their experience across contexts.

Visitors who come to Limpsfield Grange always comment on how chatty and open and reflective the girls are, and how much laughter there is. I am always surprised by this – we talk all of the time about everything at Limpsfield Grange, about autism, about feelings, about being an adult, about getting a job, about Brexit – everything! At Limpsfield Grange talking things through is how we make sense of the world.

## Promoting independence

Being independent is key to being safe and to reducing vulnerability. If autistic girls are wholly reliant on adults to tell them what to do they can be easily exploited, and this places them at risk of harm. We want the girls to be happy, healthy, empowered and included citizens, who can make choices, determine their own future and help to shape the world they live in. Developing independence enables them to be active in society, and pursue their ambitions. We want them to be satisfied with the quality of their life.

Promoting independence can be difficult, as quite often the activity you are engaging the girls in is not on their agenda. They may think it is perfectly fine that they cannot brush their teeth or wash their hair independently – it is just not important to them. So the first thing we do is create 'buy in'. We use specialist interests as the motivator, and reward the girls for trying things that they clearly have no interest in. Once a skill has been practiced a few times in one setting, then we try to transfer the activity to another setting to help the girls generalize the skill. We take lots of photos of the girls practising skills and then send the photos home, so that when the girls try something new at home that they have practised at school they have physical evidence that they have completed it successfully before.

Working in partnership with parents is key to developing and promoting independence. We ask parents to work on specific areas, including the following.

*For all ages:*

- Ensure that your daughter has regular responsibilities around the home.
- Encourage your daughter to develop her self-care skills.
- Encourage your daughter to pay for items in shops.
- Ensure that your daughter is safe on line through monitoring her online usage.
- Ensure that your daughter is using social media appropriately.
- Support your daughter to identify and manage her emotions.
- Support your daughter to develop friendships with her peers.
- Support your daughter to repair friendships when they have gone wrong.

*For specific ages:*

- Ensure that your daughter can make a snack and can make her own breakfast (KS3).
- Ensure that your daughter can prepare a light meal (KS4).
- Support your daughter to travel independently in your home area (KS4).
- Ensure that your daughter has a bank account (KS4).

At Limpsfield Grange we also set independence homework where we ask the girls to do something independently in their home or local community, and ask for photographic or video evidence. Parents, carers and families have fed back positively about this approach.

As educators we have a duty to enable the next generation to develop the right skills, tools and knowledge to thrive. At Limpsfield Grange School we want the next generation of autistic girls to take their place in a world that respects and values them. We want girls to live the life that they choose, and not live a life that is chosen for them. We want the girls to be proud of who they are, confident in knowing that they can make a contribution to society. We want them to be strong courageous and adventurous because, as Helen Keller (1940) said, 'Life is either a daring adventure or nothing.'

# References

Holliday Willey, L. (2012) *Safety Skills for Asperger Women*. London: Jessica Kingsley.

Hurley, E. (2014) *Ultraviolet Voices: Stories of Women on the Autistic Spectrum*. Birmingham: Autism West Midlands.

Keller, H. (1940) *Let Us Have Faith*. New York: Doubleday, Doran and Company.

Lash, J. P. (1980) *Helen and Teacher: The Story of Helen Keller and Anne Sullivan Macey*. New York: Delacorte Press.

Nichols, S., Moravick, G. M. and Pulver-Tetenbaum, S. (2009) *Girls Growing Up on the Autism Spectrum*. London: Jessica Kingsley.

Simone, R. (2010) *Aspergirls: Empowering Females with Asperger's Syndrome*. London: Jessica Kingsley.

Students of Limpsfield Grange and Martin, V. (2015) *M is for Autism*. London: Jessica Kingsley.

Students of Limpsfield Grange and Martin, V. (2017) *M in the Middle*. London: Jessica Kingsley.

United Nations Population Fund (2018) *Young Persons with Disabilities: Global Study on Ending Gender-Based Violence, and Realising Sexual and Reproductive Health and Rights*. New York: United Nations Population Fund. Retrieved from www.unfpa.org/sites/default/files/pub-pdf/51936_-_UNFPA_Global_Study_on_Disability_-_web.pdf (accessed 13 September 2018).

# Chapter 10

# Included or excluded?

## School experiences of autistic girls

*Jane Friswell and Jo Egerton*

This chapter begins with the premise and belief that schools do not generally exclude lightly. Many, many schools will go to great lengths to work with the most complex of children and young people to avoid exclusion. That being said, the current national picture of pupil exclusion from schools in England does not support my belief and experience of working with and supporting schools to meet the needs of children and young people with special educational needs and to keep them in school.

Why do I believe this so passionately? The answer for me is simple. Exclusion from school gives young people the message that problems can be solved by giving up or walking away. It affirms their status as a disengaged learner, whereas their entitlement is to be an engaged learner, an active participant in a school community, not a disenfranchised, peripheral non-participant. In my experience, young people who may challenge our regular systems and practices need *more*, not less, guidance from supportive and compassionate adults — and their parent carers need support too.

Formal exclusion in England is where pupils are excluded from school for either a short period ('fixed term exclusion') or permanently due to their behaviour (Brede et al. 2017).

The latest data on permanent and fixed period exclusions in England refers to 2016/2017 (Department for Education 2018a). They tell us that the rate and number of permanent exclusions have increased since the previous year's report by a small percentage of 0.02% to 0.1% of pupil enrolments, with a corresponding increase of numbers of pupils permanently excluded from 6685 to 7720 pupils. There is also a worrying increasing trend for fixed period exclusions from 4.29% of pupil enrolments in 2015/2016 to 4.76% in 2016/2017.

The national information we have available to explore the impact that school exclusion is having on girls is disappointing. The headlines are often reported in relation to boys, who are over three times more likely to receive a permanent exclusion and almost three times more likely to receive a fixed period exclusion than girls. The exclusion figures for girls as a percentage of overall exclusions have remained fairly constant since 2010, with figures varying between 20% and 23% for permanent exclusions and 25.6% and 26.4% for fixed term exclusions.

According to national data, 1685 girls were permanently excluded from school during 2016/2017; the highest prevalence of permanent exclusion featuring at the age of 14 years, with 495 girls permanently excluded in this period. This figure is 1.7 times the number of girls who are identified as permanently excluded at age 12. Alarmingly, a national total of 99,380 girls were fixed term excluded from school during this period;

the data does not indicate where repeat exclusions may have occurred. Almost 70% of this group of girls were excluded between the ages of 12 and 14 years.

## Autism and exclusion

We know little more than the information given above about girls and exclusion, which frankly is shocking. This data is alarming not only in both the proportion and incidence of exclusion of girls from our schools but also in that it tells us little else. This is a group of the school age population which is overlooked, ignored and largely invisible to policy makers and system leaders.

What we do know from Department for Education (2018a) figures is that exclusions of autistic pupils appear to be increasing. The All Party Parliamentary Group on Autism (2017) have raised concerns about the high numbers of young people on the autism spectrum being excluded from schools, seeing this as an important indication that autistic pupils' needs are not being met. With reference to the Department for Education's 2015/2016 exclusions figures (Department for Education 2017a), the *Independent* reported increases for autistic children on the previous year of 24.7% for fixed term exclusions and 36.4% for permanent exclusions – shocking statistics, even acknowledging the 10% increase in the autistic school population over that period (Kershaw 2017). We also know from Department for Education (2018a) figures that pupils who have autism as a primary diagnosis and have an SEN Statement or Education, Health and Care Plan (EHCP) are over three times more likely to receive a fixed term exclusion than pupils with no SEN; their respective 2016/2017 exclusion rates are 9.58 and 3.06 (Department for Education 2018a; Hazell 2018).

There are additional issues around the possible under-diagnosis of autistic girls, the evidence for which is reviewed in greater detail within other chapters in this book. Judith Gould (2017), in her article, 'Towards understanding the under-recognition of girls and women on the autism spectrum', considers why autistic girls are not identified at school. Explanations for this include the passive personality profiles of some girls, who present as compliant, not as having social impairments. These are girls who are shy, coy, embarrassed, naïve, innocent and unassuming. They are not disruptive and do not draw attention to themselves as many boys do. Tony Attwood, professor and world-renowned expert on Asperger syndrome and autism, states:

> Boys go into attack mode when frustrated, while girls suffer in silence and become passive-aggressive. Girls learn to appease and apologize. They learn to observe people from a distance and imitate them. It is only if you look closely and ask the right questions, you see the terror in their eyes and see that their reactions are a learnt script.
>
> (Attwood, quoted in Hill 2009)

It is possible that, within the national group of girls who are excluded from school, there may be a significant number of girls on the autism spectrum who are not showing up in the exclusion figures. This may be because: they have no diagnosis; they have an autism diagnosis which is not classed as their primary condition (so is not accounted for in the exclusion figures); or they may be misdiagnosed with overshadowing conditions. For many girls, mental and emotional well-being issues (e.g. eating disorders, anxiety disorders, etc.) will also be implicated. The exclusion experiences of these girls and their families need to be examined. It may help us as professionals to explain the symptomatic disenfranchisement of these young women from our schools (Hazell 2018). Providing a voice to the girls and families who form part of this group, and who have generously and graciously informed the working of this chapter, has been a focus of my work.

## Explanations for increased school exclusions

School leaders often explain the increasing pupil exclusions and disengagement from school with reference to the narrowed curriculum and a growing focus on testing, especially among the youngest children. The climate of austerity is another challenge that school leaders face; they regularly warn about the impact of cuts on the additional resources necessary to support pupils with the greatest level of need.

There is no doubt that cuts to school and local authority budgets have led to pastoral and mental health support services being scaled back or axed. Some schools have had to rationalize and reduce the level of support provided (e.g. additional adult support in the classroom). This clearly has an impact on the help schools can give to individual pupils as and when the need arises.

The prevalence of special educational needs (SEN) among children and young people excluded from school is high. Pupils identified with SEN account for almost half of all permanent and fixed period exclusions. Pupils in receipt of school-based SEN support arrangements are almost six times more likely to be permanently excluded from school than those pupils without SEN.

An investigation by *Schools Week* (Staufenberg 2017) suggests that the number of children leaving school to be home educated has almost doubled in recent years. Many parents of children on the autism spectrum are opting to home educate their children especially when circumstances suggest an increased risk of exclusion in relation to SEN. Figures gathered by *Schools Week* show the number of home-educated pupils rose from 15,135 in 2011/2012 to 29,805 in 2016/2017. Meleri Thomas of the National Autistic Society Cymru, interviewed by the BBC about parents of autistic pupils opting to home educate their children, commented:

> A lot of parents are finding themselves in positions where they have no options and the only thing they can do to help their children is to educate them at home even though they might not feel fully equipped to do that or want to.

> (Neal 2017)

It is not surprising, perhaps, that schools are reporting a 'bounce-back' effect from the increase of admissions of pupils arriving in their schools after a period of home education, particularly during the secondary phases of education.

We should be looking seriously at the increase in home education numbers and at the reasons for this. To what extent are schools failing these children? In many cases home education is a last resort for families who have repeatedly tried to get schools to fix school-based issues. Even if a child has poor school attendance, as professionals we should not just blame the parents for it; we should take a good, hard look at the child's experience at school because that may be the major cause of the problem. If you have a child who gets physically sick or self-harms in an attempt to avoid school, then what is it about school which is causing the problem? As for heads 'picking up the pieces' (Staufenberg 2017) when home education fails, look at the other side too, where parents are trying to deal with a child who has been severely traumatized by the school experience.

## Invisible girls

The needs of girls generally in education are overlooked, having been labelled for decades as the 'high achievers' in comparison to boys. What is obvious from the experiences of the girls on the autism spectrum and families who have contributed to this chapter, is that there seems to be a trend among schools to promote seclusion, practise illegal exclusion (Department for Education 2017a; Department for Education 2017b) and simply ignore the needs of girls who present very differently to boys with autism but whose behaviours may indicate autistic traits.

Any exclusion of a pupil, even for a short period of time, must be formally recorded. 'Informal' or 'unofficial' exclusions, such as sending pupils home to cool off, are all unlawful regardless of whether they occur with the agreement of parents or carers (Department for Education 2017b). Too many children and young people with SEN and disabilities are excluded illegally. The All Party Parliamentary Group on Autism (2017) estimate, based on Ambitious about Autism (2016) figures, that as many as 26,000 young autistic people are being unlawfully excluded each year. Not only that, but a Department for Education (2018b) survey of nearly 2000 teachers and senior leaders showed that 22% wrongly think they can encourage parents to withdraw their child from their schools, and 6% of teachers think wrongly that they can 'send pupils home to "cool off" without reporting it as exclusion' (Busby 2018). Illegal exclusion occurs also when parents are asked to take or keep pupils home from school without proper notification that it is exclusion, including picking them up from school early or at lunchtime, not coming in on certain days, or only being in school on a part-time timetable.

Ambitious about Autism (2016) found that, of a total of 745 children and young people with autism, parents and carers they had surveyed, 45% of families said their child had 'illegally been put on a reduced timetable, sent home early or asked not to come in to school on days when tests or school trips were happening' (ibid.: 11). Four hundred parents who took part in a survey for Contact a Family (2013) shared that 22% of their children were illegally excluded once a week and 15% for part of every day; more than 60% were on a part-time timetable (Murray 2013).

## School exclusion – the law and the practice

When considering school exclusions, schools must ensure that they do not discriminate against pupils on any grounds, including race, disability, gender and sexual orientation. Schools must also always comply with the principles of the Equality Act (Her Majesty's Government 2010) and are bound by the law as set out in the Act. They must also have regard to any SEN the pupil may have. A decision to exclude a child with SEN, or one who may have a Statement of SEN or an EHCP, must be taken very carefully indeed; it should be the last resort after alternatives have been tried and failed.

The head teacher and the governing board must comply with their statutory duties in relation to SEN when administering the exclusion process. This includes having regard to the Special Educational Needs and Disabilities (SEND) Code of Practice (Department for Education/Department of Health 2015). A pupil cannot be told to leave the school lawfully by a head teacher unless the formal procedures of exclusion are followed.

Since September 2012, it has become even more important for head teachers to carry out a full investigation because, even following an appeal, pupils cannot now be reinstated by an independent review panel; the panel can only quash the school's decision and direct the school's governing board to reconsider reinstating the pupil. This was a huge and controversial change to the law (Dyke 2011). Currently, the independent appeal panel's decision is binding on the parent, the child, the school governors, the head teacher/principal and the local authority.

The powers of the independent review panel include upholding the decision to exclude, recommending that the decision is reconsidered by the responsible body (the governing body) or, if the independent review panel takes the view that the responsible body's decision was flawed in light of the principles applicable for judicial review (fairness, procedural irregularity, reasonableness, proportionality), then, as mentioned above, it can quash the decision and direct that reinstatement of the pupil be reconsidered by the responsible body. There is, of course, a risk that the responsible body will reach the same decision, even after reconsideration of the matter. In the event that the pupil is not reinstated in these circumstances, the independent review panel has the power to direct that a local authority makes a financial readjustment to the school's budget or an academy makes an 'adjustment payment'.

More recent changes to school exclusion guidance include the introduction of the role of an SEN Expert. Whether or not the school recognizes that a pupil has SEN, all parents have the right to request the presence of an SEN Expert at a review meeting. The SEN Expert role is to advise the review panel, impartially, of the role of SEN in the context and circumstances of the review.

## Exclusion and seclusion – what is the difference for autistic girls?

Research on the educational experiences of autistic girls is limited. Furthermore there is almost no research on the educational experiences of autistic girls who are no longer educated at school. This is an arid area of research which perhaps explains why there is thirst for more knowledge and good practice evidence in this area. (In part, this is the mission of this book.)

Among pupils being educated in alternative provisions, 77% have recognized SEND, and are twice as likely to have mental health disorders than their mainstream peers (although this figure is likely to be an underestimate). Alluding to Office of National Statistics figures, Gill states that:

> Only half of children with clinically diagnosed conduct disorders and a third of children with similarly diagnosed emotional disorders are recognised in their schools as having special educational needs. This means the proportion of excluded children with mental health problems is likely closer to 100 per cent.
>
> (Gill 2017: 16)

It is now being considered whether educational exclusion of girls takes a different and less visible form than that of boys (ibid.). The different presentations of mental ill health in boys and girls result in different behaviours, boys being more likely to display externalized symptoms such as aggression (e.g. associated with conduct disorder), and girls being more likely to experience emotional disorders with internalized behaviours (e.g. withdrawal, self-harm) (Cole 2015; Gill 2017).

Rouse (2011) states that, for schools and local authorities, addressing the exclusion issues of girls, with their vastly lower formal exclusion figures than boys, is not a priority. However, he asserts that current exclusion figures for girls may be 'the tip of an iceberg' (ibid.: 30). He refers to 'self-exclusion' or 'hidden exclusion' among girls, aside from the recognized formal and informal exclusions triggered by rule-challenging or expectation-challenging behaviours.

Girls prompted by feelings of 'isolation and/or distress' are particularly vulnerable to self-exclusions (e.g. withdrawal, disengagement, non-attendance). This phenomenon is largely ignored, but:

> Although, these factors do not prevent the girls from accessing the school setting, they may have consequences as significant as formal disciplinary exclusion as disengagement and withdrawal may restrict an individual's access to education and support, which may lead more generally to social exclusion.
>
> (Rouse 2011: 30)

Rouse endorses Lloyd's proposal that patterns of exclusion are 'gendered' through different behaviours, different school and teacher responses and strategies, and school culture around equal opportunities, and he quotes the following findings from Osler and Vincent's work:

- 'The invisibility of girls' difficulties has serious consequences in terms of their access to help'.
- 'The nature of help on offer assumes that provision is equally available for both boys and girls'.
- 'Girls' responsiveness to sources of help is complex'.
- 'Identification of girls' needs and the subsequent provision of services are compartmentalized … [resulting in] poor coordination of services …'.
- 'The use of truancy, self-exclusion and internal exclusion were reported by the girls [as] unofficial and unrecorded exclusions'.
- 'Gender appears to be an important influence on decisions to exclude a person formally'.
- 'Bullying is a serious problem and appears to be a significant factor contributing to girls' decisions to self-exclude …'.(Rouse 2011: 24).

This list obviously resonates with the issues and behaviours of many autistic girls – their 'invisibility'; their tendency to mask and camouflage their social difficulties; their experiences of being bullied; their tendency to recede rather than confront.

## Pupil referral units and girls

We know that proportionally the number of girls in special schools/pupil referral units (PRUs) is relatively small compared to the number of boys (Brede et al. 2017; Sproston et al. 2017). This presents challenges for those girls accessing specialist provision as there are limited opportunities for them to develop appropriate peer relationships with other girls.

I recall a brief period of teaching in a special school for children with behaviour, emotional and social difficulties many, many years ago where 98% of pupils were boys, and there were only two girls on roll. The staff were predominantly male with the exception of myself and the catering and administrative staff. What chance did those two girls have in promoting their social and emotional development in an environment which was inherently male. It was unequal and inequitable.

This experience for autistic girls is often described as having a 'double whammy effect' where girls educated in specialist provision are indeed a marginalized group further hampered by the gender difference in specialist provision populations. Factor into this, the further marginalization for girls with autism, a social communication condition, in this situation; and reflect how the system itself provides yet a further barrier to inclusion and defies fundamental ethical and moral considerations.

A key issue highlighted by Sproston et al. (2017) is the lack of support ('unsuitable or non-existent'; ibid.: 8) for autistic girls transitioning to PRUs. For the autistic girls they interviewed, there were in some cases long delays between being excluded from school and accessing the PRU. Sproston et al. write:

> This lack of consideration regarding [these] transitional stages further isolated families from educational opportunities and heightened the anxiety of the girls and their parents. It is therefore recommended that ['especially for girls on the autism spectrum'], if exclusion from school is the only option, post-exclusion transition plans are developed; to help mitigate ... the substantial negative outcomes associated with school exclusion.
>
> (Sproston et al. 2017: 10–11)

For too long, as a professional community, educators have focused their effort primarily on the needs of boys in relation to underachievement and SEND, which largely is a result of the 'naughty boy' mindset which grew in the 1970s and 1980s. This pervaded our thinking around SEND and has, in my view, blinkered our ability to see what is actually happening in front of eyes in our schools with girls.

## Essential school-based support

Schools where there is a low understanding of autism and the needs of children on the spectrum may sanction autistic pupils for 'poor behaviour' when, in fact, their behaviour is the only way that the highly anxious and stressed child can communicate that their needs are not being met. Instead of punitive action, schools need to make reasonable adjustments, as mandated under the Equality Act (Her Majesty's Government 2010), to enable them to cope (All Party Parliamentary Group on Autism 2017).

Key to the effective educational and social support of autistic pupils is an organizational 'culture of understanding' (All Party Parliamentary Group on Autism 2017: 15), including autism-friendly practices. Fewer than half of teachers surveyed by APPGA said they would feel confident about supporting a child on the autism spectrum. This fact emphasizes the importance of autism as one of the topics in the new 2018 Initial Teacher Training Framework.

Girls with autism face the same academic challenges as boys but are not as vocal as boys; often they will not ask for help, will try to hide difficulties. Honeybourne's research in *Girls with Autism in the Classroom: Hidden Difficulties and How to Help* (Honeybourne 2015) identified four key issues:

- friendships and relationships;
- learning and communication;
- interpreting the world; and
- recognizing the positives.

Honeybourne carried out face-to-face interviews with 67 girls and women diagnosed on the autism spectrum, aged 14 years old and above. She asked her participants about both the positive and negative aspects of their school experiences, as well as for their suggestions on how to improve the school environment for autistic girls.

She reported that the greatest difficulties shared by the group were in the area of 'Friendships and getting on with others', contributing to the participants' 'feelings of loneliness, isolation, being a "social misfit" and related feelings of depression, worry and anxiety'. These difficulties included:

- 'Wanting/needing to spend time alone but not having the opportunity'.
- 'Struggling to meet like-minded people'.
- 'Difficulty making and maintaining friendships, and relationships with classmates'.
- 'Feeling especially isolated at break and lunch times'.
- 'Being teased or bullied'.
- 'Difficulties with group work'.(Honeybourne 2015)

One can imagine how these particular feelings captured in this study lead girls and women to seclude themselves out of a deep need for quiet and 'alone time', and also out of necessity to avoid social situations. These situations can prompt girls to respond in untypical and unique ways, which can often result in a school response which is inadequate, lacking compassion and understanding.

Sproston et al. (2017: 10) report that, in adolescence, teenage girls may externalize hitherto internalized stress, resulting in behaviours such as 'withdrawal, panic attacks or aggression, which could be misconstrued as behavioural problems ... and possibly lead to exclusion'. They highlight the importance of schools adopting 'more inclusive strategies for autistic students (especially girls) to allow them to cope without fear of retribution'.

Schools generally want to do their very best for their vulnerable pupils – I believe this assiduously, I have to. However, the needs of girls who are diagnosed and misdiagnosed with autism present a mixed and complex profile of need for most schools to identify, assess and support appropriately. So schools are on a hiding to nothing then? Not necessarily ...

Honeybourne's interviewees suggested that to help pupils on the autism spectrum schools need to:

- 'Bring structure to the unstructured'.
- 'Provide a range of activities for pupils at break and lunch times'.
- 'Provide clear guidelines for group work ...'.

- 'Allocate specific roles and make expectations clear'.
- 'Make it "ok" and "normal" for students to use a quiet space when they need some time alone; schools can be exhausting for those with ASC [autism spectrum conditions] ...'(Honeybourne 2015)

The reality though for autistic girls, diagnosed or undiagnosed, is that they experience extremely high levels of anxiety, and what we must address in schools is how we manage this compassionately and with kindness. Manage this and you will be able to manage and accommodate the girls' autism.

All staff need to recognize that despite outward signs of a girl with autism coping in any given situation; she continually manages high levels of anxiety in any situation she faces; this is exhausting and debilitating. Consider the following sober facts:

- Around half of all pupils permanently from school are suffering from a recognized mental health problem, according to a study by the Institute for Public Policy Research (IPPR), which estimates that of the 86,000-strong prison population, more than 54,000 were excluded at school.
- Those children who are permanently excluded find themselves at a significant disadvantage, with only one in a hundred going on to attain five good GCSEs, which is the typical benchmark of academic success.
- The majority will end up in prison, says the study. The IPPR says its research lays bare the 'broken system' facing excluded pupils. It flags up high levels of mental health issues among permanently excluded students – at least one in two, compared with one in 50 pupils in the wider population.
- After exclusion, the study says, there is a downward spiral of underachievement, with teachers in schools catering for excluded pupils twice as likely to have no educational qualifications.

What a depressing context in which to expect permanently excluded girls with autism operate – how do we buck this trend?

## Lived experiences of exclusion

All of the following girls were either interviewed themselves or their parents contributed by sharing their stories for them. They report mental health conditions associated with their autism, which largely manifest as high levels of anxiety. The impact anxiety has on the lives of these girls has ranged from self-harm and eating disorders to attempts to take their own lives.

### Emma

Emma is attending a new school and has been illegally excluded since October on at least 10 occasions – mainly for going to get a hug from her younger brother when she is anxious; and formally excluded on one occasion – again for seeking out her little brother.

When a child is prohibited from integrating with their peers – in Emma's experience, her younger brother – it doesn't only affect them but their parents too. SEN parents are continuously excluded just like our children.

## Lily

The following account was written by a mother who describes herself as 'the parent of a school-traumatized child':

> Within three days of my daughter starting Year 4, under a new teacher, her SEN Support Plan had been thrown out of the window, because her (supply) teacher did not agree with the contents; the plan put in place for her to move up to her new class that myself and the school SENCO had put into place was also disregarded.
>
> She was being kept in at break times three times a day because her writing was 'too slow', at eight. No one told us – her parents. I discovered this after contacting her teacher, when her behaviour was deteriorating and she was exhibiting both physical and emotional symptoms of school related stress.
>
> I spoke with her teacher, who insisted that he saw no reason that he should stop keeping our daughter in – after all 'she is allowed to eat'. We spoke with the head teacher who told us he 'would support Mr X in whichever teaching methods he chose to use'.
>
> We wrote to the school and asked them to stop keeping her in at break times for something that was out of her control and asked them to confirm where it sat in line with their 'positive' policies.
>
> All of this was to no avail – and in the middle was a little girl who was sad, unhappy, struggling and in her words 'feeling mad' and like 'a naughty girl'. Academically her work was starting to go backwards and she was not learning anything; she became more and more isolated.
>
> It eventually got to the point where we felt, as parents, we were failing to protect her and that neither she, who had spoken to her head teacher herself, or ourselves were being listened to. So we removed her from school – we had been considering home education for a while – and while initially we felt that we would only home educate her if we could do better than the school, in fact it got to the point where school, and her treatment at the hands of her teaching staff, meant that we had to remove her for her own well-being.

Parents who contributed to this chapter tell of the relentless rounds of discussions with their daughter's schools where they felt like the sole advocate for their children. The school's opportunity to champion the rights and entitlements of girls with autism is not the experience of the many families I have spoken to; in fact, quite the contrary.

It is the very nature of acting in the best interests of their daughters that parents believe ultimately leads to them feeling excluded from the in-school process of SEN Support. This I find sadly ironic given that the latest SEND Code of Practice (Department for Education/Department of Health 2014) is predicated on the principles of partnership, participation, engagement with parent carers and children.

## Lois

> Our formal complaint to the school led to a response that bore no resemblance to actual events and also that took credit for initiatives we ourselves had put into place to try to ease the pressure school was placing on her and its negative impact on our daughter's well-

being. We had also spoken with the Education Welfare Officer ourselves who simply never got back to us.

Our daughter was effectively bullied out of her school place by her own teachers and will tell anyone who listens 'school is the worst place in the world'.

It has taken nearly two years for her to recover from this experience, and at nine she is still not the world's best writer, but some of her knowledge outstrips both mine and her dad's.

## Tara

What is striking about the lived experiences of parents of autistic girls is the sad similarity where the schools have been unable or unwilling to build a relationship with their girls. Relationships are crucial to autistic girls, and as Tara, a Year 10 autistic student, tells us, 'I need to know that I'm accepted by my teachers as who I am and that they understand this, they understand me.'

We know that real and concrete learning experiences work well for most learners. However to encourage engagement in their learning autistic girls will benefit from clear links to context and visual prompts to ensure that their learning becomes embedded over time.

Tara goes on to explain:

> The really good teachers who get me and know me better than the others, they ask me questions about my interests and use this to help me to understand – like the Harry Potter diagram my English teacher drew for me to explain how to use paragraphs better.

Autistic girls want to engage with others but often find this very confusing or overwhelming which creates and exacerbates the rising anxiety many girls experience. Being alert to these, often discrete, changes in girls is a skill in itself. However, to engage our girls we have to ask them what works for them, how they would like to be supported at school and not be tempted to pathologize the differences in girls with autism and how they may present.

## Amelia

> School has a small chicken enclosure in the grounds which Amelia loves visiting. She likes to pet the chickens and she talks more to them than she does to anyone else – she has almost developed a daily dependence on handling the chickens. This works for her, for the school; or at least it was working.
>
> She was observed handling the chickens in an unkind way by an unqualified member of staff who does not know her at all. Amelia was consequently banned from visiting and handling the chickens. She doesn't understand why. No one has explained what she may have or was perceived to have done. She has been treated unfairly and her ritual visit to the chickens is no more.
>
> The chickens provided a de-stressing opportunity for her on daily basis – how can the school not recognize this? They really don't know my autistic daughter at all.

Recognizing anxiety as a characterizing feature of living with autism for girls is often overlooked at classroom level. Girls will mask their difficulties, choosing to copy the reactions and social responses of others to get themselves through the endless social situation school presents. This sets girls up for significant problems – can you imagine how incredibly difficult it must be to continually supress your natural reactions all the time? Little wonder that many parents report of the successive 'meltdowns' their daughters display when arriving home from school. Without the provision of an under-standing community, where opportunities to learn how to regulate and manage emo-tions are encouraged, we are simply excluding autistic girls from learning and living happily and staying healthy. Surely this is our prime objective as educators, to equip our girls with skills they need to lead secure and independent lives?

Those schools that choose to exclude, often without being aware of how their ignorance of the needs of autistic girls impacts their life chances, are schools that often pay lip service to core moral imperative of inclusion. Schools that are driven by results, narrow knowledge, and heavy curriculum offers, automatically operate exclusively. How are we holding these schools to account? When have we read of disciplinary con-sequences for school leaders who choose to flout the law, not make reasonable adjust-ments, not use their 'best endeavours' to do all that they can to support girls with autism?

### Michaela

> My daughter has been placed on a reduced timetable for the best part of two academic years as they found her difficult. They continually sent her home, which I soon learnt was unlawful – exact details have not been given to me and have been withheld by the acad-emy. She was not allowed to do any extracurricular activities unless I was there to supervise her. My mum was then exploited as her unpaid one-to-one as school refused to have her in as they had 'no available adult'. Her behaviours escalated once the school replaced her nan with a 'mum' (known to the school) to act as TA [teaching assistant]. She then received so many FTE [fixed term exclusions] until they permanently excluded her in June of this year.

Parents report that their daughters are not accepted for their uniqueness; they are not respected or considered as contributors to their school communities. It seems that some schools seek to homogenize their student communities and in doing so overlook the opportunity to celebrate the cool, quirkiness of our autistic girls and provide whole-school recognition of the incredible asset girls are.

Diversity of need in education requires diversity of provision and often it is this requirement of our local schools which springs the tipping point for our vulnerable girls. Local schools will struggle to work in isolation to provide for the needs of this growing group of girls nationally. What we require is an eclectic approach to securing 'what works well' approaches to establishing excellent support and intervention for autistic girls..

We have one state-funded special school for autistic girls in England: Limpsfield Grange School – a wonderful, educationally flexible and nurturing school. Head teacher Sarah Wild writes:

> The girls really want to tell people what it's like to be autistic and to help others. They've spent a long time feeling really alone and don't want other girls to feel as isolated. They're proud of their coolness and quirkiness and want other kids to feel part of a cool community.

As Kavithayini Kannadasan (2016) eloquently identifies:

- Autistic girls are non-judgmental.
- Autistic girls are honest.
- Autistic girls are rarely boring.
- Autistic girls are special.
- Autistic girls are logical.
- Autistic girls are loyal.
- Autistic girls are interesting.
- Autistic girls are wonderful.
- Autistic girls are diverse.
- Autistic girls are imaginative.
- Autistic people are unique.

As Temple Grandin (2012) says: 'Different. Not less.'

I hope we can all cherish these facts because if we can, our autism community for girls particularly would be phenomenal; and unlawful and painful school exclusion experiences will become a thing of the past; and an increasingly inclusive education will be the typical school experience for all.

## References

All Party Parliamentary Group on Autism (2017) *Autism and Education in England: A Report by the All Party Parliamentary Group on Autism on How the Education System in England Works for Children and Young People on the Autism Spectrum.* London: NAS.

Ambitious about Autism (2016) *When Will We Learn.* London: Ambitious About Autism.

Brede, J., Remington, A., Kenny, L., Warren, K. and Pellicano, E. (2017) 'Excluded from school: autistic students' experiences of school exclusion and subsequent re-integration into school'. *Autism and Developmental Language Impairments*, 2, 1–20.

Busby, E. (2018) 'One in five teachers wrongly believe "backdoor exclusions" are allowed, study finds'. *Independent*, 12 March. Retrieved from www.independent.co.uk/news/education/education-news/exclusions-teachers-off-rolling-exam-results-national-foundation-education-research-a8252436.html (accessed 9 September 2018).

Cole, T. (2015) *Mental Health Difficulties and Children at Risk of Exclusion from Schools in England: A Review from an Educational Perspective of Policy, Practice and Research 1997 to 2015.* Oxford: University of Oxford.

Contact a Family (2013) *Falling through the Net: Illegal Exclusions, the Experiences of Families with Disabled Children in England and Wales.* London: Contact a Family. Retrieved from https://contact.org.uk/media/639982/falling_through_the_net_-_illegal_exclusions_report_2013_web.pdf (accessed 9 September 2018).

Department for Education (2017a) *Permanent and Fixed-Period Exclusions in England: 2015 to 2016.* London: Department for Education. Retrieved from www.gov.uk/government/collections/statistics-exclusions (accessed 9 September 2018).

Department for Education (2017b) *Exclusion from Maintained Schools, Academies and Pupil Referral Units in England.* London: Department for Education.

Department for Education (2018a) *Permanent and Fixed-Period Exclusions in England: 2016 to 2017.* London: Department for Education. Retrieved from www.gov.uk/government/collections/statistics-exclusions (accessed 9 September 2018).

Department for Education (2018b) *Teacher Voice Omnibus Survey: March 2018*. London: Department for Education. Retrieved from www.gov.uk/government/publications/teacher-voice-omnibus-march-2018-survey (accessed 9 September 2018).

Department for Education/Department of Health (2015) *Special Educational Needs and Disability Code of Practice: 0–25 Years*. London: Department for Education/Department of Health.

Dyke, T. (2011) 'Exclusions: a school's right to decide'. *Guardian*, 21 March. Retrieved from www.theguardian.com/law/2011/mar/21/school-exclusions-independent-appeal-panels (accessed 9 September 2018).

Gill, K. (2017) *Making the Difference: Breaking the Link between School Exclusion and Social Exclusion*. London: Institute for Public Policy Research. Retrieved from www.ippr.org/publications/making-the-difference (accessed 9 September 2018).

Gould, J. (2017) 'Towards understanding the under-recognition of girls and women on the autism spectrum'. *Autism*, 21(6), 703–705.

Grandin, T. (2012) *Different. Not Less: Inspiring Stories of Achievement and Successful Employment from Adults with Autism, Asperger's and ADHD*. Arlington, TX: Future Horizons.

Hazell, W. (2018) 'Exclusions of autistic pupils up 60 per cent'. *Times Educational Supplement*, 7 June. Retrieved from www.tes.com/news/exclusions-autistic-pupils-60-cent (accessed 6 September 2018).

Her Majesty's Government (2010) 'Equality Act 2010'. Retrieved from www.legislation.gov.uk/ukpga/2010/15/contents (accessed 10 September 2018).

Hill, A. (2009) 'Doctors are failing to spot Asperger's in girls'. *Observer*, 12 April. Retrieved from www.theguardian.com/lifeandstyle/2009/apr/12/autism-aspergers-girls (accessed 9 September 2018).

Honeybourne, V. (2015) 'Autistic girls in the classroom: hidden difficulties and how to help'. 20 August. Retrieved from https://network.autism.org.uk/good-practice/evidence-base/girls-autism-classroom-hidden-difficulties-and-how-help (accessed 10 September 2018).

Kannadasan, K. (2016) 'Autism is awesome'. Retrieved from www.linkedin.com/pulse/autism-awesome-kavithayini-kannadasan (accessed 10 September 2018).

Kershaw, A. (2017) 'Worrying rise in number of children with autism being expelled or suspended from school'. *Independent*, 14 September. Retrieved from www.independent.co.uk/news/education/education-news/autism-expulsion-rate-rise-school-pupils-students-department-education-asd-a7946701.html (accessed 9 September 2018).

Murray, J. (2013) 'Children with disabilities illegally excluded from school'. *Guardian*, 18 February. Retrieved from www.theguardian.com/education/2013/feb/18/children-with-disabilities-illegally-excluded (accessed 9 September 2018).

Neal, A. (2017) 'Autism concern over home schooling rise in Wales'. Retrieved from www.bbc.co.uk/news/uk-wales-42017204 (accessed 9 September 2018).

Rouse, D. (2011) *Why Do Girls Get Excluded from School?* PhD thesis. Birmingham: University of Birmingham. Retrieved from http://etheses.bham.ac.uk/3096/1/Rouse11ApEdPsyD1.pdf (accessed 9 September 2018).

Sproston, K., Sedgewick, F. and Crane, L. (2017) 'Autistic girls and school exclusion: perspectives of students and their parents'. *Autism and Developmental Language Impairments*, 2, 1–14.

Staufenberg, J. (2017) 'Home education doubles, with schools left to "pick up pieces" when it fails'. *Schools Week*, 7 July. Retrieved from https://schoolsweek.co.uk/home-education-doubles-with-schools-left-to-pick-up-pieces-when-it-fails (accessed 10 September 2018).

# Chapter 11

# Girls who 'can't help won't'

Understanding the distinctive profile of
Pathological Demand Avoidance (PDA)
and developing approaches to support girls
with PDA

*Ruth Fidler*

## Introduction

This chapter is written in reflection of the insight and commitment of a number of professionals, inspirational young people and their families. I am privileged to have been able to work with some of these people over many years and would like to acknowledge that our current and ongoing understanding of pathological demand avoidance (PDA) is a culmination of collaboration between a number of individuals.

In this chapter we will gain an overview of the PDA profile, consider why there is particular interest in PDA among those who are interested in autistic girls, and look at strategies that can be effective in supporting girls with PDA.

There continues to be ongoing debate about the concept of PDA in terms of whether it describes a separate and distinct group, nonetheless, PDA is increasingly viewed as a profile within the autism spectrum. In 2015 The National Autistic Society updated their website to recognize it as such however there continue to be some areas within the UK and internationally where PDA is less well-known. Although this undoubtedly brings frustrations for families seeking recognition of their children's needs, the developing picture is at least moving in the right direction.

The understanding of PDA that informs this chapter is based on the original work of Professor Elizabeth Newson in the 1980s, and reflects the current views about PDA of the National Autistic Society (NAS) and the PDA Society, as well as my own professional experience.

Elizabeth Newson saw a number of children who had been referred to her for assessment at the Child Development Research Unit of Nottingham University who were described as reminiscent but not typical of other children with autism or Asperger syndrome. She recognized that although these children were not typical of the formulation of the autism spectrum at that time (World Health Organization 1992), they were similar to each other. The key differences she observed were what she described in the first peer reviewed published paper as Pathological Demand Avoidance (Newson et al. 2003).

The key differences between this group and the group of children with autism included seeming to have better social awareness, an avoidance of everyday expectations or demands, raised anxiety and being more comfortable in role play and pretending.

Elizabeth viewed PDA as part of the 'family of pervasive developmental conditions' as they were known, which we now commonly refer to as the autism spectrum (NICE

2011). Her initial figures regarding gender ratio of PDA being 50:50 were also significantly different from other presentations of autism.

Phil Christie, a specialist psychologist who worked alongside Elizabeth for many years and who continues to progress development of our knowledge of PDA, outlined initial guidelines for supporting this group of children (Christie 2007).

It is important to acknowledge that huge strides have been made in our understanding of this complex condition; however it is equally important to recognize that there is still a lot more to find out. This is what Phil Christie refers to as our 'evolving understanding' of PDA within which we need to develop:

- Greater consensus regarding diagnosis.
- Better awareness of effective strategies.
- Support networks for families.
- Better understanding of adults with PDA and long term outcomes.
- Further research, exploring, for example, social identity, anxiety and overlap with other developmental conditions.

## Why are people who are interested in girls on the autism spectrum also interested in PDA?

As our notion of autism broadens we are reviewing not only the full range of the spectrum but also the prevalence figures especially in women and girls. There remain open questions about the incidence of PDA although initial findings suggest 1:25 of individuals on the autism spectrum have a PDA profile (Gillberg et al. 2015). Due to the profile of PDA including seemingly better social skills, variability across settings such as a difference between behaviour at school and at home, and raised anxiety which leads to avoidance with a drive to control, there are often parallels drawn with other autistic girls.

Evidence is suggesting a more even gender ratio in PDA compared to in other ASD profiles (Newson et al. 2003; O'Nions et al. 2014a; O'Nions et al. 2014b; Gillberg et al. 2015). Gould and Ashton-Smith have also suggested that PDA could be more typical of a female ASD presentation (Gould and Ashton-Smith 2011).

Along with growing awareness of the issues for women and girls with autism there is also interest in promoting emotional well-being. Girls with a PDA profile are likely to experience particularly high levels of anxiety which will in turn have an increased impact on their mental health.

## What are the distinctive features of the PDA profile?

PDA seems to be dimensional in nature, affecting individuals to varying degrees (O'Nions et al. 2016). Children with PDA share some of the core features of others on the autism spectrum in terms of differences in social communication, social interaction and restricted and repetitive patterns of behaviours, activities or interests. However, there are some distinctive features described, notably that children with PDA have an extreme sensitivity to demands being placed on them. They are highly anxious and have fragile emotional well-being. They appear to have difficulties with social identity, often viewing themselves as more of an adult than a child.

> Ellie, aged 7, awarded herself the role of 'classroom manager'. In this capacity she took a lead in distributing equipment and designating pegs and pupil trays. Her teacher had to conduct careful negotiations when Ellie also tried to undertake allocating teaching groups and setting homework for other pupils.

Sensitivity to tolerating expectations, which includes those they may place upon themselves, can lead to extreme behaviour and issues with mental health.

> Charlotte, aged 17, would often go through extended periods of anxiety regarding expectations she placed on herself. For example, she was part way through a knitting project that was well within her skill level and which she wanted to finish. There were no external pressures or obstacles which prevented her doing so but she was unable to complete it. What is more, the ensuing anxiety about it led to episodes of insomnia, reduced self-care and even difficulty attending school for a time.

The most notable characteristic of PDA is a resistance to and avoidance of the ordinary demands of everyday life using approaches which are socially strategic. These may include distraction, procrastination, re-negotiation, bogus excuses or ailments, as well as more dramatic and even threatening strategies.

> When Alma, aged 9, anticipated a demand or request from her teacher, she would often start with low-level distraction or procrastination such as 'I need to show you what I found in the playground' or 'I just need to go to the toilet again.' If the expectation was not retracted and she remained sensitive to it, her strategies would become more active such as saying she felt ill, ripping up her work, throwing pens or running out of class.

The list of defining characteristics of PDA as set out by the NAS comprises:

- Resists and avoids the ordinary demands of life.
- Uses social strategies as part of the avoidance.
- Appears sociable but lacks understanding.
- Experiences excessive mood swings and impulsivity.
- Appears comfortable in role play and pretence.
- Displays obsessive behaviour that is often focused on other people.

Children and young people with PDA appear to experience an anxiety driven need to control and to avoid everyday expectations. Of course, lots of children attempt to avoid a range of everyday expectations so it is important to note we are talking about an extreme, out of the ordinary and sometimes explosive avoidance.

Moreover, children with PDA will often avoid activities that are well within their capability, that are mundane and that they are comfortable with on other occasions, such as everyday tasks like getting dressed. Interestingly they may also avoid activities that they would usually enjoy or that they had been looking forward to.

> Jade, aged 12 years, had been looking forward to going to the newly opened coffee shop near her house where they had an introductory offer on extravagant hot chocolate. She had been checking on the progress of the shop fitters and had arranged with her parents to reserve the table she preferred and take her there at a time of her choosing. When the designated day arrived she was very anxious and avoidant. She was in the end unable to get dressed and leave the house and then became so stressed about having 'let the café down' that she was not able to go an alternative day either.

Avoidance can be easily triggered in response to a variety of types of demand. An *overt demand* is when a child is asked directly to do something, e.g. 'put your shoes on and come to the door'. These are the most obvious demands and they are hard to avoid in everyday life at home and at school. A *perceived demand* is one the child is anticipating or 'reading' in a situation. This might be linked to a familiar routine at school or bedtime or might be situational such as the child recognizing 'that look' the adult has just before they ask them to do something. An *internal demand* is one that the child or young person places on themselves, such as 'I want to/should be able to feed the cat but I can't.' For some, even *praise* can be felt as a subtle demand; for example, 'You got ready for school so brilliantly yesterday' may carry an implication that the same is being expected today or tomorrow.

It is this genuine difficulty with tolerating expectations that explains one mother's description that her daughter 'can't help won't' (Christie et al. 2012: 37). What she meant was that even though there are tasks that her daughter is capable of and even sometimes willing to do, there are other occasions when she cannot help the fact that she cannot co-operate due to her high anxiety. Her mum said that reminding herself of this helped her not to take it personally and prompted her to approach her daughter with reassurance rather than frustration.

Children with PDA are not only sensitive to demands but their tolerance may vary considerably from one day or one moment to another.

Mood swings are not uncommon in other youngsters on the autism spectrum but are a particular feature of those with PDA. Linked to mood swings is impulsivity, which can lead to risk taking behaviour in areas where girls are particularly vulnerable.

> Nina, aged 18, became involved in a difficult incident when having felt snubbed by a friend she approached the friend's boyfriend at his workplace to sexually proposition him. In her agitated state she created something of a scene which not only had an impact on her wider social network but also caused considerable damage to the original friendship, which otherwise may well have been resolved.

Children with PDA have a *seemingly* better social awareness than many others on the autism spectrum. They also have an understanding of which distractions or approaches may be most effective with different people they know.

> Katie, aged 14, recognized that she could distract her teaching assistant effectively with conversation about his puppy whereas her class teacher was more easily diverted by chatting about her children.

Despite this there are still underlying difficulties with social communication and interaction meaning it may be difficult to predict and manage social situations. Some girls with PDA can be simultaneously socially vulnerable, wanting to fit in with their peers, as well as socially strategic, leading them to interact in a controlling fashion. This means they may be sending out and receiving mixed messages, which makes sustaining friendships complicated. Other girls may be hypersensitive to the distress of others and might over-process both self-doubt as well as empathy for other people. They may slip into a steep decline of rumination and blame if a social situation goes wrong, or become overly involved and disproportionately distressed or distracted by an event that has happened to someone else. Both responses can be emotionally draining for these girls.

Dr Judith Gould comments:

> The children cannot cope with strong emotions, whether in themselves or other people. Faced with emotion shown overtly they tend to become distressed, angry and negative in reaction.

(Fidler and Christie 2015: 10)

Children with PDA are more comfortable in role play than those with more straightforward presentations of autism. They may find it easier to co-operate with a request if they are in role as someone else, especially if that someone else has an adult status.

> One parent reported: 'My eight-year-old daughter with PDA coped with moving house by taking on the role of an adult. She came to sign for the keys to the new house and had tea breaks with the removal guys giving them directions about which room certain furniture should go in.'

Whereas it can sometimes be helpful to go along with a role that a child has adopted in order to gain co-operation, especially if they take on a positive role, it remains important that they do not lose sight of who they really are. Some children with PDA, and especially the girls, can become so swept away with a character that the lines between reality and pretend can become blurred.

> Tasha, aged 9, who has a keen interest in pug dogs, created a dog identity for herself as 'Lola'. She had imaginary 'dog memories' of places she had visited and things she had done. Sometimes she would be highly engaged as 'Lola' but other times would retreat into the character and would only communicate using barking or whining sounds. It could take quite some time to encourage her to re-engage as herself. Adults needed to tread a careful line between acknowledging how important 'Lola' was to Tasha and not letting this persona take over.

Another feature of the imaginative play of children with PDA, especially girls, is that although they often enjoy pretend play and are able to generate creative narratives in their games (rather than repeating a script from a book or film as many boys with autism might), they can be rather controlling.

> Alice, aged 6, enjoyed playing in an imaginary way with her friends, but would tend to direct them, such as: 'We are going to play babies. Your baby is called Gemma and she has to wear these clothes and sit there and you have to say "Shush darling" to her when I tell you she's crying ...' This type of play can be a very good way for adults to build rapport and participation with a child but it is difficult for other children to tolerate being so controlled.

Children with PDA tend to show their obsessive behaviour in different ways to those with more usual autism profiles. Instead of their personal interest being about collecting information or objects it can be more social in nature. It might be focused around, for example, celebrities or people they know in everyday life. These obsessive interests can be both positive and negative, and can be especially challenging for someone on the receiving end of a negative focus. A negative focus could come across to another child as teasing or taunting or could create obstacles for particular adults being able to work effectively with some children. Often families describe their children's avoidance itself as having an obsessive feel and some children will establish elaborate routines which are less concerned with the detail of the events but more about controlling the action.

## What difference does a PDA 'label' make?

There are professionals and parents who when they come across material about PDA, describe it as a 'light bulb moment'. They make comments such as 'This is what finally makes sense of the child I have been working with', or 'When I read about PDA it's as if someone had written a biography of my child.'

Not only is getting a label helpful in order to support families in a better understanding of their child, but it is potentially the signpost to the right interventions. After all, the fundamental purpose of a diagnosis or 'label' is to better understand a child and to link that understanding to appropriate strategies which support them to thrive. Many are the times education professionals have commented to me that they have tried the usual autism-friendly strategies and been left frustrated and confused to find that they are not effective for a child with PDA. While it is not the case that the strategies for supporting children and young people with PDA are entirely separate from those that work well for children with autism, they usually require a different and more personalized emphasis.

The PDA Society conducted an online survey in March 2018, which highlighted that:

> There is a group of autistic people for whom the conventional highly structured approaches are not only unhelpful but can lead to increased and debilitating stress ... this need for a different approach makes it essential for this group to be identified ...
>
> (PDA Society 2018: 1)

What essentially characterizes the difference in approaches is an emphasis on flexibility, collaboration and indirect strategies.

Some parents and professionals develop an effective style by trial and error, informed by instinct and personal knowledge of the child. Knowing the individual is crucial but the whole process is considerably smoother if an appropriate diagnosis can point towards recommended approaches. It is also helpful for wider family members, siblings and the full range of professionals involved from health, social care and education to understand PDA.

Getting a label that identifies differences accurately is important to young people themselves. Particularly for girls who are eager to fit in and who may have adopted a persona in order to do so, it is paramount for their long term well-being that they remain connected to, and accepting of their genuine self.

Eaton writes:

> Girls who have autism and, in particular, those who have Pathological Demand Avoidance, are often very good at masking their difficulties. They often have an inherent desire to please and to fit in with social norms for behaviour, and try very hard to maintain a 'persona' whilst in public.

> (Eaton 2018: 26)

## What sort of approaches tend to work well for girls with PDA?

Having worked in the field of autism for over 25 years, in my experience the usual style of strategies recommended for children and young people with autism, such as visual checklists, schedules and clear expectations, tend not to be as effective for those with PDA. This is because, although these usual strategies can reduce stress caused by uncertainty, they also tend to be characterized by an instructional tone and they work on the premise that providing sufficient clarity will facilitate compliance. For children and young people with PDA there is a fundamental, variable, anxiety-based difficulty with co-operation so even though there can be some benefits in helping predict events, there is still a sensitivity to expectations placed on them.

Children with PDA tend to respond best to strategies that are more personalized and flexible. These are referred to by myself and Phil Christie as 'collaborative approaches to learning' (Fidler and Christie 2019). Collaborative approaches to learning advocate creative, negotiated, individualized and indirect strategies. In practice these are developed in collaboration with all the adults involved, including parents, plus input from the young person themselves. They are approaches that are invitational, that appeal to strengths, interests, a sense of humour, and use de-personalized requests or suggestions. Providing processing time and opportunities for choice are also important features of the approach. It is central to build rapport and trust between the adults and the child since this is also a key factor in providing emotional stability and reducing anxiety, the underlying driver of the demand avoidance.

There are some well-known autism strategies that may be useful, such as visual systems, but these will need adapting so as to offer lots of opportunities for options, control and indirect presentation.

It is necessary to appreciate that the child's tolerance to demands is likely to be highly sensitive and variable. That means that adults need to stay vigilant to fluctuations and match these to their responses. An analogy of synchronizing two dials, one of which measures the child's threshold of tolerance and the other of which measures the adults' demand, can be helpful. It is described as follows:

> When things are going well and [her] anxiety is comparatively low this threshold is higher and [she] can be more accepting of demands and requests. During a more difficult time, [her] anxiety is raised and [her] threshold is lower. At these times [she] is less tolerant, feels the need to be more controlling and is easily 'tipped over the edge'.
> (Fidler and Christie 2019: 26)

Collaborative approaches to learning may lead to children having more control than is usual for their age, and may require amended expectations compared to typically developing peers, however that is not to say that there should be no boundaries or ground rules. Boundaries and ground rules should be decided with care and collaboration so they are reduced to the agreed priorities but then maintained.

The aim is not to remove all demands but to increase the occasions of co-operation while developing an increased tolerance to demands over time.

In terms of their education, girls with PDA will need learning opportunities personalized in content as well as adapted in style. Priority should be given to promoting emotional well-being and independence. For all children, but for girls in particular, emphasis is required on managing social relationships, risk taking and emotional regulation.

In 2015 the PDA Society ran its first parent conference before which they carried out a survey of parental experiences. Parents answered questions about what had helped them, commenting:

- 'Thinking of meltdowns as panic attacks and being therefore able to give reassurance and understanding.'
- 'Choose your battles. You cannot win them all.'
- 'Reduce demands to a minimum when tolerance is low.'
- 'Seeing her thrive when we adjust our parenting.'

## Summary

There continues to be active debate about the concept of PDA, which reflects our evolving understanding of the condition and calls for further research in the field. Interestingly, in my experience, it is often only when professionals meet a child with PDA that they have their own 'light bulb' moment and connect with the ways in which PDA encapsulates a distinct presentation of autism.

There is growing acknowledgement that individuals with PDA have a recognizable pattern of characteristics that are similar to each other and distinct from those of others with a more straightforward presentation of autism. Equally, there is widespread anecdotal feedback from practitioners that I and my colleagues have worked with, that approaches with a different emphasis are needed to support children with PDA.

In order to be the best reflective thinkers we can be, as parents and as practitioners, we sometimes need others to help us find new ways of thinking. Children and young people with PDA are often able to provide us with just that. As one teacher commented:

> The pupils with PDA I have taught are some of the most challenging but also the most engaging and rewarding I have ever had the pleasure of teaching … they have helped me become a better teacher because they have helped me think differently.

Despite various challenges, a parent was able to look back and reflect that the most positive aspect of parenting her daughter with PDA has been, 'the privilege of exploring the world through my amazing daughter's eyes'.

It is by valuing children with PDA that we can support them to reach their potential. This process should begin with understanding their needs and differences and using this understanding to provide effective strategies.

## References

Christie, P. (2007) 'The distinctive clinical and educational needs of children with pathological demand avoidance syndrome: guidelines for good practice'. *Good Autism Practice (GAP)*, 8, 3–11.

Christie, P., Fidler, R., Duncan, M. and Healy, Z. (2012) *Understanding Pathological Demand Avoidance Syndrome in Children: A Guide for Parents, Teachers and Other Professionals*. London: Jessica Kingsley.

Eaton, J. (2018) *A Guide to Mental Health Issues in Girls and Young Women on the Autism Spectrum: Diagnosis, Intervention and Family Support*. London: Jessica Kingsley.

Fidler, R. and Christie, P. (2015) *Can I Tell You about Pathological Demand Avoidance Syndrome? A Guide for Friends, Family and Professionals*. London: Jessica Kingsley.

Fidler, R. and Christie, P. (2019) *Collaborative Approaches to Learning for Pupils with PDA: Strategies for Education Professionals*. London: Jessica Kingsley.

Gillberg, C., Gillberg, I., Thompson, L., Niskupsto, R. and Billstedt, E. (2015) 'Extreme (pathological) demand avoidance in autism: a general population study in the Faroe Islands'. *European Child and Adolescent Psychiatry*, 24, 979–984.

Gould, J., and Ashton-Smith, J. (2011) 'Missed diagnosis or misdiagnosis? Girls and women on the autism spectrum'. *Good Autism Practice (GAP)*, 12, 34–41.

Newson, E., Le Marechal, K. and David, C. (2003) 'Pathological demand avoidance syndrome: a necessary distinction within the pervasive developmental disorders'. *Archives of Diseases in Childhood*, 88, 595–600.

O'Nions, E., Viding, E., Greven, C. U., Ronald, A. and Happé, F. (2014a) 'Pathological demand avoidance (PDA): exploring the behavioural profile'. *Autism*, 8, 538–544.

O'Nions, E., Christie, P., Gould, J., Viding, E. and Happé, F. (2014b) 'Development of the Extreme Demand Avoidance Questionnare (EDA-Q): preliminary observations on a trait measure for pathological demand avoidance'. *Journal of Child Psychology and Psychiatry*, 55, 758–768.

O'Nions, E., Gould, J., Christie, P., Gillberg, C., Viding, E. and Happe, F. (2016) 'Identifying features of pathological demand avoidance using the Diagnostic Interview for Social and Communication Disorders (DISCO)'. *European Child and Adolescent Psychiatry*, 25, 407–419.

PDA Society (2018) 'Being misunderstood: experiences of the pathological demand avoidance profile of ASD'. Retrieved from www.pdasociety.org.uk/resources/research-summary/2018-survey (accessed 16 September 2018).

World Health Organization (1992) *International Statistical Classification of Diseases and Related Health Problems* (tenth revision; ICD-10). Geneva: WHO.

# Part IV

# Autism, adolescence and social networks

## What we want the world to know

Girls of Limpsfield Grange School

### *Friends*

'I have friendships difficulties and when that happens I get in a frustrated mood very quickly.'

(Mia, Year 7)

'I struggle to make friends because people think that I am strange. It doesn't make me feel sad or anything.'

(Nicki Lee, Year 7)

'Making friends is tricky for me; I just don't know what to say.'

(Emily, Year 7)

### *Confusion and masking*

'I get really confused about lots of things and I don't understand what is going on, but no one realizes that I am confused because I hide it really well.'

(Mia, Year 7)

'I get tired a lot of the time because I have to try so hard all of the time.'

(Keshni. Year 7)

'I sometimes get really anxious about what other people are doing. I get confused when people talk about things that I don't understand.'

(Nicki Lee, Year 7)

# Chapter 12

# What do we know about the neuroscience of autism in girls and women?

## Meng-Chuan Lai

### The role of neuroscience in understanding sex, gender and autism: the essence and the myths

Understanding how the brain works is one key route to deepen our understanding of human characteristics. Neuroscience (i.e. the scientific disciplines examining how the nervous system works) has become one important perspective from which to understand autism, spanning from aetiologies to behaviours. For example, by finding out how autistic people process social information differently from neurotypical people, we may get better insight into how and why autistic individuals tend to experience and react to social situations differently compared with 'typically developing' peers (Happé and Frith 2014). So far, knowing how the brain works cannot replace other levels of understanding (e.g. cognitive and learning styles, behavioural preferences and patterns, practical daily challenges), but it provides an additional and useful lens to better capture the whole picture.

To better understand how the brains of autistic girls and women work, we should not ignore how sex and gender influence the human brain in general. Although it is well acknowledged that sex refers to biological aspects and gender refers to socially constructed characteristics (see www.who.int/mediacentre/factsheets/fs403/en), most medical and neuroscientific work to date fails to distinguish the two aspects or address them separately (Richardson et al. 2015). It is crucial to appreciate that sex and gender are intertwined; they are multi-component, involve multiple physiological and social-cultural factors, and can be dynamic and non-binary (Joel and McCarthy 2017). Most importantly, unlike the wrongly perceived notion that talking about differences between females and males implies the sexes/genders are distinct (i.e. 'sexual dimorphism'; in the neuroscience literature this usually refers to animal characteristics present in one sex but not the other), most human differences in the brain, cognition and behaviour are 'on-average' differences. In other words, sex/gender differences are merely statistical differences in terms of the means of the distributions based on sexes/genders, but there is substantial overlap across sexes/genders (McCarthy et al. 2012). Further, each individual could be viewed as a mosaic of relative maleness, femaleness and sameness (Joel and McCarthy 2017). Hence, conceptually, an appropriate understanding of autistic girls and women should be based on the appreciation that multiple sex- and gender-related factors shape their development and life experiences, and therefore brain and cognition. In fact, the same appreciation should apply to autistic males and those of other sexes/genders.

With this lens in mind, we need to be aware that our understanding of the autistic brain so far is disproportionately based on autistic males. For example, one of the largest studies on brain anatomy of autism included 1571 autistic individuals, but only 14.3% were females, giving a male-to-female ratio of 6:1 (van Rooij et al. 2018), in contrast to the 3:1 male preponderance in autism in the general population (Loomes et al. 2017). Studies examining how the brains of autistic individuals organize functionally or how they activate during a variety of cognitive tasks are even more heavily male-biased, with a ratio of 9:1 (Hull et al. 2016) and 15:1 (Philip et al. 2012), respectively. Furthermore, in all these studies, the multiple components of sex and gender are always oversimplified as a 'binary' variable of 'male' versus 'female'. This unfortunately makes it difficult to distinguish effects related to sex versus gender, and their contributing components.

Altogether, the study of how sex and gender influence the autistic brain should be considered to be in its infancy. Our neuroscientific understanding of autistic girls and women is still at a rudimentary stage.

## Three ways to understand the relations between sex, gender and autism

Despite such early-stage understanding, there have been some efforts clarifying the relations between sex, gender and autism from the perspectives of neuroscience (see Chen et al. 2017; Ferri et al. 2018; Lai et al. 2017; Lai et al. 2015; Werling 2016 for detailed reviews). Efforts to delineate similarities and differences by sex/gender in the neurobiology of autism do not yet change how autism is defined and diagnosed – autism so far is still a behaviourally defined condition. Nevertheless, such clarification opens a window to interpret some of the unique lived experiences of autistic girls and women, and to explain the male-preponderance in autism prevalence. The questions researchers ask usually follow one of the three directions described below.

### *Does autism present differently in females and males?: behaviour, cognition and the brain*

There is increasing attention paid among the autism community and researchers to understanding how autism characteristics may present differently in females and males in behaviour (Lai et al. 2015; van Wijngaarden-Cremers et al. 2014) and cognition (Hull et al. 2017), and how these may be associated with the likely under-recognition of autism in females (Kreiser and White 2014; Loomes et al. 2017). In short, on current standardized instruments, autistic females are on average measured to have lower levels of repetitive, restricted and stereotyped behaviour than males (Charman et al. 2017; Supekar and Menon 2015; van Wijngaarden-Cremers et al. 2014), but social-communication differences from autistic males vary greatly by the developmental level of the individual (Howe et al. 2015). However, anecdotal observations, qualitative research and autobiographical writings suggest that some autistic females may show more social interests and motivation, heightened sensitivity to others' emotions, intensified imagination, more friendships but with different characteristics, greater camouflaging of social difficulties and autism characteristics, and different topics of special interests, compared to the stereotypical view of autism (that applies better to males) (Lai et al. 2018a).

In a separate line of research, brain imaging studies have primarily aimed to illustrate how autistic brains may be different from neurotypical brains (usually by comparing brain metrics between groups of autistic and neurotypical individuals), disregarding or attempting to 'control for' effects specific to certain sexes/genders. Only a small number of studies have formally examined whether any autism-related brain characteristics are similar or different between males and females. It is worth noting that although some autism versus neurotypical on-average differences appear significant when examining very large samples (e.g. thousands of individuals) (van Rooij et al. 2018), in many large male-only or predominantly male samples, scientists often find it difficult to identify any consistent 'brain signature' of autism across autistic individuals (Haar et al. 2016; Hahamy et al. 2015). This is likely to be due to the complexity and heterogeneity of the autism spectrum at the level of neurobiology.

There is growing interest in uncovering how the brain features in autistic females (characterized by comparing them with non-autistic females) are the same as or different from those of autistic males (compared with non-autistic males). So far there are a small number of studies, often with small sample sizes, that show that brain features associated with autism are similar in males and females – and that females have a greater degree of brain changes. Researchers call this pattern 'quantitative sex-modulation', implying that the neural mechanisms leading to autism are largely shared between the sexes, but that females require more brain changes to demonstrate recognisably autistic behaviours than do males, owing to the presence of other protective mechanisms (Lai et al. 2017). On the other hand, there are many more studies, often with larger sample sizes (hence with better statistical power), showing that the brain features of autism substantially vary by sex; a pattern called 'qualitative sex-modulation', which implies that there are unique, sex-specific 'neural pathways' to autism (ibid.). These scenarios can co-occur. It is possible that some brain regions or circuitries show qualitative sex-modulation, some demonstrate quantitative sex-modulation, and the rest of the brain is not affected by one's sex when it comes to the neurobiology of autism.

Not surprisingly, given the great variation among individuals in different studies, there is still a lack of consistency about where in the brain, or what aspect of the brain, shows quantitative and/or qualitative sex-modulation. One exception is the orbito-frontal cortex (which is involved in several social, emotional and decision-making processes), for which several studies have implicated sex differences in autism-related changes: in the way cortical tissue is folded, in connections to other brain regions and in neural activity while thinking about oneself versus others (Lai et al. 2018b; Nordahl et al. 2015; Schaer et al. 2015).

Do these preliminary findings of sex-modulation of the autistic brain explain differences seen in behaviour and cognition? This is what scientists are investigating. For example, one study shows an association between restricted and repetitive behaviour and regions in the brain involving motor function (Supekar and Menon 2015). Another example is a positive correlation between camouflaging and neural activation of the orbitofrontal cortex when thinking about oneself versus others in autistic women but not autistic men (Lai et al. 2018b). However, so far there are very few studies like these, and limited evidence that addresses links between brain and behaviour. Clarifying the relations between brain, cognition and behaviour in the light of sex/gender differences in autism needs to be the focus of future investigation.

## Are sex and gender involved in the vulnerability and protective processes for the emergence of autism?: evidence of a 'female protective effect'

The male-preponderance of autism prevalence reflects that, in general, it is more difficult for females than males to 'pass the threshold' of autism diagnosis. Scientists call this the 'female protective effect' (FPE; see also Chapter 2, this volume). Based on the knowledge that the occurrence of autism is substantially associated with genetic factors (Sandin et al. 2017; Tick et al. 2016), one would predict that for individuals to be autistic, they would require substantial 'genetic loads' (i.e. having more inherited genetic markers or new genetic changes associated with autism than neurotypical individuals in general). Because of FPE, females will require even more of a genetic load to be autistic. Large-scale family-based studies have mostly supported the FPE hypothesis, by showing that siblings of autistic females are more likely than siblings of autistic males to have high autistic traits or an autism diagnosis (Palmer et al. 2017; Robinson et al. 2013; Werling and Geschwind 2015). What remains unclear, however, is what exactly are the mechanisms that underlie FPE. Scientists are actively investigating the biological bases of FPE, which may involve interactions among gene regulation and expression, prenatal hormonal environment, immune responses, gut bacteria, metabolism, etc. (Ferri et al. 2018; Werling 2016).

Longitudinal studies following infants who have an older sibling with autism (and hence a raised likelihood of autism themselves due to genetic effects; known as 'infant-sibling' studies) suggest that certain aspects of FPE relate to early cognitive development. Infant girls who have older siblings with autism show enhanced attention to social scenes (including faces) compared to infant boys who have older siblings with autism, and infant boys and girls who have neurotypical older siblings (Chawarska et al. 2016); this suggests that increased social attention may serve as a mechanism of FPE in early development by providing increased access to social experiences. In another infant-sibling study, previously identified 'early autism markers' (i.e. social-communication behaviours and eye gaze patterns in infancy) predict later autism characteristics only in boys but not in girls, suggesting that there are certain moderating factors that may serve as FPE mechanisms during early child development (Bedford et al. 2016).

What is also interesting is that in the general population, the association between different domains of autistic traits is stronger in males than in females (Ronald et al. 2011). In addition, autistic traits are associated with social and affective cognitive processes in males but not in females (Kothari et al. 2013; Matsuyoshi et al. 2014; Rhodes et al. 2013; Valla et al. 2010).

Altogether, these suggest the possibility that FPE mechanisms involve differences in social behaviour and cognition early on and across the lifespan. In general, females have a more 'fractionable' cognitive architecture than males; for females, the different aspects of autism (social and communication difficulties, rigid and repetitive behaviours and interests) seem to hold together less tightly. Females are also more resilient in early years to entering an atypical developmental trajectory leading to an autism diagnosis, even with existing heightened genetic predisposition.

Another potential way to uncover FPE mechanisms is based on our understanding of the normative sex/gender differences in the brain in the neurotypical population. On average, males and females differ in how brain regions are co-ordinated in terms of neural signals (Biswal et al. 2010; Satterthwaite et al. 2015), in the connection pattern of white matter fibres (Ingalhalikar et al. 2014) and in the size of specific brain regions (Ruigrok et al. 2014). If some of these reflect the brain bases of FPE, we would expect that certain autistic brain characteristics also appear in these brain circuitries or regions. For instance, there are brain regions that are connected to the rest of the brain in a more extensive way in neurotypical females than in neuro-typical males. If neurotypical people also tend to show more connections in these same brain regions compared to autistic people, the connectivity of such regions could be taken as an indicator of how the FPE (as well as vulnerability) in autism is underpinned in the brain. An example is the so-called 'default network', a brain circuit linking midline and lateral structures, which critically underlies cognitive processes of understanding one's own and others' thoughts and emotions, which has been shown to meet this expectation based on studies with autistic males (Floris et al. 2018). A definitive answer awaits further studies with autistic females and replicated findings.

Finally, it will be important to know if FPE has any 'residual' impact on the brain and cognition of autistic females, especially those at the border of clinical diagnosis. How might the presence of FPE alter the developmental trajectory or cognitive-behavioural presentation of autism? The answer may provide clues to be leveraged for novel inter-vention and support.

### Do developmental processes associated with sex and gender also contribute to the emergence of autism and the lifespan development of autistic individuals?: possible convergence of mechanisms

A related question surrounds the extent to which the mechanisms underlying FPE (and those underlying the higher vulnerability in males) for autism come from mechanisms associated with the typical development of sex and gender (Ferri et al. 2018; Lai et al. 2015). The 'convergence' of autism and sex-related factors has been implicated in studies involving human brain (Lai et al. 2017), hormone-related processes (Baron-Cohen et al. 2015; Kosidou et al. 2016), the intersections between hormones and immune processes in the womb (McCarthy and Wright 2017), and their interaction with genetic factors (Park et al. 2017). These findings suggest that several aspects of sex differences, spanning genetics, hormones, immunity and the brain, may be causally (but not deterministically) linked to the emergence of autism.

By contrast to sex, gender-related processes have barely been studied (Cheslack-Postava and Jordan-Young 2012). For example, it is still unclear how gendered contexts (i.e. socio-cultural background that is influenced by gender expectations and stereotypes, such as dress, play material and the way children are encouraged to interact with others, etc.) contribute to the early emergence of autistic characteristics, whether and when one is recognized as having autism, how one modifies one's behaviour associated with autism and how autism is diagnosed (Kreiser and White 2014; Lai et al. 2015). There is also insufficient understanding of how autism intersects with an individual's identity devel-opment in relation to gender and sexuality, given the emerging findings of greater gender and sexual fluidity and diversity in autistic people (Dewinter et al. 2017; George and Stokes 2017).

Several components of sex and gender seem to converge with mechanisms underlying the emergence of autism and the autistic individual's development across the lifespan. The exact interrelation between autism, sex and gender, however, can only be clarified when we have a much better understanding of both the life experiences and the neurobiology of autistic individuals across all sexes and genders.

## Concluding remarks

Better understanding of girls on the autism spectrum requires focusing on both life experiences and the various neurobiologies of autism, across individuals of all sexes and genders. To achieve this goal, it is important to acknowledge that sex and gender are multi-component and involve multiple intertwining physiological and socio-cultural factors. The clarification of how components of sex and gender have impacts on the emergence, presentation and lifespan development of autism will provide greater clarity of how we can enhance the well-being of autistic individuals, particularly girls and women.

## References

Baron-Cohen, S., Auyeung, B., Norgaard-Pedersen, B., Hougaard, D. M., Abdallah, M. W., Melgaard, L.et al. (2015) 'Elevated fetal steroidogenic activity in autism'. *Mol Psychiatry*, 20, 369–376.

Bedford, R., Jones, E. J., Johnson, M. H., Pickles, A., Charman, T. and Gliga, T. (2016) 'Sex differences in the association between infant markers and later autistic traits'. *Molecular Autism*, 7, 21.

Biswal, B. B., Mennes, M., Zuo, X. N., Gohel, S., Kelly, C., Smith, S. M., *et al.* (2010) 'Toward discovery science of human brain function'. *Proceedings of the National Academy of Sciences USA*, 107, 4734–4739.

Charman, T., Loth, E., Tillmann, J., Crawley, D., Wooldridge, C., Goyard, D.et al. (2017) 'The EU-AIMS Longitudinal European Autism Project (LEAP): clinical characterisation'. *Molecular Autism*, 8, 27.

Chawarska, K., Macari, S., Powell, K., DiNicola, L. and Shic, F. (2016) 'Enhanced social attention in female infant siblings at risk for autism'. *Journal of the American Academy of Child and Adolescent Psychiatry*, 55, 188–195.

Chen, C., van Horn, J. D. and Consortium, G. R. (2017) 'Developmental neurogenetics and multimodal neuroimaging of sex differences in autism'. *Brain Imaging and Behavior*, 11, 38–61.

Cheslack-Postava, K. and Jordan-Young, R. M. (2012) 'Autism spectrum disorders: toward a gendered embodiment model'. *Social Science and Medicine*, 74, 1667–1674.

Dewinter, J., De Graaf, H. and Begeer, S. (2017) 'Sexual orientation, gender identity, and romantic relationships in adolescents and adults with autism spectrum disorder'. *J Autism Dev Disord*, 47, 2927–2934.

Ferri, S. L., Abel, T. and Brodkin, E. S. (2018) 'Sex differences in autism spectrum disorder: a review'. *Current Psychiatry Reports*, 20, 9.

Floris, D. L., Lai, M.-C., Nath, T., Milham, M. P. and Di Martino, A. (2018) 'Network-specific sex differentiation of intrinsic brain function in males with autism'. *Molecular Autism*, 9, 17.

George, R. and Stokes, M. A. (2017) 'Gender identity and sexual orientation in autism spectrum disorder'. *Autism*, 11(1), 131–141.

Haar, S., Berman, S., Behrmann, M. and Dinstein, I. (2016) 'Anatomical abnormalities in autism?'. *Cerebral Cortex*, 26, 1440–1452.

Hahamy, A., Behrmann, M. and Malach, R. (2015) 'The idiosyncratic brain: distortion of spontaneous connectivity patterns in autism spectrum disorder'. *Nat Neurosci*, 18, 302–309.

Happé, F. and Frith, U. (2014) 'Annual research review: towards a developmental neuroscience of atypical social cognition'. *Journal of Child Psychology and Psychiatry*, 55, 553–557.

Howe, Y. J., O'Rourke, J. A., Yatchmink, Y., Viscidi, E. W., Jones, R. N. and Morrow, E. M. (2015) 'Female autism phenotypes investigated at different levels of language and developmental abilities'. *J Autism Dev Disord*, 45, 3537–3549.

Hull, J. V., Jacokes, Z. J., Torgerson, C. M., Irimia, A. and van Horn, J. D. (2016) 'Resting-state functional connectivity in autism spectrum disorders: a review'. *Frontiers in Psychiatry*, 7, 205.

Hull, L., Mandy, W. and Petrides, K. V. (2017) 'Behavioural and cognitive sex/gender differences in autism spectrum condition and typically developing males and females'. *Autism*, 21, 706–727.

Ingalhalikar, M., Smith, A., Parker, D., Satterthwaite, T. D., Elliott, M. A., Ruparel, K.*et al.* (2014) 'Sex differences in the structural connectome of the human brain'. *Proceedings of the National Academy of Sciences USA*, 111, 823–828.

Joel, D. and McCarthy, M. M. (2017) 'Incorporating sex as a biological variable in neuropsychiatric research: where are we now and where should we be?'. *Neuropsychopharmacology*, 42, 379–385.

Kosidou, K., Dalman, C., Widman, L., Arver, S., Lee, B. K., Magnusson, C. and Gardner, R. M. (2016) 'Maternal polycystic ovary syndrome and the risk of autism spectrum disorders in the offspring: a population-based nationwide study in Sweden'. *Mol Psychiatry*, 21, 1441–1448.

Kothari, R., Skuse, D., Wakefield, J. and Micali, N. (2013) 'Gender differences in the relationship between social communication and emotion recognition'. *Journal of the American Academy of Child and Adolescent Psychiatry*, 52, 1148–1157 e2.

Kreiser, N. L. and White, S. W. (2014) 'ASD in females: are we overstating the gender difference in diagnosis?'. *Clinical Child and Family Psychology Review*, 17, 67–84.

Lai, M.-C., Ameis, S. H. and Szatmari, P. (2018a) 'Young women on the autism spectrum'. In N. Gelbar (ed.), *Adolescents with Autism Spectrum Disorder* (pp. 289–319). Oxford: Oxford University Press.

Lai, M. C., Lombardo, M. V., Chakrabarti, B., Ruigrok, A. N., Bullmore, E., Suckling, J.*et al.* (2018b) 'Neural self-representation in autistic women and association with "compensatory camouflaging"'. *Autism*.

Lai, M.-C., Lerch, J. P., Floris, D. L., Ruigrok, A. N., Pohl, A., Lombardo, M. V. and Baron-Cohen, S. (2017) 'Imaging sex/gender and autism in the brain: etiological implications'. *J Neurosci Res*, 95, 380–397.

Lai, M.-C., Lombardo, M. V., Auyeung, B., Chakrabarti, B. and Baron-Cohen, S. (2015) 'Sex/gender differences and autism: setting the scene for future research'. *Journal of the American Academy of Child and Adolescent Psychiatry*, 54, 11–24.

Loomes, R., Hull, L. and Mandy, W. P. L. (2017) 'What Is the male-to-female ratio in autism spectrum disorder? a systematic review and meta-analysis'. *Journal of the American Academy of Child and Adolescent Psychiatry*, 56, 466–474.

Matsuyoshi, D., Kuraguchi, K., Tanaka, Y., Uchida, S., Ashida, H. and Watanabe, K. (2014) 'Individual differences in autistic traits predict the perception of direct gaze for males, but not for females'. *Molecular Autism*, 5, 12.

McCarthy, M. M., Arnold, A. P., Ball, G. F., Blaustein, J. D. and De Vries, G. J. (2012) 'Sex differences in the brain: the not so inconvenient truth'. *J Neurosci*, 32, 2241–2247.

McCarthy, M. M. and Wright, C. L. (2017) 'Convergence of sex differences and the neuroimmune system in autism spectrum disorder'. *Biol Psychiatry*, 81, 402–410.

Nordahl, C. W., Iosif, A. M., Young, G. S., Perry, L. M., Dougherty, R., Lee, A.*et al.* (2015) 'Sex differences in the corpus callosum in preschool-aged children with autism spectrum disorder'. *Molecular Autism*, 6, 26.

Palmer, N., Beam, A., Agniel, D., Eran, A., Manrai, A., Spettell, C.*et al.* (2017) 'Association of sex with recurrence of autism spectrum disorder among siblings'. *JAMA Pediatrics*, 171, 1107–1112.

Park, B. Y., Lee, B. K., Burstyn, I., Tabb, L. P., Keelan, J. A., Whitehouse, A. J. O.*et al.* (2017) 'Umbilical cord blood androgen levels and ASD-related phenotypes at 12 and 36 months in an enriched risk cohort study'. *Molecular Autism*, 8, 3.

Philip, R. C., Dauvermann, M. R., Whalley, H. C., Baynham, K., Lawrie, S. M. and Stanfield, A. C. (2012) 'A systematic review and meta-analysis of the fMRI investigation of autism spectrum disorders'. *Neuroscience and Biobehavioral Reviews*, 36, 901–942.

Rhodes, G., Jeffery, L., Taylor, L. and Ewing, L. (2013) 'Autistic traits are linked to reduced adaptive coding of face identity and selectively poorer face recognition in men but not women'. *Neuropsychologia*, 51, 2702–2708.

Richardson, S. S., Reiches, M., Shattuck-Heidorn, H., LaBonte, M. L. and Consoli, T. (2015) 'Opinion: Focus on preclinical sex differences will not address women's and men's health disparities'. *Proceedings of the National Academy of Sciences USA*, 112, 13419–13420.

Robinson, E. B., Lichtenstein, P., Anckarsater, H., Happé, F. and Ronald, A. (2013) 'Examining and interpreting the female protective effect against autistic behavior'. *Proceedings of the National Academy of Sciences USA*, 110, 5258–5262.

Ronald, A., Larsson, H., Anckarsater, H. and Lichtenstein, P. (2011) 'A twin study of autism symptoms in Sweden'. *Mol Psychiatry*, 16, 1039–1047.

Ruigrok, A. N., Salimi-Khorshidi, G., Lai, M.-C., Baron-Cohen, S., Lombardo, M. V., Tait, R. J. and Suckling, J. (2014) 'A meta-analysis of sex differences in human brain structure'. *Neuroscience and Biobehavioral Reviews*, 39, 34–50.

Sandin, S., Lichtenstein, P., Kuja-Halkola, R., Hultman, C., Larsson, H. and Reichenberg, A. (2017) 'The heritability of autism spectrum disorder'. *Journal of the American Medical Association*, 318, 1182–1184.

Satterthwaite, T. D., Wolf, D. H., Roalf, D. R., Ruparel, K., Erus, G., Vandekar, S.*et al.* (2015) 'Linked sex differences in cognition and functional connectivity in youth'. *Cerebral Cortex*, 25, 2383–2394.

Schaer, M., Kochalka, J., Padmanabhan, A., Supekar, K. and Menon, V. (2015) 'Sex differences in cortical volume and gyrification in autism'. *Molecular Autism*, 6, 42.

Supekar, K. and Menon, V. (2015) 'Sex differences in structural organization of motor systems and their dissociable links with repetitive/restricted behaviors in children with autism'. *Molecular Autism*, 6, 50.

Tick, B., Bolton, P., Happé, F., Rutter, M. and Rijsdijk, F. (2016) 'Heritability of autism spectrum disorders: a meta-analysis of twin studies'. *Journal of Child Psychology and Psychiatry*, 57, 585–595.

Valla, J. M., Ganzel, B. L., Yoder, K. J., Chen, G. M., Lyman, L. T., Sidari, A. P.*et al.* (2010) 'More than maths and mindreading: sex differences in empathizing/systemizing covariance'. *Autism Research*, 3, 174–184.

Van Rooij, D., Anagnostou, E., Arango, C., Auzias, G., Behrmann, M., Busatto, G. F.*et al.* (2018) 'Cortical and subcortical brain morphometry differences between patients with autism spectrum disorder and healthy individuals across the lifespan: results from the ENIGMA ASD Working Group'. *Am J Psychiatry*, 175, 359–369.

Van Wijngaarden-Cremers, P. J., van Eeten, E., Groen, W. B., van Deurzen, P. A., Oosterling, I. J. and van der Gaag, R. J. (2014) 'Gender and age differences in the core triad of impairments in autism spectrum disorders: a systematic review and meta-analysis'. *J Autism Dev Disord*, 44, 627–635.

Werling, D. M. (2016) 'The role of sex-differential biology in risk for autism spectrum disorder'. *Biology of Sex Differences*, 7, 58.

Werling, D. M. and Geschwind, D. H. (2015) 'Recurrence rates provide evidence for sex-differential, familial genetic liability for autism spectrum disorders in multiplex families and twins'. *Molecular Autism*, 6, 27.

# Chapter 13

# Mental health and girls on the autism spectrum

*Tina Rae and Grace Hershey*

## Introduction

If autism in girls remains undiagnosed, they are at high risk of developing mental health difficulties such as anxiety, depression, self-harm and eating disorders. This also impacts upon their ability to engage in the learning process and, in turn, achieve their full potential. We are also aware of the fact that women and girls can and do learn to act neurotypically in social settings. Diagnosticians can therefore perceive someone who presents as able, who has reciprocal conversation and who uses appropriate affect and gestures, as not fulfilling the criteria presented in the international classification systems. This results in diagnosis being missed and girls and young women are left to adopt social roles which are based on intellect rather than social intuition. The camouflaging that they engage in alongside the repressing of their autistic behaviour, is totally exhausting and is perhaps a direct cause of the high statistics of women on the continuum with mental health problems (Yaull-Smith 2008). In this chapter we will therefore focus upon the mental health disorders and risks experienced by girls and young women with ASD, and also discuss an intervention specifically designed to support them in managing both internal and external pressures and stressors.

## Mental health difficulties

### The concept of mental health

Mental health affects all aspects of a child's development including their cognitive abilities, their social skills as well as their emotional well-being. Building emotional resilience is key and many psychologists believe that there are core attributes seen in mentally healthy children and young people (Weare 2000):

- The capacity to enter into and sustain mutually satisfying personal relationships.
- A continuing progression of psychological development.
- An ability to play and to learn appropriately for their age and intellectual level.
- A developing moral sense of right and wrong.
- The capacity to cope with a degree of psychological distress.
- A clear sense of identity and self-worth.

With good mental health, children and young people do better in every way. They enjoy their childhoods, can deal with stress and difficult times, are able to learn better, do better at school, navigate the online world they grew up in so they benefit from it, and enjoy friendships and new experiences.

There is also a growing understanding and recognition that mental health is more than the absence of mental illness and that good mental health underpins everything we do, how we think, feel, act and behave. It is an essential and precious individual, family, community and business resource that needs to be protected and enhanced.

People with higher levels of good mental health and well-being have better general health, use health services less, live longer, have better educational outcomes, are more likely to undertake healthier lifestyles (including reduced smoking and harmful levels of drinking), are more productive at work, take less time off sick, have higher income, have stronger social relationships and are more social (Lyubomirsky et al. 2005; National Institute for Clinical Excellence 2009). Higher levels of mental well-being are also associated with reduced levels of mental ill-health in adulthood (Keyes et al. 2010).

Given this level of evidence as to the more positive outcomes in all aspects of life for those with good mental health, it is clearly vital that we ensure more vulnerable populations such as girls and young women with ASD have the necessary support to effectively manage and maintain their own well-being. This is particularly important given the fact that there is now such an awareness of the increased risk and raised levels of mental ill health in those with ASD generally (Crane et al. 2018; Simonoff et al. 2008).

### The role for professionals supporting young people

As the UK Department for Education (DfE) stated in their report, *Mental Health and Behaviour in Schools*, one of the means by which schools can promote their pupils' mental health is by:

> Providing pupils with inner resources that they can draw on as a buffer when negative or stressful things happen helps them to thrive even in the face of significant challenges. This is especially true for children who come from home backgrounds and neighbourhoods that offer little support … Activities that bolster mental health operate under a variety of headings, including 'emotional literacy', 'emotional intelligence', 'resilience', 'character and grit' 'life skills', 'violence prevention', 'anti-bullying', and 'coping skills'.
>
> (Department for Education 2014: 19)

### The complex world of today's children and young people – the need for early identification and intervention

The online world has created incredible opportunities for young people to explore, experiment, socialize, create and educate themselves in ways which were previously undreamt of. But it has also exposed children to the risk of harm, including seeing extreme pornography and sexting (Martellozzo et al. 2016).

While on line resources can also have a positive and informative role in young people's lives, this kind of pressure, early sexualization, 24-hour access to social media, alongside the range of peer pressures and academic pressures probably all contribute to the mental and emotional problems that young people experience in this complex social context.

Navigating the complexities of this context is stressful for all children and young people but there are concerns for the young women on the continuum, who do not necessarily have the skill set of analysing and accurately interpreting the content and behaviour of others online, to manage this without experiencing high levels of stress and anxiety. These difficulties include anxiety disorders, social phobias, self- harm and eating disorders. Of most concern to many professionals has been the prevalence of self-harm behaviours within this group.

## Self-harm

Of all the areas of mental health promotion, suicide and self-harm are probably the most challenging for both professionals and the target groups involved. There is sadly little research on the topic of self-harm in those with Autism – including in girls and young women – but the limited research does point strongly to increased risk for this group in adolescence (Culpin et al. 2018; Hedley et al. 2018). Among 6091 participants in one longitudinal study, children with autism and autistic traits had higher depressive symptom scores than the general population at age 10 years, remaining elevated in an upward trajectory until age 18 years. Social communication impairment was associated with depression at 18 years and was substantially mediated by bullying. It is therefore not surprising that the risk of suicide attempts is also significantly increased in this group (Chen et al. 2017). However, in the latter study, although patients with ASD were seen to have an increased risk of suicide attempts compared with those without ASD there remains a need for further studies to clarify the underlying pathophysiology between ASD and suicidality and to elucidate whether prompt intervention for ASD may indeed reduce this risk.

If suicide rates are to be reduced and the damage that stems from self-harm is to be ameliorated, then it is essential that these issues are addressed in a coherent manner with both those supporting these vulnerable teenagers and the students themselves.

Coleman suggests that 'it is most helpful to consider self-harm as a continuum, ranging from behaviour which has a strong suicidal intent (e.g. some kinds of overdose) to behaviour which is intended to help the person stay alive (e.g. cutting)' (Coleman 2004: 6). Coleman adds that the problem with the term 'deliberate self-harm' is that it has an implication of wilfulness about it, which may be unhelpful to young people if they believe they have little control over their behaviour.

It is important to point out that self-harm is at the opposite end of the continuum in terms of suicidal intent. Cutting, itself, is frequently a way or means of being able to stay alive as opposed to achieving death. Generally, forms of self-mutilation are an attempt to gain release from severe emotional tension or distress. This form of self-abuse may also be a means of the young person redirecting the anger that they feel, i.e. they may hate their abuser but be unable to express that hatred towards that individual and this form of mutilation provides them with an outlet for these feelings.

Overall, self-harm refers to a range of behaviours along a continuum ranging from low to high suicidal intent. In general, young people who tend to mutilate or cut themselves are likely to have a lower suicidal intent whilst those who take an overdose may have a higher suicidal intent. However, it is important to note that although few of those who engage in cutting will attempt suicide, most young people who attempt suicide have previously self-harmed and self-harm can be seen to considerably raise the risk of suicide attempts (Olfson et al. 2018).

What is important is that the young person accesses appropriate assessment procedures within the context of a mental health organization. Part of this assessment would include identifying risk factors which are similar to those identified with suicide. However, risk factors for self-harm also include physical, sexual or emotional abuse, low self-esteem and anxiety and difficulties in relationships. Ensuring that girls and young women on the continuum are effectively screened for such risk factors would seem to be an essential given the fact that there is a direct link between their condition and mental health needs and difficulties.

## Systems for assessment and screening

For young people experiencing mental health difficulties, support needs to come from all areas of their lives. The DfE recognized in their guidance, *Mental Health and Behaviour in Schools* (Department for Education 2014) that 'in order to help their pupils succeed, schools have a role to play in supporting them to be resilient and mentally healthy'. For this to be achieved it is vital that school staff feel they are appropriately skilled and are aware of the resources, and wider services, available to support them.

In order to effectively support young people with a variety of mental health needs in the school environment it is essential to reach all areas of the school environment (Time to Change 2017). Schools need to take a 'whole school' approach in order to support students effectively. An authentic 'whole school' approach means involvement from everyone in the school community; from governors, all staff, pupils, parents and outside agencies (Weare 2015). A genuine whole school approach is the most effective way to implement changes to ethos and practice thus having the most impact on students with mental health needs; in turn it will have the most impact on girls with autism who also have mental health needs.

The DfE identified in their guidance (Department for Education 2014) that there are two key elements to identifying children who are at risk of mental health problems: 'effective use of data' and 'an effective pastoral team'. By using data systems commonly used in the school environment, such as behaviour records, attendance records and attainment levels, changes can be monitored and this may lead to the identification of children who are experiencing difficulties with their emotional and mental well-being. Having an identified member of staff for a young person to speak to ensures that at least one member of staff can notice any changes in a student's presentation and act on this in accordance with the school's policies. These two elements also provide information and evidence to support students who may need to be referred on to Child and Adolescent Mental Health Services (CAMHS). This information provides a clear profile of a child, which can be shared with local CAMHS to help students receive the most appropriate support may take the form of CBT, Mindfulness interventions, MBSR, etc.

## Using therapeutic approaches in the school context

So how do we support ASD girls within the school context – on both an individual and on a group level? Ultimately, we know that there is a need to focus upon interventions to support the development of self- help and self- management strategies. We know that specific therapeutic approaches, such as cognitive behavioural therapy (CBT) and tools from positive psychology, can be adapted for use with girls on the autistic continuum.

It is a given that all young people frequently experience anxious and negative thoughts and doubts. These messages will often reinforce a state of inadequacy and/or low levels of self-esteem. The process of CBT helps to support young people in reconsidering these negative assumptions. It also allows them to *learn how* to change their self-perceptions in order to improve their mental and emotional state – this is the key aim of this kind of intervention.

### Using CBT – the evidence base

Initially research and clinical applications of CBT were with adult populations as it had been proposed that young children have not developed the meta-cognitive skills needed for taking part in CBT, with these skills only developing at the 'formal operational stage' of development (Bolton 2005). Research shows that although abilities may not be as refined as in adolescents, children from seven or eight years of age have the ability to form simple theories, appraise their thoughts, understand that thoughts can be controlled and can change behaviour (Flavell and Green 1999; Sodian et al. 1991).

Some researchers argue that children have the inferential skills needed to access CBT as young as 4 or 5 years old (Muris et al. 2007), while others propose that theory of mind (i.e. ability to attribute mental states, or infer what others are thinking) is the most important skill needed to be able to take part in the therapy (Stallard 2005). While it is generally agreed that young people are able to take part in CBT, the nature of the therapy tends to be different to that with adults. CBT with young people tends to have more of a focus on behavioural components, as cognition (working with thoughts) develops later in childhood (Stallard 2005).

CBT has been applied in educational settings in several ways. Whole school approaches that draw on cognitive behavioural approaches include the Social and Emotional Aspects of Learning (SEAL) curriculum. Such approaches aim to promote the emotional well-being of all students, and prevent mental health difficulties developing. CBT approaches have been applied successfully in whole class interventions to reduce anxiety. There is evidence that school based small group and individual sessions using cognitive behavioural approaches, including problem solving and working with thoughts and behaviours, are effective mental health interventions (Department for Education 2014). There is also increasing evidence as to the success of such interventions to treat anxiety specifically among children and adolescents with ASD (Luxford et al. 2017; Kester and Lucyshyn 2018).

In our practice, we have found that a key set of tools can effectively be introduced to young people in schools in order to support the development of effective thinking and promote levels of self-confidence and resilience. This approach and philosophy aims to utilize strategies from cognitive behaviour therapy, mindfulness, resilience theory and positive psychology (MacConville and Rae 2012) in order to achieve such a goal. These evidence based interventions can provide us with tools to encourage and maintain effective thinking which will, in turn, promote well-being overall.

## Support and intervention within a group

In order to translate this thinking and approach into a group intervention for girls on the autism continuum in the high school context we began with a specific focus upon the rationale for setting up group interventions and some of the practical considerations around delivery and content. In designing the course contents, reference was initially made to the report of the American Psychological Association's Task Force on the sexualization of girls, which concludes that it is vital for psychologists, educators, carers and community organizations to work together in order to encourage the development of curricula which enhance self-esteem based upon young people's abilities and character as opposed to their appearance (American Psychological Association 2007). The report also advocates increasing public awareness and the development of policy in this area to reduce sexualized images of girls in all forms of media and products, and the development of positive portrayals of girls and young women as strong, competent and non-sexualized. This is particularly pertinent to young women on the autism spectrum who may be considered more at risk in terms of absorbing influences in the media and in terms of engaging in obsessional routines regarding eating habits and self-care.

## Impact of the media – an ongoing issue

The media provides us with a great deal of evidence of the sexualization of women, including music videos, television, magazines, films, music lyrics, sports media, video games, internet and advertising (Krassas et al. 2001). These media images also further emphasize a narrow and unrealistic notion of physical beauty which has evident implications for the development of girls' and young women's self-esteem and self-image (O'Donohue et al. 1997). This is particularly pertinent to girls and young women with ASD who may become fixated by specific images and media personalities and over anxious in terms of achieving the perfect body/appearance or life style. This, in turn, can lead to increased risk of eating disorders such as anorexia and bulimia.

## Pressure through interpersonal relationships

Girl's relationships can also be seen as a source of sexualization. This is particularly the case for some of our young women on the continuum whose relationships are extremely intense. Other girls almost take on the role of a female lover and muse and the obsessional behaviours displayed towards them can be a very real source of stress and anxiety. The need to present as the perfect, beautiful and sexual being can become all-consuming for the girls with ASD and needs to be challenged in a sensitive but pro-active manner so as to ensure that these irrational and obsessive behaviours are both recognized and cognitively reframed by the girls themselves.

Parents/carers may also present girls and young women with the message that being physically attractive is one of the most important goals for them to achieve and some will provide access to plastic surgery in the attempt to reach the ideal (Brown and Gilligan 1992). Research also shows that teachers can encourage girls to play at being sexualized adult women (Martin 1998) or maintain the belief that girls from specific ethnic backgrounds are hypersexual and therefore unlikely to achieve any real academic success in school (Rolon-Dow 2004).

It is also evident that male and female peers contribute to this process. Peer pressure from both genders has been found to contribute to girls conforming to standards of thinness or sexiness (Eder 1995; Nichter 2000). A key concern is also the particular ways in which the process encourages boys to sexually objectify and harass girls. This kind of behaviour is also 'normalized' by the girls themselves via the process of self-objectification – the process whereby girls and young women learn to think of and treat them themselves as objects of other people's (mainly boy's and men's) desires (McKinley and Hyde 1996). For the girl on the autism continuum, this poses a very real risk as they attempt to navigate the boy's responses and behaviours and this, again, provided us with the rationale for including these topics within our intervention.

## The impact of sexualization

The unrealistic expectations on girls and young women to achieve the 'ideal' in terms of appearance has led to an increase in eating disorders and the number of young women having breast implants at an increasingly early age (Zuckerman and Abraham 2008). Exposure to gender-stereotypical ideas and images also contributes to sexist attitudes and beliefs and sexual harassment and violence against women (Kilbourne and Lazarus 1987). Sexual objectification can also be seen to enable and encourage a range of oppressions including employment discrimination and sexual violence alongside the trivialization of women's roles and accomplishments in the workplace (Fredrickson and Roberts 1997).

This evidence base provided us with the rationale for developing our intervention with a specific focus on girls on the autism continuum whom we regarded to be most at risk of accepting and 'buying in' to this narrative and also being at risk of making incorrect and sometimes risky and inaccurate judgements about the sexual behaviours of others and putting themselves at risk (Visser et al. 2017). Rae and Piggott's (2014) programme was used as inspiration for developing both the structure and content of this intervention.

Each group session would typically last for an hour to an hour and a half. However, in the special school context we would usually allocate a whole afternoon session which enabled additional time for each activity and specifically for processing ideas and new concepts. The majority of the groups incorporated girls and young women with a range of special educational needs including ASD, ADHD and sensory difficulties. Navigating this complexity required two facilitators both experienced in the application of therapeutic approaches and differentiating for a range of needs. It is important to note that two facilitators were allocated to each group to enable one to deliver the content and one to observe the process and be available to provide individual support as and when required.

## Aims of the group intervention

The aim of the 12-session programme we devised and delivered was to build a therapeutic environment that allowed and promoted autonomy, emotional resilience and open communication for girls on the autism spectrum. This statement can be broken down into three main objectives:

1   Promote emotional resilience within the group members.
2   Assist in the develop of the skills associated with positive communication.
3   Support group members with a view to further developing self-regulation and awareness.

The contents of the sessions clearly reflected the concerns and themes arising from the discussions between the facilitators and their observations of the specific needs of the group of girls in terms of maintaining their mental health and supporting the development of skills to navigate the complex world of teenage girl in a social media, 'selfie' dominated context.

The activities therefore aimed to:

- Promote personal and social skills development
- Develop pupils' self-esteem and self-awareness
- Empower young people to explore the many aspects of sexuality and healthy personal relationships
- Encourage pupils to accept personal responsibility for keeping the mind and body safe and healthy
- Help pupils to evaluate and access confidently a range of local and national sources of information, support and advice
- Address contemporary issues that are relevant to young people, including:
- Consent in teenage relationships and recognizing safe versus potentially exploitative relationships.
- The consequences of, and law relating to, sexual behaviour.
- The range of sexual attitudes, relationships and behaviours in society.
- Exploring attitudes to teenage conception and pregnancy.
- Exploring attitudes towards sexuality.
- Body image, obesity, self-respect, aspiration.
- The media portrayal of young people.
- The effects and risks and legal consequences of the use of psychoactive substances (i.e. legal highs) and performance (e.g. steroids) and image enhancing substances.
- Understanding and strengthening intergenerational relationships.
- Understanding mental health as a concept and the stigma attached to having been given such a label.
- Exploring the nature of stress and anxiety and understanding methods to minimize the impact of these.
- Understanding the nature of and triggers to self-harming behaviours in young people.
- Understanding how to maintain mental health using tools from a range of evidence based therapeutic approaches including CBT and mindfulness.

### Making it all 'ASD friendly'

We were very aware throughout the intervention process of the need to ensure that the activities and structure were all ASD friendly. In brief, this meant reflecting upon key elements such as content and style of delivery. Each session had to ensure that the following elements were considered:

- *Reinforcement* – this was essential in terms of allowing copious opportunities for over learning key skills and concepts
- *Explicit language* – our language needed to be very clear and explicit at all times
- *Concrete examples* – were needed in each session so as to facilitate comprehension
- *Role play* – was used to practice key social skills and problem-solve challenges met in the real world of relationships with both genders

- *Social stories* – we also used as a key tool for developing awareness and behaviour change
- *Structure and routine* – each session was structured in the same way so as to reduce anxiety
- *Modelling obsession versus habit* – we used case studies to show how obsessions about a boy/girl/pop star/media personality could become an unhealthy habit
- *Reading others' intentions* – we used role plays in order to try to develop skills in reading behaviours
- *I do not have to copy that* – we used this as a mantra throughout the sessions to reinforce the importance of taking control and not being manipulated by images in the media/others' behaviours and choices
- *Self-awareness* – 'if I do not feel comfortable what should I do?' – we used real life examples of other girls' experiences of being used/exploited due to not 'reading it right' and supported the development of problem solving skills by using structured frameworks
- *The session structure was also made explicit at the start of each session and any changes were discussed and prepared for at the outset.*

The sessions were structured as follows:

1   Welcome.
2   Group rules.
3   Talk time.
4   Ice breaker.
5   Core activity/activities and additional activities.
6   Reflections and feedback.
7   Target setting.
8   Compliments to close.
9   Relaxation.

### A few reflections to note

When trialling this intervention we were keen to ensure that we developed the evidence base. This involved us in taking pre and post measures in order to identify the outcomes of the intervention for each girl and to also highlight adaptations for future work in the delivery of the programme. Having now delivered this programme in both a special and mainstream context, it is very important to highlight a few points that may impact delivery by facilitators in the future. It is very important that the facilitator(s) make themselves aware of the contents and aims of each of the sessions in the programme so as to ensure that their selection (if they choose not to deliver all of the sessions in sequence) is entirely appropriate to the target group. It may be appropriate to select a more focused set which focus on key areas such as relationships or self-image. This will also need to be planned with time constraints in mind as some institutions may not be able to allocate sufficient time in any one or two term block to actually deliver all of these sessions in sequence.

We would also strongly advise that any such group intervention needs to consider the vulnerabilities of each member of the group. The intervention was most successful when run with a group of girls who were all diagnosed with ASD as this allowed for a sense of a supportive community to develop in which the girls felt confident about discussing issues and problems openly. When delivering to a more mixed group we felt that there was always the potential for our ASD girls to become the victims of bullying or to be scapegoated to varying degrees.

The resource has provided the impetus to develop further programmes (Rae 2016a; Rae 2016b) which incorporate CBT and mindfulness approaches, which we hope will provide a genuinely meaningful experience for the target groups in terms of really addressing their concerns and anxieties while also providing them with a range of tools and strategies to more effectively maintain and further develop their overall well-being and mental health.

### Developing a diagnostic and supportive framework for staff in schools – fostering communication

For schools to have a process and framework to identify children who may need such interventions within the school environment is hugely beneficial. Frameworks can also be used to share information with local CAMHS and support referrals for young people. It is also important for schools to have an understanding of their local CAMHS referral criteria and pathway so they are able to support the young person and their family with this (Prever 2006).

The Department of Health's *Future in Mind* report outlines the need for improved communication between schools and CAMHS (Department of Health 2015). It is necessary for schools to have a clear process to identify those young people most at need of further support. This process should include communication with services such as CAMHS to ensure young people are supported by all professionals involved. However, it is important to remember that support needed for young people, including girls with autism, may not always come from local CAMHS. Voluntary, community sectors or local authority services, including those services that work specifically with young people with autism, may be most appropriate to work alongside schools with providing support to young people around their emotional and mental health. There is also some anecdotal evidence that some CAMHS services have taken the view that ASD young people present with Neurodevelopmental conditions are which are outside of their brief or that they do not have specialist therapists who can effectively support such young people. This is a concern which demands further investigation and follow up in our view.

The DfE's *Mental Health and Behaviour in Schools* advises that 'schools can use the Strengths and Difficulties Questionnaire (SDQ) to help them judge whether individual pupils might be suffering from a diagnosable mental health problem and involve their parents/carers and the pupil in considering why they behave in certain ways' (Department for Education 2014). The SDQ can facilitate professionals thinking about the child and their mental health. Tutt (2016) reminds us that the scales within the SDQ help us to identify emotional symptoms, conduct problems, hyperactivity/ inattention, peer relationship problems and pro-social behaviour. The score provided by the SDQ can be used to identify whether a referral to local CAMHS is appropriate. The SDQ is widely available for schools to use and provides a common language and the basis for collaborative approaches for subsequent assessments and interventions between CAMHS and schools. The Development and Well-being Assessment (DAWBA), which is a more detailed parent, teacher or self- report questionnaire covering all major diagnoses in mental health, as well as ASD and ADHD, is also used by professionals in both educational and clinical contexts.

## Conclusions

Developing this common language between educationalists, clinicians and parents and young people seems to us to remain an essential in terms of developing appropriate pathways and access to support for our most vulnerable young people. Engaging with services that work specifically with young people with autism can also support the development of whole school systems for identification and intervention which truly meet the needs of our girls and young women on the continuum. As stated previously, all young people are exposed to a range of pressures including early sexualization, potentially 24-hour access to social media, alongside a range of peer pressures and academic pressures, which all contribute to the mental and emotional problems that they experience in this complex social context. As Eaton states:

> Many girls and young women did not (and still do not) get a diagnosis of their difficulties and there is growing evidence that they will have an increased risk of experiencing issues with friendships and relationships, be prone to bullying and harassment, and may well experience significant mental health problems.
>
> (Eaton 2017: 9)

This is now in no doubt, but we now also understand more fully the more nuanced responses, interventions and support systems that need to be in place for our young people on the continuum. However, this remains a work in progress and demands more research and engagement with the young people themselves in order to develop interventions and systems that are both preventative and remedial for girls on the autism spectrum.

## References

American Psychological Association (2007) *Report of the APA Task Force on the Sexualisation of Girls.* Washington, DC: American Psychological Association.

Bolton, D. (2005) 'Cognitive behaviour therapy for young people and adolescents: some theoretical and developmental issues'. In P. J. Graham (eds), *Cognitive Behaviour Therapy for Young People and Families* (2nd edn, pp. 9–24). Cambridge: Cambridge University Press.

Brown, L. M. and Gilligan, C. (1992) *Meeting at the Crossroads: Women's Psychology and Girls' Development.* Cambridge, MA: Harvard University Press.

Chen, M.-H., Pan, T.-L., Lan, W.-H., Hsu, J.-W., Huang, K.-L., Su, T.-P.*et al.* (2017) 'Risk of suicide attempts among adolescents and young adults with autism spectrum disorder: a nationwide longitudinal follow-up study'. *Journal of Clinical Psychiatry*, 78(9), e1174–e1179.

Coleman, J. (2004) *Teenage Suicide and Self-Harm: A Training Pack for Professionals.* Brighton: Brighton Trust for the Study of Adolescence.

Crane, L., Adams, F., Harper, G., Welch, J. and Pellicano, E. (2018) '"Something needs to change": mental health experiences of young autistic adults in England'. *Autism*, in press (doi: doi:10.1177/1362361318757048).

Culpin et al. (2018)

Department for Education (2014) *Mental Health and Behaviour in Schools*. London: Department for Education.

Department of Health (2015) *Future in Mind: Promoting, Protecting and Improving our Children and Young People's Mental Health and Well Being*. London: NHS England.

Eaton, J. (2017) *A Guide to Mental Health Issues in Girls and Young Women on the Autism Spectrum: Diagnosis, Intervention and Family Support*. London: Jessica Kingsley Publishers.

Eder, D. (1995) *School Talk: Gender and Adolescent Culture*. New Brunswick, NJ: Rutgers University Press.

Flavell, J. H. and Green, F. L. (1999) 'Development of intuitions about the controllability of different mental states'. *Cognitive Development*, 14(1), 133–146.

Fredrickson, B. L. and Roberts, T. A. (1997) 'Objectification theory: toward understanding women's lived experience and mental health risks'. *Psychology of Women Quarterly*, 21, 173–206.

Hedley, D., Uljarević, M., Wilmot, M., Richdale, A. and Dissanayake, C. (2018) 'Understanding depression and thoughts of self-harm in autism: a potential mechanism involving loneliness'. *Research in Autism Spectrum Disorders*, 46, 1–7.

Kester, K. R. and Lucyshyn, J. M. (2018) 'Cognitive behavior therapy to treat anxiety among children with autism spectrum disorders: a systematic review'. *Research in Autism Spectrum Disorders*, 52, 37–50.

Keyes, C. L. M., Dhingra, S. S. and Simoes, E. J. (2010) 'Change in level of positive mental health as a predictor of future risk of mental illness'. *American Journal of Public Health*, 100(12), 2366–2371.

Kilbourne, J. and Lazarus, M. (1987) *Still Killing Us Softly: Advertising's Image of Women*. Northampton, MA: Media Education Foundation.

Krassas, N., Blauwkamp, J. M. and Wesselink, P. (2001) 'Boxing Helena and cosseting Eunice: sexual rhetoric in Cosmopolitan and Playboy magazines'. *Sex Roles*, 44, 751–771.

Luxford, S., Hadwin, J. A. and Kovshoff, H. (2017) 'Evaluating the effectiveness of a school-based cognitive behavioural therapy intervention for anxiety in adolescents diagnosed with autism spectrum disorder'. *Journal of Autism and Developmental Disorders*, 47(12), 3896–3908.

Lyubomirsky, S., Sheldon, K. M. and Schkade, D. (2005) 'Pursuing happiness: the architecture of sustainable change'. *Review of General Psychology*, 9(2), 111–131.

MacConville, R. M. and Rae, T. (2012) *Building Happiness, Resilience and Motivation in Adolescents: A Positive Psychology Curriculum for Well-being*. London: Jessica Kingsley.

Martellozzo, E., Monaghan, A., Adler, J. R., Davidson, J., Leyva, R. and Horvath, M. A. H. (2016) *I Wasn't Sure It Was Normal to Watch It: A Quantitative and Qualitative Examination of the Impact of Online Pornography on the Values, Attitudes, Beliefs and Behaviours of Children and Young People*. London: NSPCC.

Martin, K. A. (1998) 'Becoming a gendered body: practices in pre-schools'. *American Sociological Review*, 63, 494–511.

McKinley, N. M. and Hyde, J. S. (1996) 'The Objectified Body Consciousness Scale'. *Psychology of Women Quarterly*, 20, 181–215.

Muris, P., Mayer, B., Vermeulen, L. and Hiemestra, H. (2007) 'Theory of mind, cognitive development, and young people's interpretation of anxiety related physical symptoms'. *Behaviour Research and Therapy*, 45(9), 2121–2132.

National Institute for Clinical Excellence (2009) *Social and Emotional Well Being in Secondary Education*. London: National Institute for Clinical Excellence.

Nichter, M. (2000) *Fat Talk: What Girls and Their Parents Say about Dieting*. Cambridge, MA: Harvard University Press.

O'Donohue, W., Gold, S. R. and McKay, J. S. (1997) 'Children as sexual objects: historical and gender trends in magazines'. *Sexual Abuse: Journal of Research and Treatment*, 9, 291–301.

Olfson, M., Wall, M., Wang, S., Crystal, S., Bridge, J. A., Liu, S. M. and Blanco, C. (2018) 'Suicide after deliberate self-harm in adolescents and young adults'. *Pediatrics*, 141(4), e20173517.

Prever, M. (2006) *Mental Health in Schools: A Guide to Pastoral and Curriculum Provision*. Victoria, VIC: Hawker Brownlow Education.

Rae, T. (2016a) *Building Positive Thinking Habits: Increasing Self-Confidence and Resilience in Young People through CBT*. Buckingham: Hinton House Publishers.

Rae, T. (2016b) *Bouncing Back and Coping with Change: Building Emotional and Social Resilience in Young People Aged 9–14*. Buckingham: Hinton House Publishers.

Rae, T. and Piggott, E. (2014) *Supporting the Well Being of Girls: An Evidence Based Programme*. London: Routledge.

Rolon-Dow, R. (2004) 'Seduced by images: identity and schooling in the lives of Puerto Rican girls'. *Anthropology and Education Quarterly*, 35, 8–29.

Simonoff, E., Pickles, A. and Charman, T. (2008) 'Psychiatric disorders in children with autism spectrum disorders: prevalence, comorbidity, and associated factors in a population-derived sample'. *Journal of the American Academy of Child and Adolescent Psychiatry*, 47(8), 921–929.

Sodian, B.Zaitchik, D. and Carey, S. (1991) 'Young people's differentiation of hypothetical beliefs from evidence'. *Young Person Development*, 62(4), 753–766.

Stallard, P. (2005) 'Cognitive Behaviour Therapy with prepubertal young people'. In P. J. Graham (eds), *Cognitive Behaviour Therapy for Children and Families* (2nd edn, pp. 22–33). Cambridge: Cambridge University Press.

Time to Change (2017) 'A whole-school approach'. Retrieved from www.time-to-change.org.uk/get-involved-schools/school-leaders/whole-school-approach (accessed 16 September 2018).

Tutt, R. (2016) *Rona Tutt's Guide to SEND and Inclusion*. London: Sage.

Visser, K., Greaves-Lord, K., Tick, N. T., Verhulst, F. C., Maras, A. and van der Vegt, E. J. (2017) 'An exploration of the judgement of sexual situations by adolescents with autism spectrum disorders versus typically developing adolescents'. *Research in Autism Spectrum Disorders*, 36, 35–43.

Weare, K. (2000) 'Work with young people is leading the way in the new paradigm for mental health – commentary'. *International Journal of Health Promotion*, 4(4), 55–58.

Weare, K. (2015) *What Works in Promoting Social and Emotional Well-Being and Responding to Mental Health Problems in Schools? Advice for Schools and Framework Document*. London: National Children's Bureau.

Yaull-Smith, D. (2008) 'Girls on the spectrum'. *Communication*, Spring, 30–31.

Zuckerman, J., and Abraham, R. (2008) *Teenagers and Cosmetic Surgery: Focus on Breast Augmentation and Liposuction*. Washington, DC: National Research Centre for Women and Families.

# Chapter 14

# Friendships on the autism spectrum

*Felicity Sedgewick and Liz Pellicano*

Friendships are a crucial part of our development as social individuals, from childhood through to adulthood, and can make us happier and healthier across the lifespan (Antonucci and Akiyama 1987; Berkman and Syme 1979). They allow us to develop social skills (Schaffer 1996) and provide critical social and emotional support, building resilience and adjustment (Demir and Urberg 2004; Dumont and Provost 1999). Difficulties in this area of social development have been associated with maladaptive behaviours and worse-than-expected adult outcomes (Bagwell et al. 1998). As with many areas of research, there is much less known about the friendships of autistic girls than about the friendships of autistic boys. Nevertheless, we do know that there are notable and consistent differences in the friendships of neurotypical girls and boys, and so it is possible that such differences are also apparent in the friendships and social relationships of young autistic people.

## What do we know about gender differences in the friendships of neurotypical teens?

Among neurotypical girls, friendships are more supportive and less defined by power struggles than those of boys (De Goede et al. 2009). Young women's friendships are based more on talking, especially about personal problems, and emotional sharing than young men's, who instead focus on shared activities (Aukett et al. 1988; Caldwell and Peplau 1982; McNelles and Connolly 1999). There are also gender differences in which aspects of someone's personality boys and girls focus on when choosing friends. Boys tend to focus on attributes that are linked to high social status, whereas girls tend to seek out people with attributes that help them to maintain close relationships with a few friends (Benenson 1990). Boys are more likely to have large groups of less emotionally intimate same-sex friends, whereas adolescent girls tend to have a few very close friends (Aukett et al. 1988). Girls have been shown to experience more friendship jealousy than boys, in that they are more likely to feel negatively towards other children who they feel might 'steal' their best friend (Parker et al. 2005). This may be because girls are more 'exclusive' in their friendships than boys, being less likely to accept an extra person into an existing friendship group (Eder and Hallinan 1978). This reluctance to accept new friends into an established relationship might be linked to the emotional closeness which is so important for girls (Johnson 2004; Rose 2002), as sharing highly personal information leaves an individual vulnerable if the new person turns out to be untrustworthy.

Differences in friendship behaviours by gender may be a result of different socialization patterns. Parents typically encourage gendered play – for example, co-operative pretend play with girls and active physical play with boys – which may later have a significant role in developing friendship patterns (Lindsey and Mize 2001). Furthermore, it has been found that typically girls reach complex social and linguistic development stages earlier than boys, which may allow them to form relationships based on co-operative play and shared conversation more easily (Barbu et al. 2011).

## What about friendships in those on the autism spectrum?

Autistic children and teenagers often find making and maintaining friendships difficult (American Psychiatric Association 2013), predominantly due to challenges with social communication. Although there is much variation in autistic children and young people's friendship experiences, they are more likely to be on the periphery of the social networks in mainstream school classrooms (Kasari et al. 2011) compared with their neurotypical peers. As discussed later in this chapter, they are also more likely to be the victims of bullying (Rowley et al. 2012), which may be more prevalent than previously thought (Humphrey and Symes 2010).

Perhaps as a result of the well-recognized challenges with social communication faced by autistic individuals, there is a common perception that some autistic children, young people and adults do not *want* to have friends. Anecdotal reports and increasing empirical evidence, however, suggest otherwise. Autistic children and young people report having friends and best friends (Bauminger et al. 2008), and have a desire to play with, and chat to, their neurotypical peers (Travis et al. 2001). This motivation for social contact was highlighted by Calder et al. (2013), who studied autistic and non-autistic young people in mainstream primary schools. They found significant variation in the children's motivation for making and keeping friends. While some young autistic people desperately wanted friends, others had limited social connections but preferred things this way: 'I am happy with my life right now. I am not friendly and talkative, but I am not not friendly. I am somewhere in the middle' (ibid.: 12).

## What about the friendships of autistic girls?

Differences in the friendship experiences of autistic boys and girls are perhaps unsurprising, given that it is well known that neurotypical girls and boys have distinct friendship experiences, as discussed above. Head et al. (2014) found that autistic girls aged 10–16 years had friendships they rated as being of higher quality than autistic boys and, furthermore, scored similarly to boys *without* autism (on the Friendship Questionnaire). This finding was supported by parental reports of the children's relationships, suggesting that autistic girls have better social skills and higher social motivation than autistic boys. Similarly, when examining children's friendship patterns, Dean et al. (2014) showed that autistic boys were more likely to be actively excluded and rejected by their peers, whereas autistic girls were more connected with peers. Girls on the autism spectrum also had mostly neurotypical female friends, while autistic boys were generally rejected by neurotypical boys. The authors suggested that the neurotypical friends of autistic girls helped to prevent their active exclusion from the social networks of their neurotypical peers, allowing them to maintain their greater connectedness and number of relationships.

It has been shown that autistic girls have more complex language use compared to age- and IQ-matched boys on the spectrum (Goddard et al. 2014). Additionally, autistic girls tend to have intense interests that revolve around people/animals rather than objects/things and are more similar to those of same-age and gender peers (e.g. celebrities, pop music, drawing) (Attwood et al. 2006; Hiller et al. 2014). Their imaginative play is also more gender-typical than that of boys (Knickmeyer et al. 2008). Such differences could have implications for their later interactions with their neurotypical peers, which may make it more likely for girls to be able to engage effectively with them.

Some studies have shown that autistic girls have friendships, especially best-friendships, which are very like those of neurotypical girls and very different to those of autistic boys. For example, we have carried out several studies looking at social motivation (how interested people are in friendships), friendship ratings and friendship experiences in autistic girls in both special and mainstream schools. We asked adolescent autistic girls, autistic boys, non-autistic girls and non-autistic boys to complete the Friendship Qualities Scale (FQS) (Bukowski et al. 1994), which asks adolescents to rate how true a range of statements are about them and their best friend. We also carried out semi-structured qualitative interviews with the adolescents about their friendships, including questions such as 'What do you do with your friends?' and 'How do you know when someone is your friend?'.

In special schools, we found that adolescent boys and girls on the autism spectrum differed with respect to their peer relationships, particularly in regard to their experiences of conflict within these relationships, with girls having closer and more secure friendships than boys, but also experiencing more conflict (Sedgewick et al. 2016). Using the Social Responsiveness Scale (second edition; SRS-2; Constantino 2012), teachers reported that the autistic girls in their classes had fewer social difficulties and higher levels of social motivation than the autistic boys. The reduced social motivation seen in the autistic boys in this study is consistent with other research which showed that (mostly male) adolescents on the autism spectrum report lower scores on the Friendship Motivation Questionnaire (Richard and Schneider 2005), suggesting that they have lower levels of internal motivation for initiating and maintaining friendships.

The autistic girls in this sample talked about how their friendships were focussed on other people (e.g. what they had been doing, what they liked) rather than on actions or objects (e.g. games or lessons) as the autistic boys described. This suggests that the girls were more interested in people generally, and engaging with those people socially, than the autistic boys in the study. Head et al. (2014) also reported that autistic girls showed greater interest in the relationships of other people, as well as in their own direct relationships with others, compared with autistic boys. These findings resonate with work reporting that autistic children (mostly boys) are more likely to focus on 'active' rather than 'affective' components of relationships (Bauminger and Kasari 2000) and with that of Dean et al. (2014), described above, on friendship patterns.

In mainstream schools, Sedgewick et al. (2018b) found very similar patterns. Autistic girls rated their best-friendships similarly to neurotypical girls, and these friendships were very different to those of autistic boys. The autistic girls' friendships were closer, more secure, more supportive, and they spent more time together. In interviews, autistic girls talked about their friends in similar ways to neurotypical girls, saying that their friends are 'there for them' and are 'people I trust'. Where there were differences, however, were in the nature of their social networks. Autistic girls tended to have one or two intense best-friendships and not to have the wider social group that was a key feature for their neurotypical counterparts. They would want to spend much, or all, of their time with their best friends, either physically or through constant messaging. This intensity also meant that conflict within these friendships could be devastating.

Autistic girls tended to take a very uncompromising approach to conflict resolution. They would either see things as totally their fault and do anything and everything they could to fix the friendship, or they would see the other person as entirely to blame and decide to withdraw from the friendship completely because it was ruined and could never be mended. Overall, however, autistic girls had friendships which they were happy with and which worked for them, and these friendships helped them to navigate the complexities of the social world of high school and adolescence.

Online interactions and social media also play a major role in girls' friendships, regardless of whether they are autistic. Social media often acts as a way to reinforce offline friendships and to make them stronger. For example, you might like your best friend's photos to show that you are following them, to appear popular and to boost your closeness to someone. The number of 'likes' a photo or post receives is often seen as a key measure of how popular someone is and how someone feels. These concrete measures of social status can appeal to autistic girls, as they are a very unambiguous way of seeing how people are responding to you without the complexities and nuances of face-to-face interactions and high-school social hierarchies. Interestingly, there is also a developing range of online social obligations to maintain friendships and relationships, similar to that of the obligation, say, to sit with your best friend at lunch in order to stay friends. For example, liking your friend's posts is crucial, but so is knowing what not to do. For example, you should not respond if a friend's boyfriend comments on your post because that could be seen as interfering in their offline relationship. Overall, though, autistic girls found social media to be a very positive thing for their friendships, especially as it allowed them to communicate in a written format. Written, online conversations can be easier than keeping up with group conversations in person because it provides the young person with the time to think about exactly what to say and how to say it, as well as giving a clear record of what everyone else had said or was saying.

Despite the closeness of their friendships, and a general sense of satisfaction, all the girls in the study by Sedgewick et al. (2018b) had high levels of friendship insecurity, regardless of whether they were autistic. Both autistic and neurotypical girls discussed worrying that their friends did not really like them or that they were in some way not good enough for their friends. This anxiety could result in them withdrawing from friendships, as they would simply assume that the other person could not possibly really want to be their friend, sometimes in the face of evidence to the contrary. Autistic girls also tended to interpret neutral or even positive social situations as negative, such as someone saying, 'I like your top' as being sarcastic and teasing them, which also contributed to their difficulties knowing how their peers saw them and where they stood with people. The insecurity some girls felt about their friendships also played into their conflicts, with accusations of interfering in friendships, stealing friends or not being honest about whether they were friends.

Both autistic and neurotypical girls alluded to wanting to fit in, but in different ways. For example, neurotypical girls talked about dating to look cool, and when asked most said that the people they knew who dated did so to fit in with the popular crowd. Equally, autistic girls talked about friends who 'let you be yourself' or 'don't mind that

I'm a bit weird', which neurotypical girls did not, implying that autistic girls feel they must control how they appear to people around them, but feel reassured that they can relax with true friends. This camouflaging by autistic girls and women is seen in many situations (Dean et al. 2017; Lai et al. 2017; Parish-Morris et al. 2017), but it is important to note that neurotypical girls can do it too, particularly in social situations. Adolescence is a time when most young people have a strong focus on fitting in and being liked by their peers, and this may be a driving factor behind behaviours for autistic girls, such as suddenly becoming fascinated with make-up or a certain book or TV show fandom, as they think this will help them get on with the other girls they know.

This desire to fit in can also lead to competition with friends, which is something that neurotypical girls talked about in particular (Sedgewick et al. 2018b). Several neurotypical girls talked about the feeling of competing with their friends, both academically and socially, and trying to gain and maintain a place in the social hierarchy of secondary school. Autistic girls, in contrast, did not talk about this competition at all, suggesting that they were possibly unaware of the dynamics between their neurotypical peers or were so disengaged from the process that they did not think it was relevant to their social lives. While in many ways this can be a good thing, as it means that many autistic girls are not buying into the processes which are so frequently cited as having a negative impact on the mental health of teenage girls, it may also mark them out as odd in comparison to their neurotypical peers and therefore increase their difficulties in making friends beyond the people they already know.

## What about bullying?

There is significant evidence that autistic children are more likely to be bullied than their neurotypical peers due to their social vulnerabilities (Sofronoff et al. 2011), with prevalence rates of up to 94% in some studies (Hebron and Humphrey 2014; van Roekel et al. 2010). It is not just traditional forms of bullying to which autistic young people are subjected, with bullying online, through social media and through mobile phones (known as cyber-bullying) being similarly common (Kowalski and Fedina 2011). These high rates and variety of forms of bullying have been linked to a range of features of autism. For example, research has shown that difficulties with social communication, mental health issues, co-occurring attention-deficit/hyperactivity disorder (ADHD), having friends, and anger regulation are all linked to higher rates of bullying of autistic young people (for reviews, see Schroeder et al. 2014; Sreckovic et al. 2014).

Interestingly, autistic children with higher levels of social skill may be more likely to be bullied (Rowley et al. 2012). This is possibly because having fewer social difficulties generally leads to peers having higher expectations of them, for which an autistic child can be 'punished' for failing to meet. This explanation seems especially probable considering other research showing that autistic children and young people are more likely to be bullied than children with intellectual disability (Zeedyk et al. 2014). It is also the case that autistic young people who display more internalizing behaviours (such as being quiet or anxious) are more likely to be bullied than those who display externalizing behaviours (such as difficulties with anger management) (Zablotsky et al. 2013), which is key since autistic girls are likely to be anxious and to internalize their difficulties. Appearing more socially able, both through camouflaging behaviours and the gendered differences between autistic boys and girls discussed above, means that autistic girls may be particularly vulnerable to being bullied by their neurotypical peers, more so than autistic boys.

## But it is not just the obvious bullies…

In Sedgewick et al.'s studies, autistic girls reported significantly less conflict in their best-friendships than non-autistic girls (Sedgewick et al. 2016; Sedgewick et al. 2018b; Sedgewick et al. 2018b), but also discussed many instances of what can be termed as 'relational conflict' (Nichols et al. 2009), including gossiping, interfering in relationships, excluding individuals socially and 'stealing' friends.

Although there is a wealth of work on bullying (Hong and Espelage 2012), little research has been conducted on the impact of conflict *within* the friendships and peer relationships of autistic children and adolescents – and particularly of autistic girls. Conflict within friendships is also known as 'relational conflict', 'relational aggression', or 'relational bullying' (Murray-Close et al. 2007). This type of conflict is more commonly associated with girl–girl relationships and includes the stereotypical, vindictive behaviour of teenage girls – gossiping, spreading rumours and isolating both individuals and small groups. These behaviours can have negative impacts similar to those of more overt bullying but, critically, take place within relationships typically categorized as 'friendships'. This categorical (friends, who should be nice to you) and behavioural (someone being unpleasant or bullying) mismatch can lead to difficulties for any adolescent who must try to make space for unkind behaviours within the concept of a 'friend', but may be especially puzzling for teenagers on the autism spectrum. Research has highlighted how the nature of gender differences in friendship networks, as described above, plays into the frequency of relational aggression and the significant impact it has on girls' friendships, as these tighter and more intimate relationships can be more easily manipulated and exploited (Lagerspetz et al. 1988). The challenges of friendship formation and maintenance may be especially significant for autistic girls, who are potentially more likely to experience relational conflict than autistic boys, just as neurotypical girls are more likely to experience relational conflict than neurotypical boys (Bowie 2007).

For autistic adolescents, who can struggle to understand unwritten rules, especially in relation to complex social situations in secondary school, comprehending and coping with the subtle and insidious relational aggression of girls may be particularly difficult. Such behaviours require a flexible approach to friendship, which may be challenging for autistic adolescents. Indeed, it has been shown that autistic adolescents can have a 'fixed and active' definition of friendship, focussed on doing specific things with 'someone you hang out with' (Bauminger and Kasari 2000; Calder et al. 2013) rather than emotional closeness, which may leave autistic adolescents vulnerable to social manipulation. They may take people at 'face value' and so assume that others' intentions are both consistent and genuine. They might also be less likely to have supportive friends who can act as a social feedback system as to whether particular behaviours or interactions are to be expected or if someone is actually being mean to them (Steward 2013).

Our recent research on the bullying experiences of autistic girls compared to both neurotypical girls and to autistic and neurotypical boys has shown that autistic girls have far more problems with their wider peer group than do any of the other research participant groups (Sedgewick et al. 2018b). In line with what happens for neurotypical boys and girls, autistic boys faced 'overt' conflict – shouting, pushing, name-calling – while autistic girls faced 'relational conflict'. Yet autistic girls were subject to such conflict much more frequently than autistic boys were subjected to more obvious behaviours. In semi-structured interviews, when asked about how their friends treated them, several autistic girls talked about 'friends' who would leave them out of things, upset them or suddenly 'drop them' when someone 'cooler' came along. These are all difficult things to experience for anyone, but were particularly confusing for autistic girls, who often said that they were still friends with these girls despite their treating them badly and, sometimes, despite the fact that they had not spoken in quite a long time.

Unfortunately, autistic girls also struggled to know how to handle conflict effectively in their friendships, using different conflict resolution strategies to their neurotypical peers. For major disagreements (as opposed to minor bickering), neurotypical girls described waiting, then talking to their friend to resolve the issue. For them, conflict resolution was a reciprocal process with joint problem-solving. In contrast, as described above, autistic girls described an 'all-or-nothing' approach. This again left them vulnerable to both social manipulation – if you think everything is your fault, the other person can make you do things to fix it – and to social isolation – if you stop talking to your friends every time you fall out, you can end up with no friends. That said, the use of more flexible conflict resolution strategies seemed to increase as girls got older, meaning that disagreements were managed in a more nuanced way and their friendships were perceived to be stronger as a result. This is also a process which has been seen in autistic women, who describe having much greater self-assurance in their relationships in adulthood than they did in adolescence and who, consequently, are much happier with their relationships (Sedgewick et al. 2018b).

## What are the key things to know?

Although the friendship issues that autistic girls face may appear overwhelming in their complexity, there are three essential points to take from this chapter for those offering support to autistic girls.

First, autistic girls have friendships that are different to those of autistic boys and more similar to those of neurotypical girls, so being female is more important in predicting types of social experiences than being autistic.

Second, autistic girls are having to deal with the same social expectations and behaviours as neurotypical girls, yet many of these social expectations are difficult for them to understand and manage.

Third, many autistic girls find friendships that work for them, especially as they get older. Therefore, supporting girls in developing positive friendships is more important than worrying about them having the 'right' friendships.

We need more research on how the unique challenges faced by autistic girls and young women with regard to their friendship experiences extend into adulthood (though see Sedgewick et al. 2018a), including in more intimate relationships, and how any such challenges might impact on their social and emotional wellbeing. We also need more research into friendships between autistic young people, who may socialize in different ways to their neurotypical peers. Supporting autistic girls in the development of their more complex and subtle social skills will enable them to engage with their peers in adolescence and beyond – in the ways that they wish to, which work for them, and with who they choose as friends.

# References

American Psychiatric Association (2013) *Diagnostic and Statistical Manual of Mental Disorders* (5th edn). Washington, DC: APA.

Antonucci, T. C. and Akiyama, H. (1987) 'An examination of sex differences in social support among older men and women'. *Sex Roles*, 17(11), 737–749.

Attwood, T. (2006) *The Complete Guide to Asperger's Syndrome*. London: Jessica Kingsley.

Aukett, R., Ritchie, J. and Mill, K. (1988) 'Gender differences in friendship patterns'. *Sex Roles*, 19 (1–2), 57–66.

Bagwell, C. L., Newcomb, A. F. and Bukowski, W. M. (1998) 'Preadolescent friendship and peer rejection as predictors of adult adjustment'. *Child Development*, 69(1), 140–153.

Barbu, S., Cabanes, G. and Le Maner-Idrissi, G. (2011) 'Boys and girls on the playground: sex differences in social development are not stable across early childhood'. *Plos One*, 6(1), e16407.

Bauminger, N. and Kasari, C. (2000) 'Loneliness and friendship in high-functioning children with autism'. *Child Development*, 71(2), 447–456.

Bauminger, N., Solomon, M., Aviezer, A., Heung, K., Gazit, L., Brown, J. and Rogers, S. J. (2008) 'Children with autism and their friends: a multidimensional study of friendship in high-functioning autism spectrum disorder'. *Journal of Abnormal Child Psychology*, 36(2), 135–150.

Benenson, J. F. (1990) 'Gender differences in social networks'. *Journal of Early Adolescence*, 10(4), 472–495.

Berkman, L. F. and Syme, S. L. (1979) 'Social networks, host resistance and mortality: a nine-year follow-up study of Alameda County residents'. *American Journal of Epidemiology*, 109(2), 186–204.

Bowie, B. H. (2007) 'Relational aggression, gender and the developmental process'. *Journal of Child and Adolescent Psychiatric Nursing*, 20(2), 107–115.

Bukowski, W. M., Hoza, B. and Boivin, M. (1994) 'Measuring friendship quality during pre-and early adolescence: the development and psychometric properties of the Friendship Qualities Scale'. *Journal of Social and Personal Relationships*, 11(3), 471–484.

Calder, L., Hill, V. and Pellicano, E. (2013) '"Sometimes I want to play by myself": Understanding what friendship means to children with autism in mainstream primary schools'. *Autism*, 17(3), 296–316.

Caldwell, M. A. and Peplau, L. A. (1982) 'Sex differences in same-sex friendship'. *Sex Roles*, 8(7), 721–732.

Constantino, J. N. (2012) *Social Responsiveness Scale*, 2nd edition (SRS-2). Old Tappan, NJ: Pearson Clinical, Western Psychological Services.

De Goede, I. H., Branje, S. J. and Meeus, W. H. (2009) 'Developmental changes in adolescents' perceptions of relationships with their parents'. *Journal of Youth and Adolescence*, 38(1), 75–88.

Dean, M., Harwood, R. and Kasari, C. (2017) 'The art of camouflage: gender differences in the social behaviors of girls and boys with autism spectrum disorder'. *Autism*, 21(6), 678–689.

Dean, M., Kasari, C., Shih, W., Frankel, F., Whitney, R., Landa, R.*et al.* (2014) 'The peer relationships of girls with ASD at school: comparison to boys and girls with and without ASD'. *Journal of Child Psychology and Psychiatry*, 55(11), 1218–1225.

Dumont, M. and Provost, M. A. (1999) 'Resilience in adolescents: protective role of social support, coping strategies, self-esteem and social activities on experience of stress and depression'. *Journal of Youth and Adolescence*, 28(3), 343–363.

Eder, D. and Hallinan, M. T. (1978) 'Sex differences in children's friendships'. *American Sociological Review*, 43(2), 237–250.

Goddard, L., Dritschel, B., Robinson, S. and Howlin, P. (2014) 'Development of autobiographical memory in children with autism spectrum disorders: deficits, gains and predictors of performance'. *Development and Psychopathology*, 26(1), 215–228.

Head, A. M., McGillivray, J. A. and Stokes, M. A. (2014) 'Gender differences in emotionality and sociability in children with autism spectrum disorders'. *Molecular Autism*, 5(1), 19.

Hebron, J. and Humphrey, N. (2014) 'Exposure to bullying among students with autism spectrum conditions: a multi-informant analysis of risk and protective factors'. *Autism*, 18(6), 618–630.

Hiller, R. M., Young, R. L. and Weber, N. (2014) 'Sex differences in autism spectrum disorder based on DSM-5 criteria: evidence from clinician and teacher reporting'. *Journal of Abnormal Child Psychology*, 42(8), 1381–1393.

Hong, J. S. and Espelage, D. L. (2012) 'A review of research on bullying and peer victimization in school: an ecological system analysis'. *Aggression and Violent Behavior*, 17(4), 311–322.

Humphrey, N. and Symes, W. (2010) 'Perceptions of social support and experience of bullying among pupils with autistic spectrum disorders in mainstream secondary schools'. *European Journal of Special Needs Education*, 25(1), 77–91.

Johnson, H. D. (2004) 'Gender, grade and relationship differences in emotional closeness within adolescent friendships'. *Adolescence*, 39(154), 243.

Kasari, C., Locke, J., Gulsrud, A. and Rotheram-Fuller, E. (2011) 'Social networks and friendships at school: comparing children with and without ASD'. *Journal of Autism and Developmental Disorders*, 41(5), 533–544.

Knickmeyer, R. C., Wheelwright, S. and Baron-Cohen, S. B. (2008) 'Sex-typical play: masculinization/defeminization in girls with an autism spectrum condition'. *Journal of Autism and Developmental Disorders*, 38(6), 1028–1035.

Kowalski, R. M. and Fedina, C. (2011) 'Cyber bullying in ADHD and Asperger syndrome populations'. *Research in Autism Spectrum Disorders*, 5(3), 1201–1208.

Lagerspetz, K. M., Björkqvist, K. and Peltonen, T. (1988) 'Is indirect aggression typical of females? Gender differences in aggressiveness in 11- to 12-year-old children'. *Aggressive Behavior*, 14(6), 403–414.

Lai, M.-C., Lombardo, M. V., Ruigrok, A. N., Chakrabarti, B., Auyeung, B., Szatmari, P. and MRC AIMS Consortium. (2017) 'Quantifying and exploring camouflaging in men and women with autism'. *Autism*, 21(6), 690–702.

Lindsey, E. W. and Mize, J. (2001) 'Contextual differences in parent–child play: Implications for children's gender role development'. *Sex Roles*, 44(3–4), 155–176.

McNelles, L. R. and Connolly, J. A. (1999) 'Intimacy between adolescent friends: Age and gender differences in intimate affect and intimate behaviors'. *Journal of Research on Adolescence*, 9(2), 143–159.

Murray-Close, D., Ostrov, J. M. and Crick, N. R. (2007) 'A short-term longitudinal study of growth of relational aggression during middle childhood: associations with gender, friendship intimacy and internalizing problems'. *Development and Psychopathology*, 19(1), 187–203.

Nichols, S., Moravcik, G. M. and Tetenbaum, S. P. (2009) *Girls Growing Up on the Autism Spectrum: What Parents and Professionals Should Know about the Pre-teen and Teenage Years*. London: Jessica Kingsley.

Parish-Morris, J., Liberman, M. Y., Cieri, C., Herrington, J. D., Yerys, B. E., Bateman, L. *et al.* (2017) 'Linguistic camouflage in girls with autism spectrum disorder'. *Molecular Autism*, 8(1), 48.

Parker, J. G., Low, C. M., Walker, A. R. and Gamm, B. K. (2005) 'Friendship jealousy in young adolescents: individual differences and links to sex, self-esteem, aggression and social adjustment'. *Developmental Psychology*, 41(1), 235.

Richard, J. F. and Schneider, B. H. (2005) 'Assessing friendship motivation during preadolescence and early adolescence'. *Journal of Early Adolescence*, 25(3), 367–385.

Rose, A. J. (2002) 'Co-rumination in the friendships of girls and boys'. *Child Development*, 73(6), 1830–1843.

Rowley, E., Chandler, S., Baird, G., Simonoff, E., Pickles, A., Loucas, T. and Charman, T. (2012) 'The experience of friendship, victimization and bullying in children with an autism spectrum disorder: associations with child characteristics and school placement'. *Research in Autism Spectrum Disorders*, 6(3), 1126–1134.

Schaffer, H. R. (1996) *Social Development*. Oxford: Blackwell Publishing.

Schroeder, J. H., Cappadocia, M. C., Bebko, J. M., Pepler, D. J. and Weiss, J. A. (2014) 'Shedding light on a pervasive problem: a review of research on bullying experiences among children with autism spectrum disorders'. *Journal of Autism and Developmental Disorders*, 44(7), 1520–1534.

Sedgewick, F., Crane, L., Hill, V. and Pellicano, E. (2018a) 'Friends and lovers: the relationships of autistic women'. *Autism in Adulthood*, in press.

Sedgewick, F., Hill, V. and Pellicano, E. (2018b) '"It's different for girls": gender differences in the friendships and conflict experiences of autistic and neurotypical adolescents'. *Autism*, in press (doi: doi:10.1177/1362361318794930).

Sedgewick, F., Hill, V., Yates, R., Pickering, L. and Pellicano, E. (2016) 'Gender differences in the social motivation and friendship experiences of autistic and non-autistic adolescents'. *Journal of Autism and Developmental Disorders*, 46(4), 1297–1306.

Sofronoff, K., Dark, E. and Stone, V. (2011) 'Social vulnerability and bullying in children with Asperger syndrome'. *Autism*, 15(3), 355–372.

Sreckovic, M. A., Brunsting, N. C. and Able, H. (2014) 'Victimization of students with autism spectrum disorder: a review of prevalence and risk factors'. *Research in Autism Spectrum Disorders*, 8(9), 1155–1172.

Steward, R. (2013) *The Independent Woman's Handbook for Super Safe Living on the Autistic Spectrum*. London: Jessica Kingsley Publishers.

Travis, L., Sigman, M. and Ruskin, E. (2001) 'Links between social understanding and social behavior in verbally able children with autism'. *Journal of Autism and Developmental Disorders*, 31 (2), 119–130.

Van Roekel, E., Scholte, R. H. and Didden, R. (2010) 'Bullying among adolescents with autism spectrum disorders: prevalence and perception'. *Journal of Autism and Developmental Disorders*, 40 (1), 63–73.

Zablotsky, B., Bradshaw, C. P. and Stuart, E. A. (2013) 'The association between mental health, stress and coping supports in mothers of children with autism spectrum disorders'. *Journal of Autism and Developmental Disorders*, 43(6), 1380–1393.

Zeedyk, S. M., Rodriguez, G., Tipton, L. A., Baker, B. L. and Blacher, J. (2014) 'Bullying of youth with autism spectrum disorder, intellectual disability, or typical development: victim and parent perspectives'. *Research in Autism Spectrum Disorders*, 8(9), 1173–1183.

# Chapter 15

# Help us make our own way

## Talking to autistic women and girls about adolescence and sexuality

*Gillian Loomes*

## Introduction

Adolescence is a pivotal time. A time filled with uncertainty, with possibilities and potential; exhilarating and terrifying. A time when, as young people, we begin to develop a sense of 'self', and of our place in the world: to make our own mark, and to begin the work of shaping the kind of person we want to be. It is also a time when we begin to understand how we relate to others around us, and to start the process of constructing our adult social identities based upon these relationships – of which undoubtedly some of the most significant such identities are our sex, our gender, and our sexuality; and an associated understanding of the types of intimate relationships we may wish to pursue as we enter adulthood. Adolescence can be a time of fluidity; of precariousness; of experimenting with the options available to us and weighing up the possibilities we are offered. We may encounter risks as we jump from the cliff edge, and hope to find a soft landing; and we may make mistakes, falling flat on our face and trusting that there is someone to pick us up.

So what of adolescence for those of us who are autistic? How do autistic girls experience this transition process of becoming autistic women? What are the key issues? And how can we be supported to navigate them? What skills and resources do we need, to ease this transition into autistic womanhood? Recent years have seen the emergence of a wide range of discourse (threads of written and spoken communication and debate) to which we turn in attempting to answer these, and other questions that intrigue and challenge us. From earlier publications addressing issues of sexuality from 'puberty and beyond' (Newport and Newport 2002); to instructional, 'guide' materials on dating (Murry Ramey and Ramey 2008); long-term relationships (Hendrickx 2008; Stanford 2002); and marriage (Slater-Walker and Slater-Walker 2002). We come to such publications as consumers, in the hope that we may be able 'to learn how to apply theoretical information' (Murry Ramey and Ramey 2008: 12).

It is certainly a common experience among young autistic girls and women to consume autism-related discourses greedily, as a means of building our identity and expressing our experience of the world. So the power of such discourses should not be underestimated, especially for those of us who have lived an initial period of our lives with the sense that we are misunderstood by those around us, and the profound sense of failing to belong or to 'fit in' that goes along with such experiences. Indeed, the titles of many books written by autistic women speak strongly to these themes – titles such as *Martian in the Playground* (Sainsbury 2009) and *Pretending to be Normal* (Holliday-Willey

2014) reveal a strong sense of feeling 'different' in the (non-autistic) world. This search for narrative and the construction of identity is a significant, though historically under-recognized aspect of autistic experience. I have described it like this:

> From our very earliest attempts at communication, we are often told that our sensory and emotional expressions are wrong. We are told that cuddles are supposed to be pleasant, even if to us they are painful. We are told that busy, loud environments that hurt every part of our bodies and make us either run, curl up or lash out are 'fun'. We are told that it's important to look at people's eyes when we talk to them, even if to us this is painful. We are told that the ways in which we do conversation are wrong. We are told that the ways in which we do friendships are wrong. We are told that our passions and enthusiasms are wrong. We are told that we are wrong.
>
> (Loomes 2016)

When we consider autistic adolescence in these terms, it becomes brutally apparent that access to information about autism is crucial to the development of our sense of 'self' as a socially connected human, with a socially constructed identity. So the key issue then becomes, what discourses do we encounter in this search for information? There are documented accounts of the pain experienced by young autistic people on encountering dehumanizing descriptions of autism. One such account is the case study of 'Ben', who attempted suicide as a result of low self-esteem and hopelessness, having been exposed to negative discourses of autism as a young man.

> I'm in so much pain because I know I'm going to be alone forever. What kind of a life is that?
> I read a study. Like 70% [of people with autism] expressed interest in sex and stuff, but only about 10 or 15% are expected to have like any kind of relationship. And even a smaller number are expected to like get married and stuff.
>
> (Bagatell 2007: 424)

Imagine approaching life, facing the road yet to be travelled, and feeling that you will be alone on that road forever. Imagine living in a world that tells you that this is your fate: that there is no hope of companionship or intimacy for you, for people like you. That those things, things that are such integral structures in the social world, things such as marriage that many young people envisage as part of their future – as *normal*, are not for you.

In circumstances such as Ben's, authoritative academic accounts can seem at the same time to provide answers to our questions about why we are 'abnormal', and to set our destinies in stone – to seal our fate. The bold, black letters on white paper or computer screen provide us with a glimpse of what we can expect. Of what the word 'autistic' means for our future, while at the same time seeming to remove our agency in claiming our own future and shaping the world around us. And, as Ben's account illustrates, it can be a grim sight.

The suggestion that autistic people should engage in such a narrative search in the quest for an autistic identity is one that has historically been rejected, almost to the point of ridicule. My own experience of diagnosis informed me in no uncertain terms, that to have such a sense of 'self' as to recognize one's difference, and one's social 'deficits' negated the very concept of autism – it served as proof that one was 'mildly autistic', or 'high functioning'. But, as more autistic people are sharing accounts of experiences such as Ben's, and, conversely, of moments of extreme joy in 'finding their tribe' through autism-related discourse, it is becoming clear that such experiences are far from uncommon. And it seems that two key questions arise from this recognition:

1   What discourses do autistic girls and young women encounter as they construct their identity?
2   How can we create space for communities of autistic 'voice' on which young autistic women and girls can draw, and to which they in turn can contribute?

## My approach

This chapter is not a 'self-help' book, or a 'guide' to adolescence for autistic women and girls. I am not seeking to contribute to the growing body of this sort of literature. I do not doubt for a moment that we need access to information about autism. But my aim here is different. What I am concerned with here is how, precisely, we might go about *using* the information to which we have access. I am interested in discussing *how* autistic girls might approach adolescence, and how we might build positive autistic identities. So I am going to begin by setting out what I see as the 'problem' with the current situation: that young autistic women experience significant barriers in the processes of identity-building I have explored so far, arising from a lack of appropriate discourses on which they can draw in order to construct their own positive sense of autistic 'self'. I am then going to suggest ways in which we may foster the conditions in which we may develop and harness autism-related discourses authored *by* autistic women, *for* autistic women, and construct our own 'voice'.

### The problem: attempting a jigsaw with the pieces missing

As I have indicated, the problem as I see it, is that while our ability to construct meaningful social identity relies upon being able to draw upon, and orchestrate discourses around us, young autistic women and girls who approach adolescence and attempt to do this around their autistic social identities find that there simply are not appropriate authoritative discourses on which they can draw. It is the frustration of this unsatisfactory construction process that I describe in the following poem:[1]

### Jigsaw identity: autistic woman

An oxymoron

A collision

A painful, confused elision

Jigsaw-work-in-progress

The 'autistic' piece

Girls aren't autistic

Male disorder; male terrain

Extreme Male Brain

'Autie hands'

Holding up to the light

Staring, squinting, looking, measuring

Autistics and lesbians

That 'and'

Autistic boys; poster boys

Blonde boys; white boys

Peering through frosted glass

Where are all the girls?

Autie hand raised


The 'woman' piece

Not being but doing

How? Why?

Boys' clothes and dungarees and hairy legs

So 'unfeminine', must try harder

But 'feminine' is tight and hugging and scratchy and stilted and false

It's 'masking'

And 'ethics of care'

I care about justice


Compromises, sacrifices, acceptances

What looks good, what feels good

Sometimes an 'and', sometimes a 'versus'

But from the compromises, sacrifices, acceptances

Comes a boldness of spirit

That says, 'I am'

Autistic woman

Autie hand raised


The pieces don't always fit

And that line, that join tells a thousand stories

War stories, survival stories

Trace your finger over it and let it talk

The pieces don't always fit

But they're my pieces

Mine

Hard fought-for and hard won

I will not labour to throw my pieces away

I will not sacrifice them

No surrender

Instead, I will smooth them, shape them; ease them till they fit

Comfortable and neat

Trace your finger over the line and let it talk

This is labour I will accept

The birth of autistic feminism

Claiming the pieces

Owning the pieces

And making them fit

What I express in the poem 'Jigsaw identity' is a central feature of my autistic, female experience – a sort of identity 'homelessness' as neither my 'autistic' status nor my 'woman' status seemed to be confirmed and supported by the relevant discourses I found in my own avaricious search for information, and a sense of belonging. I could not find the right pieces, and the pieces I had were a grating, jarring, uncomfortable fit.

## The pieces: considering 'autistic' and 'woman'

Autism has historically been a man's world. The research set out in the germinal paper 'Autistic disturbances of affective contact' (Kanner 1943) involved four times as many boys as girls, and Hans Asperger originally believed that the condition he described as 'autistic psychopathy' could not affect girls (National Autistic Society 2018). More recently, a study of autistic adults living in households in England found a diagnosis rate of 1.8% among boys and men, compared with 0.2% for women and girls (Brugha et al. 2009). There are various suggested explanations for the impact of sex on rates of autism diagnosis: including the theory that autism is an exaggeration of typical gender differences (Wing 1981); the 'extreme male brain theory' that autism is caused by the effects of fetal testosterone (Baron–Cohen 2002); or that genetic factors mean that males are more likely to inherit autism than females (Skuse 2000). Each of these accounts suggests that different rates of diagnosis of autism between the sexes arise due to differing prevalence rates – with more boys than girls actually developing autism. However, alternative theories have emerged, pointing to more socially situated reasons for these differences – namely, that girls are more likely to be able to 'camouflage' their autistic traits than boys, meaning that while they are autistic, they are not identified and diagnosed as such (Dean et al. 2017). Related to this, it has been suggested that teachers are less likely to report autistic traits in girls than they are in boys (nasen 2016).

Whatever the 'truth' of the role of sex in autism and diagnosis, there are many potential consequences for autistic girls and women arising from it. Issues include barriers to accessing appropriate support and resources, lost educational and employment opportunities, and difficulties in establishing and maintaining satisfying relationships. What I am interested in here though, is the impact of sex and gender-related autism discourses on the ability of adolescent autistic girls and women to form autistic identities.

> I remember the disability coordinator at university explaining to me why autism was thought to be 'rare' in girls and women. She said that it could be because of biological factors, or it could be because society is more protective of girls, and less likely to identify behaviours as problematic. This was worrying though. Girls being autistic was rare, so maybe I wasn't actually autistic. Maybe I wasn't properly autistic. Not properly autistic, not properly normal, not properly anything …
>
> (Gillian Loomes, account of personal experience)

We have already seen, in Ben's story (Bagatell 2007), that we use discourses in order to construct identity. But it is challenging to say the least to build identity without the bricks of such discourse with which to work. Autistic girls and women encounter this difficulty given the lack of discourses detailing theoretical and empirical accounts of autism relating specifically to women and girls. But it is worse than that. In addition to this lack of discourse with which to construct identity, autistic women and girls face an additional hurdle in the form of authoritative discourses detailing how autism is predominantly a male experience. And these discourses are powerful; they come from authoritative sources: academic research in peer reviewed journals. As Foucault tells us, discourses exist in complex power relationships (Foucault 1977; Foucault 1980). This means in practice that authoritative discourses based on academic and clinical research is likely to be more influential and persuasive than the narratives of autistic women themselves. And this causes us a profound problem. The historical omission of autistic girls and women from authoritative accounts of autism renders us 'voiceless', and presents significant barriers to our development of identity. I will return to this issue, and consider what we might do about it. Firstly though, I want to focus on the 'woman' part of the identity jigsaw.

## The 'woman' piece

Autistic girls and women do not exist in a social vacuum. We inhabit a social world, where our autistic status exists alongside, and interacts with our other identities. Of course, this means that autistic young women and girls are susceptible to, and impacted by discourses that seek to define, and to set the parameters of womanhood. We are fed the 'beauty myth' (Wolf 1991), and expected to conform with conventions of dress and appearance that are directly contrary to our sensory needs and preferences. We are at significantly greater risk of sexual violence than our non-autistic female counterparts (Bargiela et al. 2016). We often struggle with the 'hidden curriculum' of womanhood – whether and how to apply make-up, whether and when to begin removing body hair, how to develop and maintain intimate relationships (especially where such relationships are non-heterosexual and therefore not necessarily an explicit part of school-based and social curricula). Such struggles can lead to bullying, and to accusations that we are not 'proper women'.

What is important to recognize though, is that far from being intrinsic aspects of autism, these are experiences that are shared by other groups who have encountered the constraining boundaries of 'proper womanhood'. Lesbian women of colour (Lorde 1984), older women (MacDonald and Rich 1984) and other groups have successfully developed their own 'voice', in order to challenge the restrictive boundaries they encounter, and establish their own identity as 'woman'. As autistic women, I suggest we need to do the same.

In order to do this, we need to know that the gendered and sex-related discourses we encounter in the social world are not neutral. They are socially and politically charged, and they direct us in certain directions, or they invite us to resist. Such socio-political currents impact on everyone, and have been discussed at length, notably in key feminist writing such as that of Adrienne Rich on 'Compulsory heterosexuality and lesbian existence' (Rich 1980). Ways of being (such as heterosexuality) are presented as 'natural' or 'normal', but they are in fact culturally defined institutions constructed within, and imposed upon society. We need to think about what this means in the context of autism. We know that autistic girls and women engage in 'camouflaging' (Skuse 2000) and 'pretending to be normal' (Holliday-Willey 2014) in order to attempt to navigate a social world where it seems we do not belong. But when your life is based on attempts to fit in, to 'get it right', according to incomprehensible social rules, you become vulnerable. And what of autistic people who do not, or who cannot comply with such social rules? What of queer autistic women? What of disabled autistic women? Autistic women of colour? What of the damage done in our shattering attempts to be 'normal' in the absence of a suitable, authoritative 'script'?

Autistic adolescent girls and women deserve to be offered an autistic-feminist political identity in order to escape the binds of socially enforced conformity with discourses that masquerade as 'normal'. As those within the Neurodiversity movement are fond of saying 'non-compliance is a social skill'. It is one we need to teach, to learn, and to practise. So how do we do this? How do we find our 'voice'? And how do we speak out?

## Social spaces: vocal places

The psychologist asked me to tell him about my experiences of 'relationships' and about my sexuality. I stared in his direction, like a rabbit caught in headlights, with no idea what to say. There were various possible ways that I might have chosen to voice the fact that, until that point, in my early twenties, my experiences of sex and relationships with boys and men had ranged from boring and unfulfilling, to painful and traumatic. What I really wanted to say to the psychologist was, 'I actually don't really like men. I'm attracted to women. I think I might be gay.' But I found, in that moment, with the hot, stuffy air of the psychologist's office hanging between us, and engulfed in silence, I just couldn't say it. I couldn't make the words come. I didn't know how to explain the 'truth' of my sexuality, without risking his disbelief at my autism.

'Oh, well that explains it then! You're not autistic after all! Lucky you! You're just gay!'

But I needed him to believe in my autism. It was the reason I was here, begging for the psychologist's help. So I filled that weighted pause with something plausible, but not true. Well, not my chosen 'truth'. Not the narrative I would have created to sum up that aspect of my life. I fell back on what I thought I knew of autism to present an account of why I felt I struggled in relationships. I said what I thought was expected of me. I followed the script. And it was a 'truth' of sorts. But that moment was a discursive crossroads, where I was presented with multiple choices in terms of how I may have constructed my 'self', and my sexual identity. And I took the easy road – the straight road.

(Gillian Loomes, account of personal experience)

So, in order to build their identity, young autistic women and girls need access to discourses that speak to our lives and our experiences. Crucially, these discourses need to be sufficiently authoritative to be able to transcend the power of academic discourses that have written us out of autistic history. But how do we achieve this? How do we create spaces where autistic women can find our 'voice', and can share our world, without fear that what we share will be used against us, in a painful claim that we are 'only mildly autistic' or 'not proper women'. I want to take my experience in a psychologist's office, as an autistic woman in my early twenties, in order to map out the potentialities and contingencies that formed the terrain of this discursive space. And I want to consider how those of us who are autistic girls and women might navigate this terrain, and how those who support us might enable us to do so.

Let me begin, then, by exploring my encounter in the psychologist's office. This experience taught me something fundamental about how identity works, and about how we produce our identities in interaction by presenting the details called for by the physical and social space. Markova (2018) talks about this phenomenon in the context of social research, arguing that interviews take place in specific socio-cultural conditions where participants select and deselect specific features of the conditions they are discussion about, according to what they consider relevant or irrelevant, thereby creating new meanings of the issues in question. This was exactly my encounter in the psychologist's office, as I was constrained by what I believed was expected of me. At the time, I did not have available to me a sufficiently authoritative discourse of 'autistic lesbian' on which I could draw in order to present this identity in my conversation with the psychologist. I therefore felt under pressure to prioritize one or the other, and I chose to prioritize my autistic identity as that was the one most closely connected with my perceived need for psychological intervention, and my possible right to such intervention. Autistic women and girls come in all shapes, sizes, and colours of the rainbow, and if we are going to give adolescents the tools with which to build a sense of 'self', and a social identity that reflects all aspects of our lives, we need to develop discourses reflecting our heterogeneity, and, crucially, these discourses must be authoritative. And in order for the 'voices' of autistic women and girls to be authoritative, as authors of our own experiences and identities, we may need to bring about a radical shift in hierarchies of power in relation to knowledge of autism. This is without doubt a daunting task, but it is a crucial one, if future generations of autistic young women are to inherit a world where 'autistic' and 'women' can sit together as proud identity claims.

## Building conversation: thoughts, recommendations, next steps

In this chapter, we have explored the ways in which discourses are used in the shaping of socially situated identities. I have shown that for young autistic girls and women, there is a lack of appropriate authoritative discourses on which to draw in order to construct their identities, both as 'autistic' and as 'women'. I have suggested that this renders us essentially 'voiceless' and vulnerable. So we have work to do. As autistic women and girls, and as those who support us, we need to think about how we can produce the spaces in which discourses can be produced about how we experience autism in the social world. And we need to create the conditions in which such discourses can be authoritative, so that our 'voice' can be heard. This is a massive undertaking. Here are some things we may consider as we build our strategies:

- We need to consider the spaces in which we discuss (and, in so doing, construct) our identities. And we need to be mindful of the power hierarchies operating in these spaces. For example, if we are talking about our autistic identity in an assessment of need, with a view to accessing support services, the things that we will say (and the identity we will construct) will be based on aspects of ourselves (and of autism) that are relevant to our support needs, and that are most likely to meet our objective of obtaining the support we need. The assessment and the assessor hold a kind of power over us that influences how we exercise our 'voice' and construct and express our autistic identity. We need to recognize, to name, and to theorize this power in order that we can challenge its constraints. And we need to create opportunities for egalitarian discussion about autism, and about the experiences of autistic women.
- We need to recognize, articulate, and theorize the distinctions between talking about 'what autism is' (e.g. in clinical research), and about the socially situated experiences of autistic women and girls. There is a place for both types of discourse, but when they are confused, and not recognized for what they are, and the work they do, things can become very messy.
- We need to develop opportunities for autistic women to contribute individually and collectively to discussion and debate affecting women as a whole (e.g. reproductive rights, responses to gender-based violence). This is important as, following examples set by others, such as Black women, and lesbians, autistic women can contribute to the development of an intersectional, heterogeneous narrative of womanhood, challenging the constraints of traditional stereotypes and the normative values of the established social order. Such endeavours will in turn provide the discursive threads that can be gathered by future generations of autistic young women, and woven into the tapestry of their own identities, and of those of the autistic community.
- Finally, and perhaps most audaciously, we need to think critically about the role and impact of diagnosis as a gatekeeper to our community, and the function that diagnosis plays in our understanding of autism as a social identity (Loomes 2017). I have discussed above the ways in which girls and women have been historically frozen out of, and rendered 'voiceless' in, authoritative accounts of autism. But I argue further that the very assumptions upon which diagnosis is premised – as a search for the definitive nature and cause of 'disease'– result in circumstances in which the arts of identity construction and community-building masquerade as a science rooted in positivistic quests for empirical 'truth'. As such, diagnostic frameworks provide scripts by which the narratives of those girls and women who include autism in their social identity are constrained; or, conversely, we find that we are bonded to discourses that may not represent our lived 'truth' with the result that we are rendered essentially 'voiceless' – unable to articulate experiences that fall outside of the constraints of the diagnostic framework, and in a precarious position that risks the discrediting of our autistic social identity. Instead of a model of 'diagnosis', with its associated epistemological and ontological assumptions, I wonder if we can move towards a

framework of identity that describes socially situated models of autism, as experienced by women. And that enables individuals to locate their place within such models, while identifying the strengths that they encounter, and recommending the provision of supports, strategies, and community involvement as appropriate. Such an approach would represent a bold paradigm shift for our community. I do not pretend that it would be easy. But I do argue forcefully that a socially situated account of autism, recognizing the social conditions in which we live, and in which our autistic identities are shaped and produced, will enable us to find our 'voice' both individually and collectively, and will ensure that the adolescent experiences of future generations of autistic young women are considerably less painful, confused, isolated, and frightening than those who have gone before. Such a goal is socially and politically imperative. We have work to do!

And so I will bring this chapter to a close, by stating that it is my sincere hope and firm intention that these thoughts may contribute to an emerging, and blossoming autistic, feminist 'voice', that will inspire future generations of autistic girls and young women, and to which they may in turn contribute, in the development of individual and collective identity. For too long, autistic girls and women have experienced a double oppression of stifling, silencing narratives that dismiss or discredit our autistic experiences, and that challenge our status as women. We need to nurture the development, both of adolescent individuals, and of our wider autistic feminist community. I suggest that this nurturing will be found in social spaces, and vocal places, and I look forward to working together to create and sustain such places.

## Note

1   Written for and performed at the Intimate Lives Conference, University of Birmingham, UK, July 2018. The conference focused on issues of sex, gender, and sexuality as experienced by the autistic community, and established a network for discussion around these issues.

## References

Bagatell, N. (2007) 'Orchestrating voices: autism, identity and the power of discourse'. *Disability and Society*, 22(4), 413–426.

Bargiela, S., Steward, R. and Mandy, W. (2016) 'The experiences of late-diagnosed women with autism spectrum conditions: an investigation of the female autism phenotype'. *Journal of Autism and Developmental Disorders*, 46, 3281–3294.

Baron-Cohen, S. (2002) 'The extreme male brain theory of autism'. *Trends in Cognitive Sciences*, 6 (6), 248–254.

Brugha, T., McManus, S., Meltzer, H., Smith, J., Scott, F. J., Purdon, S.*et al.* (2009) *Autism Spectrum Disorders in Adults Living in Households throughout England: Report from the Adult Psychiatric Morbidity Survey 2007*. Leeds: NHS Information Centre.

Dean, M., Harwood, R. and Casari, C. (2017) 'The art of camouflage: gender differences in the social behaviours of girls and boys with autism spectrum disorder'. *Autism*, 21(6), 678–689.

Foucault, M. (1977) *Discipline and Punish*. London: Allen Lane.

Foucault, M. (1980) *Power/Knowledge*Brighton: Harvester.

Hendrickx, S. (2008) *Love, Sex and Long-Term Relationships: What People with Asperger Syndrome Really, Really Want*. London: Jessica Kingsley.

Holliday-Willey, L. (2014) *Pretending to be Normal*. London: Jessica Kingsley.

Kanner, L. (1943) 'Autistic disturbances of affective contact'. *Nervous Child*, 2, 217–250.

Loomes, G. (2016) 'A very short blog about being autistic in the world'. *The Questioning Aspie*, 27 August. Retrieved from https://thequestioningaspie.wordpress.com/2016/08/27/what-i-want-you-to-know (accessed 5 September 2018).

Loomes, G. (2017) 'It's only words: a critical insider perspective on the impact of diagnosis in the construction of autistic social identity'. *Good Autism Practice*, 18(1), 20–24.

Lorde, A. (1984) *Sister Outsider*. Berkeley, CA: Crossing Press.

MacDonald, B. and Rich, C. (1984) *Look Me in the Eye: Old Women, Aging and Ageism*. London: Women's Press.

Markova, I. (2018) '"Giving voice": opening up new routes in the dialogicality of social change'. *Journal of the Theory of Social Behaviour*, 47, 279–285.

Murry Ramey, E. and Ramey, J. J. (2008) *Autistics' Guide to Dating*. London: Jessica Kingsley.

nasen (2016) *Girls and Autism: Flying under the Radar*. Tamworth: nasen. Retrieved from www.nasen.org.uk/resources/resources.girls-and-autism-flying-under-the-radar.html (accessed 5 September 2018).

National Autistic Society (2018) 'Gender and autism'. Retrieved from www.autism.org.uk/about/what-is/gender.aspx (accessed 5 September 2018).

Newport, J. and Newport, M. (2002) *Autism, Asperger's and Sexuality: Puberty and Beyond*. Austin, TX: Future Horizons.

Rich, A. (1980) 'Compulsory heterosexuality and lesbian existence'. *Signs: Journal of Women in Culture and Society*, 5(4), 631–660.

Sainsbury, C. (2009) *Martian in the Playground: Understanding the Child with Autism*. London: Sage.

Skuse, D. H. (2000) 'Imprinting, the X chromosome, and the male brain: explaining sex differences in the liability to autism'. *Pediatric Research*, 47(1), 9–16.

Slater-Walker, C. and Slater-Walker, G. (2002) *An Asperger Marriage*. London: Jessica Kingsley.

Stanford, A. (2002) *Asperger Syndrome and Long-Term Relationships*. London: Jessica Kingsley.

Wing, L. (1981) 'Sex ratios in early childhood autism and related conditions'. *Psychiatry Research*, 5, 129–137.

Wolf, N. (1991) *The Beauty Myth: How Images of Women are Used against Women*. London: Vintage.

# Part V

# Autistic girls
## Looking to the future

## What we want the world to know

Girls of Limpsfield Grange School

### Autism and gifts

'Having autism is stressful but you need to suffer for the good gifts such as recognizing different patterns and textures and being honest.'

(Scarlett, Year 9)

'I've always been interested in what it is like to be someone else, to share their perspective and to think their thoughts.'

(Lauren, Year 9)

'Everyone thinks it is a bad thing to be autistic. I'd like everyone to just try a little bit to understand autism, instead of just pretending.'

(Carrie, Year 7)

### Things need to change

'Quite regularly the term autistic is used on the internet as an insult. This is really offensive to those of us who are autistic – like myself. Autism is not a joke and it is not something to be ashamed of or embarrassed by.'

(Leila, Year 7)

'The world needs to change the way it looks at autistic people. People just see our autism. They see a communication disorder, but it is not like there is anything wrong with us. We just find it harder to communicate, that's all!'

(Daisy, Year 10)

'Mainstream schools need to teach their kids that autism isn't an illness or a disease. It's a difference. That would have such a positive impact on autistic people – they would feel like they belonged.'

(Molly, Year 10)

# Chapter 16

# Girls for the future

## Transitions and employment

*Jo Egerton, Helen Ellis and Barry Carpenter*

---

> My hopes for having a career or working life have faded. I could have done with some
> help earlier in my life to direct me into a suitable career.
>
> (An intellectually able autistic woman, quoted in Baldwin and Costley 2016: 490)

This chapter focuses on the periods of transition that lead up to and shape the early-career planning decisions made by young autistic women for their futures. This chapter begins with a personal reflection by one of the authors on her experiences as a young autistic woman transitioning through school into the world of work. The issues that she raises extend into the sections that follow, as the chapter explores research findings around post-secondary transition and employment.

In the context of national and international employment statistics for autistic women, the chapter emphasizes the need for employers to recognize the value that autistic employees can bring to their workforce, and identifies the barriers to employment that currently thwart the successful inclusion of autistic women within the workforce. Employers need to remove barriers to their inclusion, and establish a mutually enabling working environment for autistic women and their neurotypical colleagues. Currently, there is a very long way to go.

The chapter then concludes by considering two evidence-based approaches that might smooth the transition experiences of autistic girls emerging into adulthood, and enable the professionals working with them to offer improved support towards realizing their aspirations.

## Transitions – hurdle by hurdle

*Helen Ellis is an autistic advocate and self-advocate, a member of the Westminster Autism Commission and of the All Party Parliamentary Group on Autism (APPGA) Advisory Group. She shares her vivid recollection of her transitions in the following paragraphs.*

Within the journey from childhood to adulthood there are many transitional stages of life, each teaching us key skills and each presenting their own unique set of problems and hurdles to overcome.

The most focused-on transition is often the primary school to secondary school transition; the huge leap in the education system from cosy, one-level schools, with a single class teacher and lots of room to run and play, up to the chaotic environment of a multi-level, huge, sprawling, campus-style building, with different teachers and class mates for each subject.

Personally, I managed to avoid a lot of the anxiety-filled change at this point in my life due to the simple fact that I had been enrolled in the tertiary system – I joined my middle school at the start of Year 5 and left at the end of Year 8. This, to me, was perfect; I was able to make the switch from the one class teacher to multi-subject teachers seamlessly because I was already familiar with the faces and names of the staff, I did not have to learn a new route to school or even a new building; all I had to do was ensure that I remembered to go outside to the language building instead of turning left towards the Year 6 wing!

I would wholeheartedly advocate for the middle school system to be employed across the country for autistic pupils. The reduction of stress and anxiety in that key 11–12 years age bracket made the tempestuous time of puberty at least vaguely bearable for me, especially with the oldest pupils in the school being only 13 years old. It also meant that when we did transition to upper school we were not treated as the 'kiddies' of the school at 11 years old but instead were fairly left alone as 13-year-olds only a few years younger than the 16-year-olds in Year 11. (The sixth form was a separate entity whose students spent most of their time annoyed with anyone in uniform regardless of year group.)

One of the hardest parts about the transition from primary level education to secondary was one I did not manage to avoid however; the switch from class teacher to subject teachers. It was easier for me through already knowing a lot of the staff, and I did have the advantage of having a maths teacher for a father, so I was familiar and comfortable with the idea of subject specialists, but it still threw me for a while: getting used to rapidly switching between subjects not just in cerebral thinking but also in location.

It may seem a simple task, but having to both mentally 'leave' science and reset the brain to 'drama' as well as actually vacating the science lab and moving through the school to the drama studio was a new and tricky concept for me. There were times I often only managed the physical movement (as I was swept along by my classmates) and arrived to the next lesson still thinking about the last thing mentioned in the previous lesson – especially if that last thing was a shouted instruction of homework after the bell rang!

I cannot count the number of times I got the homework task completely wrong because I was trying to process the instruction at the same time as dealing with packing my bag up and joining the melee of bodies going out the door. This was always made ten times worse on the days I had my period as I had half my mind on my internal clock monitoring how long it had been since I last changed my pad and whether I was at risk of leaking!

The mini transitions from lesson to lesson were always problematic in school – the overwhelming nature of the exit-crush, the excitable chattering of peers finally allowed to talk to each other, the dizzying overload of input from movement and processing delay as I tried to remember where I was going and why.

And this only got worse as I progressed through the stages of education, with each year of secondary school and then further education meaning that the peers in one class were all going off to different subjects in the next lesson; I would leave my maths A level class to go to chemistry, but others were going to French or history while I was being joined in the lab by those coming from a free period where they had been working on a biology project.

Oddly this did not alter much at university level as a lot of the degree had set modules so class cohorts remained the same from one lecture to another. However, within a shared house or along a residential hall corridor, there could be students from all the different faculties, an issue that can deeply affect those on medical courses when they get thrown into shifts – particularly when having to cope with night shifts while living next door to a permanent party room!

The transition to adulthood and independence is a lot more complicated than just a change in education style and level however; it is a seismic shift towards fully fledged adult life – self-study, independent living, autonomy in major life decisions.

Every step of the prior educational journey is structured: year group to year group; primary to secondary; set lessons and subjects. Suddenly the choice is overwhelming – sixth form and A levels or college and BTEC courses or apprenticeships or the world of work …

And with each choice you find yourself spinning further away from friends and peers. Even if you did not get on with classmates in school, suddenly the lack of any familiarity is terrifying. Choosing the next step on the path to adult life is perhaps the most complicated and high-anxiety choice of a person's lifetime; it comes at a time in life when we crave newness and the chance to prove our independence but we lack the depth of experience and context to necessarily make the right long term choices.

The friend whom you grew up with, hitting all the major milestones together, is off on a seven-year medicine course heavy on exams and twelve-hour shifts, while you are contemplating a sociology course that is a straight three-year BA degree with heavy self-study at the other end of the country.

The university experience is fantastic if it goes right but there are many potential problems in leaving home for higher education, not least the fact that, as their students are legal adults, the university and other services will only deal directly with the person in question and not their parents – I had to hand deliver consent forms I had created to various departments authorizing my mother to be told information and to be contacted if I stopped responding (as I often got so overwhelmed by situations that I ignored them completely).

This transition to being a legal adult is hard to navigate, especially for autistic adults who need support in managing their time, money and workloads. In these situations a parent can literally know nothing until their child comes home having been kicked out for failing to submit any work or gets summoned to court for missing payments.

A lot more needs to be done earlier in education to prepare children for what adulthood truly means, and more needs to be done by universities and colleges to understand the adjustments that need to be put in place for autistic students – we are not the best at asking for help even when it is desperately needed!

And all forms of education need to improve on how they prepare people for the transition to the working world; careers advice needs to be more proactive, especially for people like me who fall in love with ideas of careers but do not fully understand all they entail and so get burnt trying to survive in those worlds.

The world of work is unlike anything school prepares you for really. Suddenly you find yourself in a situation where not only are you battling with others for a single vacancy (which is so different to the all-in-this-together mentality of exams and coursework in education) but if you get the job you may find yourself working with people of varying interests and lives that do not match yours. Even within a local job that does not involve a long commute there can be a range of ages, home towns, family set ups and political views to get used to.

Entering the employment field from university can also mean a rapid readjustment to a 9–5 day having had minimal hours of timetabled lectures on undergraduate programmes. Learning to adapt to the working day and the fact that others may work different hours to you can be a struggle for autistic people. I still occasionally go looking for a colleague on the day she works from home even though I have known that fact for over six months.

The office management structure and unofficial social hierarchies can cause huge issues for autistic people to adjust to. The transition from a class of people learning from one person in charge at the front to answering to multiple people in a command chain can create confusion and unintentional offense as the employee may not realize that they are talking to their manager's manager or a high level director, and so refuse to do the task until the manager they know instructs them to!

The transition to the world of work generally takes a fair amount of time to adjust to, but with so many employers wanting a 'hit the ground running' appointee and having little to no patience with teaching a new recruit all the things they need to know, it can become a toxic experience for autistic people. Inductions are often stacked full of instructions and training that the organization needs you to have, but skip over key knowledge that would make the transition from 'new person' to 'employee' so much easier for someone. When I started my last job I was confident enough to ensure that I got responses to my questions about the 'tea round' and answering another person's phone as well as the standard queries about how to book leave and what to do if severe weather prevents me commuting in.

In essence, every transition is different and stressful. This is true for everyone not just autistic people, but ultimately the transitions that we, as autistic people, go through between the ages of 11 and 25 years are huge and have the potential to be incredibly traumatic if not handled correctly.

## A major hurdle

As Helen Ellis has powerfully described above, leaving school is a major hurdle for any child. The transition from that school environment with all of its familiar people, routines, structures, rules and memories — good and bad — is a time of worry and concern for any young person, even if it is tinged with the excitement of a 'new adventure.'

For the girl with autism the perspective on leaving school may be very different. Feelings of abandonment may be evoked; the loss of that teacher who always showed kindness by letting you enter the classroom once everyone else was settled in their place; that teaching assistant (TA) who would spend time with you explaining the incomprehensible emotional aspects of English literature; the learning mentor who, every Thursday, would host a lunch club for 'girls like you', where you could talk excitedly about your latest special interest.

Feelings of loss… your friends were few, often younger than you, but friends they were and you spent time together playing the games you wanted to play or politely looking at the thousand photographs of horses on your mobile phone. Why do they get to stay at school with all of its familiar smells and textures and colours that you have learnt to manage over the years? Just because you have reached 18 years old, it seems so unfair that you are ejected into that busy world with routines you do not understand, with noises that are frightening, with people you do not know, who talk quickly and make facial expressions that you cannot comprehend, and where everyone and everything moves so fast.

Indeed, some young women with autism would challenge the assumption that 18 years of age is the right time to leave school. Sainsbury (2000), in her well-known book *Martian in the Playground*, describes it as 'ludicrous' to make that assumption. For her the post-school option was university, but even that brought an 'incredulous reaction' (ibid.: 122) in some quarters (she went on to gain a first class degree from New College, Oxford). She states that for her, as for other high-functioning adults with autism, university was the first chance 'to experience formal education as enjoyable and to discover themselves as competent', with routines and flexibility that accommodated unique and creative learning styles.

In a similar vein, the world-famous Temple Grandin writes:

> ... the really big challenge for me was making the transition from high school to college... In order to deal with such a major change ... I needed a way to rehearse it, acting out each phase in my life by walking through an actual door, window or gate.

(Grandin 1995: 18)

## Autism, employment and the law

Internationally, the political aspiration for people with disabilities to enter employment following the end of formal education is enshrined in law in an increasing number of countries. Being in work is recognized as 'important for social inclusion and economic independence' (Australian Bureau of Statistics 2017). It is also a predictor of improved cognitive performance, physical and mental health and well-being, and has been shown to promote a sense of personal dignity and to enhance quality of life for people on the autism spectrum (Hendricks 2010; Reine et al. 2016; Sung et al. 2015).

In the UK, the transition elements of the Children and Families Act 2014 and the associated *Special Educational Needs and Disabilities Code of Practice* (Department for Education/Department of Health 2014) are strengthened for autistic people by the Adult Autism Strategy statutory guidance in which the Government commits to:

> ... ensure that employment is promoted as a positive outcome for the majority of children and young people with autism who have [Education, Health and Care] EHC plans, [and] that routes to employment are fully explored during the reviews of those plans from ... age 13–14 onwards.

(Department of Health 2015)

However, despite these intentions, as the Department of Health acknowledges, adults on the autism spectrum are 'significantly underrepresented in the labour market' (Parkin et al. 2016: 22), although there are currently UK Government initiatives exploring solutions (Department for Work and Pensions/Department of Health 2017). The UK's employment rate for all disabled adults is 50.7% against 81.1% for adults not classified as having a disability (Powell 2018). However, National Autistic Society figures (National Autistic Society 2016), based on a national survey of 2080 autistic adults of working age, estimate that only 32% of autistic adults are in some kind of paid work (a percentage effectively static since 2007), and that of those only 16% are working full time. While not directly comparable, USA figures show that 58% of young autistic adults were employed during their early 20s compared with 95% of those with other disabilities (Roux et al. 2015), and the Australian Bureau of Statistics (ABS 2017) figures for 2015 indicate 40.8% workforce participation (people employed or seeking work) of autistic people compared with 53.4% of working age people with disability.

Even for autistic adults who are employed, there are issues. Fifty-one per cent of those surveyed by the National Autistic Society believed they were over-skilled for the job they were employed to do, and 40% were working for fewer hours than they would like. Additionally, 79% of autistic adults surveyed who were on out-of-work benefits said that they wanted to work. While recognizing that paid employment may not be appropriate for all these people, the National Autistic Society pointed out:

> Employers need information and incentives to encourage them to recruit autistic employees and make necessary reasonable adjustments. Everyone … needs better information to enable them to understand how autistic people experience the world and relate to it so that they can better support them.
>
> (National Autistic Society 2017: 2)

Auticon, an award-winning IT business originating in Germany, employs 15 IT consultants, all autistic, who work on prestigious contracts (e.g. with GlaxoSmithKline). Harris (2017) writes that Auticon's founder, Dirk Müller-Remus, was 'appalled by the often dismal opportunities available to autistic people', described by Auticon's UK chief executive, Ray Coyle, as 'Some of the most loyal, capable and dedicated employees I've had', who, 'In the right role and with the right support … significantly outperform a neurotypical person doing the same job'. He appreciates their innovatory skills as 'invaluable', ascribing these to the autistic employees' 'totally different cognitive process and … completely different perspective' alongside 'the capacity to concentrate on a single task for long periods, an appreciation of systems and patterns, [and] an amazing facility with IT'. Other organizations that regularly employ intellectually able autistic people (e.g. government intelligence and security services, Proctor and Gamble's research centre, the US's *The Atlantic* magazine) would agree. Yet, prior to their employment by Auticon, all the IT consultants had had long spells in unemployment (Harris 2007).

However, of all Auticon's 15 autistic consultants at that time, only one was a woman. As Ray Coyle told Harris, 'We can do better than that'.

## Gender disparities around employment

Girls on the autism spectrum and girls with disabilities face similar gender discriminations to their neurotypical peers, but perhaps to a greater extent due to reduced exposure to gender-stereotype-challenging role models and iconoclasm in popular culture. While it seems that gender is not significant in competitive employment[1] rates among autistic young people (Kaya et al. 2016; Sung et al. 2015), there are conflicting reports about gender associated employment outcomes (e.g. likelihood of finding work; number of hours worked, pay, etc.) (Lindsay et al. 2018). Across a range of studies, variously in relation to competitive, supported and integrated employments, findings suggest that among young adults on the autism spectrum, being older, being white, being male, not being on benefits, having post-secondary education, having had job placements and sustained casual work experience prior to leaving school, and having preparatory (e.g. c. v. preparation, mediation with prospective employers) and on-the-job employment support increases the likelihood of employment (Chiang et al. 2013; Lindsay et al. 2018; Migliore et al. 2012; Sung et al. 2015).

Lindstrom et al., working in the USA, reported that women of working age with disabilities, irrespective of disability type, are 25% less likely to secure jobs than males with disabilities (Lindstrom et al. 2012; Lindstrom et al. 2013). They are more likely to earn less and work fewer hours than male counterparts, and to be clustered in low paying, female-associated occupations (e.g. caring, clerical work), restricting their career development and occupational opportunities. They suggested that these gender-associated discrepancies were due to both individual and structural barriers such as 'low self-esteem, limited self-efficacy, and a lack of self-advocacy skills' as well as family and community attitudes.

There is a double discrimination for females with disabilities seeking employment (Lindstrom et al. 2012; Reine et al. 2016), and a triple discrimination for females with disabilities from culturally and linguistically diverse (CLD) communities (Powers et al. 2008). First there are gender associated discriminations already described. Then there is disability discrimination: autistic adults who showed more autistic symptoms or who had a secondary condition were less likely to have paid employment than those who showed fewer symptoms and had no secondary conditions, irrespective of their functional ability (Chiang et al. 2013). The third discrimination, around race/culture, occurs for females with disabilities from CLD communities. Not only were numbers of CLD women with disabilities in paid employment lower than those of their male counterparts and non-CLD peers, but also girls with disabilities from these communities were more likely to say that less was expected of them than their non-CLD peers due to community attitudes to both their disability and their gender.

Parent and teacher support, prior to and during transition, while being predictors of good employment outcomes, can also unintentionally limit the career opportunities accessed by girls with disabilities if career advice and support is not truly personalized. Girls' career options can be restricted by gender stereotyping of school-based advice, vocational training and job experience offers, and by parents' safety concerns for girls. Expectations of boys with disabilities are more likely to include their getting a job, living away from the family home, and having a family. However, despite gender bias, Lindstrom et al. found that:

> Young women with learning disabilities who display high levels of self-determination, motivation, and self-efficacy are more likely [than those who do not] to achieve their career goals and express overall satisfaction within their chosen occupations.
>
> (Lindstrom et al. 2018: 11)

## Preparing young people for employment

Young people emerging into adulthood from adolescence make many important decisions such as leaving or continuing education, and independence from their family or caregivers. This period of 'uncertainty, decisions and transitions' (Huntley 2013: 116) between adolescence and adulthood, together with puberty, provides particular challenges for autistic young people, who struggle with change.

Part of this is the challenge of moving from education into further or higher education and employment. Prefacing her interviews with young autistic people and their parents in her study, *Aspirations and Outcomes for People with Autism Spectrum Disorders in Emerging Adulthood*, Huntley (2013: 79–80) writes that for young autistic people who are 'able to find education, employment or self-employment that fits with their interests, skills and needs'. success is possible. However, the earlier educational experiences of her autistic interviewees, all under the age of 25 years, impacted on their success. One mother, interviewed along with her daughter, stated:

> I think if she'd had the right support… she could have had a really good job now really. She'd probably have to do a job on her own, not with a team, but she's very bright and I think she could have got quite high qualifications.
>
> (MO08, quoted in Huntley 2013: 79)

The National Autistic Society advises that 'Autistic people need support throughout their lives to help them access and prepare for employment opportunities' (National Autistic Society 2017: 2). Leaving secondary or post-secondary education should be the culmination of education-based support programmes that orientate young people on the autism spectrum towards employment and employer expectations. To do this effectively, schools need greater awareness of the workplace experiences and perspectives of female autistic adults and to learn from them so they can better prepare the autistic young women of the future. This is important. When preparation to enter the world of work or post-secondary education is inadequate, it increases the likelihood of poor employment trajectories, including frequent job losses and uneven work histories, as well as decreasing confidence, motivation and self-esteem (Griffith et al. 2012).

The current under-identification of girls on the autism spectrum, leading to lack of support for and attention to their specific needs, may have critical implications for their post-school success. One important finding from Lindstrom et al.'s research was that:

> …lack of disability [self-]awareness created an additional barrier to postschool success for young women with disabilities… Without a clear understanding of [their] disability limitations or accommodations needed, it was difficult for young women to articulate their needs and make a plan to succeed in either academic or employment environments. The college women in our study…spoke of the need to learn to ask for help and persistently advocate for appropriate supports and services.
>
> (Lindstrom et al. 2018: 114)

## Developing aspirations

Lindstrom et al. (2012: 116) describe how career aspirations and options of young people with disabilities are closely linked to the various stages of forming a vocational self-identity, starting with 'who they are and who they would like to become'. This is achieved through a wide variety of experiences and opportunities for self-discovery, and support to assimilate this to a developing sense of self.

The following case study illustrates the developing career aspirations of one group of Year 10 girls. Limpsfield Grange School is a local authority maintained school for girls with communication and interaction difficulties. It takes a positive, long-term approach to planning for adulthood jointly with their pupils, promoting high expectations for employment (Neustatter 2015).

In July 2018, 17 Year 10 girls on the autism spectrum (aged 13–16, most 14 or 15 years old) from Limpsfield Grange School completed a 10-question 'Interests, skills and career plans' survey. The survey was developed by one of the chapter authors to find out how far the pupils had thought through their future in relation to five 'tasks' which promote successful transition:

- *Knowledge of and confidence in their interests and skills*: 16 of the 17 pupils articulated a range of very different interests and skills that represented their strengths, achievements and personal characteristics they were proud of. Only one pupil (age 15 years) lacked the confidence to respond to these questions.
- *Identifying post-secondary education and employment pathways*: Sixteen pupils had ideas about their post-secondary career steps (chosen from a five-option list). Only one 14-year-old pupil made no choice of next move, noting that she was 'unsure of the future'.
- *Developing clear career aspirations; associations with skills and interests*: Four pupils did not yet have firm career aspirations (unsurprisingly, this included the two youngest); two pupils responded with generic areas associated with their interests, while the remaining eleven had very specific aspirations, three including an 'Option B' in case their preferred career was unachievable, and one two-step plan. In just over half the group (nine) there was a link between their top three interests and/or skills and their career choice.
- *Recognizing how they felt about the future*: This is important as acknowledging feelings is a first step to managing them; and the school environment gives pupils the opportunity to learn how to manage feelings around change with support. Five girls did not know or were unsure how they felt; three described themselves as 'worried', 'nervous', 'anxious' and/or 'scared'; four described excitement mixed with anxiety; while three were entirely positive. Two gained reassurance from faith/hope – one in her abilities and the other in her back-up plan.
- *Reflecting on career plans and offering advice to others*. Finally, applying advice and giving advice arguably demonstrate (a) pupils' increasing ability to accept and implement another point of view to achieve an improved outcome, and (b), in being able to offer advice, a growing sense of self-efficacy in and ownership of their career planning process. Five of the six pupils who neither remembered being given advice, nor felt they could offer any, described nervousness or lack of certainty about their feelings about the future (the sixth described themselves as 'happy'). There were five who did not remember receiving advice, but shared suggestions for others transitioning in the future; three of these pupils noted that they felt worried or did not know how they felt about the future; one was nervous but excited, while the other expressed 'strong hopes'. The remaining six remembered receiving advice and offered their own; all felt positively about post-secondary transition; four of these pupils said they felt excited (albeit two mixed with nervousness), and the other two expressed hope or faith in their career aspirations.

The summarized range of careers advice offered by pupils from their experience is pertinent for others; although it is derived from their messages and wording, it is not verbatim:

- Do what you love or enjoy; have interests – this makes it easier to choose a career.
- Be confident and resilient; try your best; never give up.
- Think and have ideas about your future; choose wisely; work hard.
- Keep an alternative career idea in mind in case your first choice is not possible.
- We are all here for a reason; if you fail in your aspiration, do not worry as you will come out stronger.
- This school treats pupils 'a whole different way' to mainstream schools.

These young people's varying levels of self-knowledge, confidence, aspirations and planning have, to different degrees, enabled them to begin constructing the strong foundation on which they will build their future career success. Interestingly, there was little indication that pupil age had any impact on responses. Responding to a final invitation to share further thoughts, five young women made comments that were specifically relevant to their individual career aspirations. It is perhaps fitting to close this analysis with a sentence opener from of them; she wrote: 'I'd rather have a job linked to my passions than ...'. Everyone finishing that sentence would do so differently – as such, it provides a powerful discussion springboard for considering true career aspirations and fulfilling lives.

## Creating a vocational identity

The recommendations in this section carry through the themes and tasks of the case study above. The importance of creating a vocational identity has been addressed by Lindstrom et al. in the PATHS curriculum, designed to better prepare young women for the world of work and currently under trial in the USA (Lindstrom et al. 2013; Lindstrom et al. 2018). Among the activities for young people with disabilities advised by Lindstrom et al. (2012) to support building a personalized, vocational identity and extend aspirations are:

- Creating a personal interest inventory as a basis for career exploration.
- Identifying skills development pathways that reflect their occupation interests.
- Interacting with high earning female role models with disabilities, or those who have non-traditionally female roles.
- Clarifying their long- and short-term career goals, and understanding the connection between their goals and their personal interests, strengths, needs and motivation.
- Developing the skills and strategies to navigate, direct and (ultimately) self-direct their own occupational planning and exploration.
- Enrolling on 'occupation-specific vocational courses or participat[ing] in community work experience' (Lindstrom et al. 2012: 109); young women with disabilities were less likely to do this than their male counterparts.
- Seeking mentored opportunities.

However these activities needed to be supported by personal development skills training in preparation for workplace expectations (Hendricks 2010; Lai et al. 2011; Lindstrom et al. 2012; Sung et al. 2015), including the following:

- Addressing communication, assertiveness and social difficulties (including appropriate behaviour and personal hygiene expectations).
- Learning executive function skills which can be taught and scaffolded, such as organization, scheduling, task sequencing.
- Support to learn appropriate employment-orientated social behaviours, including strategies for coping and waiting, anger management and leisure behaviours.
- Learning to identify, describe, self-reflect and build on their own strengths and successes.
- Developing strong self-advocacy skills, together with the self-confidence to use them, enabling young women to voice their own ideas, preferred options and choices, challenge others' stereotypic and inappropriate expectations (low or high), and challenge workplace harassment or bullying should it occur (23% of Baldwin and Costley's interviewees experienced bullying).

Certain within-work interventions (Baldwin and Costley 2016; Hendricks 2010; Sung et al. 2015) improved the likelihood of employment for young autistic people and successful job retention. They included:

- Collaborative transition planning between education providers and vocational support organizations or employers.
- Workplace support (e.g. external support, environmental adjustment, personal support from managers and colleagues).
- On-the-job training, and supports to promote skills mastery such as personal digital assistants (PDAs), video-based instruction, audio cuing; the increased independence from job coaches, co-worker, mentors, etc., while helpful, may prevent social interaction with colleagues.
- 'Fall-back support' enabling autistic young adults to try again.
- Greater expenditure in service provision, including job placement assistance, longer support periods, etc.

PATHS-2 (Lindstrom et al. 2018) supports the areas raised above. During trials, they found that young women completing their course displayed increased self-acceptance and confidence in 'specific career development knowledge and skills'.

## Supporting young autistic people with learning difficulties

The voices that we have heard so far in this chapter are those of girls with autism who are intellectually able, at the end the autism spectrum formerly characterized by 'Asperger syndrome'. Originally it was thought, based on Kanner's (1943) study of 'a new syndrome of autism', that all children on the autism spectrum were fundamentally intelligent. Wing and Gould (1979) in their Camberwell study, were the first to prove this assumption wrong by recognizing and demonstrating that autism and severe learning difficulties (SLD) could occur together. Such children would now meet the criteria for Complex Learning Difficulties and Disabilities (CLDD) identified in the research of Carpenter et al. (2011). Carpenter et al. (2015: 13) speak of the 'new autisms' which give a different lens through which to view the child's needs profile, and this would certainly be true of girls with autism and learning difficulties.

Beyond Words' series of employment-themed wordless books (funded by the UK Department of Work and Pensions) introduces employment knowledge, understanding, skills and attitudes though pictures in a way that is accessible to people with a range of severe learning and communication difficulties (www.booksbeyondwords.co.uk). As part of a book club hosted by a facilitator, the books' illustrations are used to invite the participation of a small group in collaboratively creating a story that reflects their experiences and concerns around a given situation. The case study below describes how such a book club worked in a school environment.

## Case Study: *Choosing My First Job*

Nasreen, Jasmine and Amanda were all Year 13 students in a school for children with moderate learning difficulties (MLD). For each, autism was a part of their diagnosis, giving rise to overlapping and compounding learning difficulties (Carpenter et al. 2015).

As a part of their Transition Programme they were considering work options. They had received talks from various employers; for example from day nurseries, cafés, garden centres, etc. Each had left them with an easy-to-read leaflet. The three students had some basic reading skills, but their comprehension was patchy. In situations where there were uncertain outcomes, their anxiety would often prevent logical thought and response, and an inability to respond to the words they read.

To overcome these difficulties the three young women were introduced to *Choosing My First Job* (Banks et al. 2018). The book depicted key scenes in a story sequence of young people involved, as they were, in searching for jobs. Faced by the young people in the illustrations, each of the girls was able to describe the jobs illustrated, talk about the characters and relate the work activities to their own aspirations. Through detailed observations it was noted that levels of engagement increased; the girls were 'curious' about the job roles, responsive to questions and discussion, and persistent in their handling of the book and interpretation of the story. By the end of the session, their anxiety levels had decreased, and participation had increased.

Innovative interventions such as the example given here are crucial if we are to unlock the interests and potential of girls of all abilities across the autism spectrum.

As part of the 'Autism in Pink' project (http://autisminpink.net), funded by the European Union's Lifelong Learning Programme across four countries, young autistic adults explored employment and security. Some had full-time paid work; others capitalized on creative skills or worked in supported environments. Some spoke for themselves; others had advocates speaking on their behalf based on what the advocates knew of them. Discussions in the UK (Autism in Pink 2014) weighed up the challenging work issues – sensory overload, the difficulties of communication – against the financial security that bought short-term pleasures and long-term peace of mind. One of the authors of this chapter, Helen Ellis, who took part in the 'Autism in Pink' project, explained that for her:

> It's knowing within myself that I have some control over my future. I'm in a job now that I feel confident I can say if I want to move on somewhere else I will get a good reference, I have the experience to go find something. I'm no longer depending on other people to help me out in that way.

## Conclusion

Adulthood is an emergent status realized through the gradual acquisition of certain rights, privileges and responsibilities (May 2000). For young people with autism such a natural progression cannot be taken for granted, and the process of acquisition is fraught with challenge and complexity.

'Acquisition' is a major dynamic within the process of transition. There are so many new skills to acquire that it can be daunting and overwhelming for the girl with autism; Williams (1996: 249) recalls 'endless questions that I did not understand'. This may trigger overwhelming anxiety, that 'wild-savage beast that prowls beside me taking me hostage' (Students of Limpsfield Grange School and Martin 2015: 18) as they cross the transitional abyss, leaving the secure school structures of the adolescent years and reaching for the unknown, the unfamiliar.

While pathways from school to the adult world are not always clear for girls with autism, Helen Ellis and the students of Limpsfield Grange, both in their writing and contribution to this chapter, express the paradox of transition. Anxiety is a dynamic within that paradox, but where girls can be enabled through whatever means to engage with aspiration then their intrinsic motivation can be liberated and dreams turned into realities.

## Acknowledgements

The authors would like to thank the young people and their staff at Limpsfield Grange School, Surrey, and The Westminster School, Worcestershire, for their contributions to this chapter.

## Useful websites

www.mentallyhealthyschools.org.uk
www.bbc.com/teach/class-clips-video/pshe-ks2-ks3-when-i-worry-about-things/z7jyd6f
www.engagement4learning.com
www.barrycarpentereducation.com

## Note

1 'Competitive employment' is 'employment in an integrated setting or self-employment that is performed on a full-time or part-time basis for which an individual is compensated at or above the minimum wage' (Sung et al. 2015).

## References

Australian Bureau of Statistics (2017) 'Disability, ageing and carers, Australia: summary of findings 2015'. Retrieved from www.abs.gov.au/ausstats/abs@.nsf/Lookup/4430.0Main%20Fea tures752015 (accessed 1 September 2018).

Autism in Pink (2014) 'Autism in Pink Documentary (English)'. Retrieved from www.youtube.com/watch?v=E-FvExDAqh8 (accessed 17 September 2018).

Baldwin, S. and Costley, D. (2016) 'The experiences and needs of female adults with high-functioning autism spectrum disorder'. *Autism*, 20(4), 483–495.

Banks, R., Carpenter, B. and Ramalingham, D. (2018) *Choosing My First Job*. London: Books Beyond Words.

Carpenter, B., Egerton, J., Bloom, T., Cockbill, B., Fotheringham, J. and Rawson, H. (2011) *The Complex Learning Difficulties and Disabilities Research Project: Developing Meaningful Pathways to Personalised Learning* (project report). London: Specialist Schools and Academies Trust.

Carpenter, B., Egerton, J., Cockbill, B., Bloom, T., Fotheringham, J., Rawson, H. and Thistlethwaite, J. (2015) *Engaging Learners with Complex Learning Difficulties and Disabilities*. London: Routledge.

Chiang, H.-M., Cheung Y. K., Li, H. and Tsai L. Y. (2013) 'Factors associated with participation in employment for high school leavers with autism'. *Journal of Autism and Developmental Disorders*, 43(8), 1832–1842.

Department for Education/Department of Health (2014) *Special Educational Needs and Disabilities Code of Practice: 0–25 Years*. London: Department for Education/Department of Health.

Department for Work and Pensions/Department of Health (2017) *Improving Lives: The Future of Work, Health and Disability*. London: Department for Work and Pensions.

Department of Health (2015) *Adult Autism Strategy: Statutory Guidance for Local Authorities and NHS Organisations to Support Implementation of the Autism Strategy*. London: Department of Health.

Grandin, T. (1995) *Thinking in Pictures: My Life with Autism*. New York: Random House.

Griffith, G. M., Totsika, V., Nash, S. and Hastings R. P. (2012) '"I just don't fit anywhere": support experiences and future support needs of individuals with Asperger syndrome in middle adulthood'. *Autism*, 16(5), 532–546.

Harris, J. (2017) 'How do you solve the trickiest problems in the workplace? Employ more autistic people'. *The Guardian*, 9 October. Retrieved from www.theguardian.com/society/2017/oct/09/autism-working-spectrum-capable-employees-talent (accessed 28 August 2018).

Hendricks, D. (2010) 'Employment and adults with autism spectrum disorders: challenges and strategies for success'. *Journal of Vocational Rehabilitation*, 32, 125–134.

Huntley, Z. (2013) *Aspirations and Outcomes for People with Autism Spectrum Disorders in Emerging Adulthood*. DClinPsy thesis. London: University College London. Retrieved from http://discovery.ucl.ac.uk/1404348/1/Zoe_Huntley_E-thesis_vol_1_copyright_free_NS.pdf

Kanner, L. (1943) 'Autistic disturbance of affective contact'. *Nervous Child*, 2, 217–250.

Kaya, C., Chan, F., Rumrill, P., Hartman, E., Wehman, P., Iwanaga, K., et al. (2016) 'Vocational rehabilitation services and competitive employment for transition-age youth with autism spectrum disorders'. *Journal of Vocational Rehabilitation*, 45(1), 73–83.

Lai, M.-C., Lombardo, M. V., Pasco, G., Ruigrok, A. N. V., Wheelwright, S. J., Sadek, S. A., et al. (2011) 'A behavioral comparison of male and female adults with high functioning autism spectrum conditions'. *PLoS One*, 6(6), e20835.

Lindsay, S., Cagliostro, E., Albarico, M., Srikanthan, D. and Mortaji, N. (2018) 'A systematic review of the role of gender in securing and maintaining employment among youth and young adults with disabilities'. *Journal of Occupational Rehabilitation*, 28, 232–251.

Lindstrom, L., Harwick, R. M., Poppen, M. and Doren, B. (2012) 'Gender gaps: career development for young women with disabilities'. *Career Development and Transition for Exceptional Individuals*, 35(2) 108–117.

Lindstrom, L., Doren, B., Post, C. and Lombardi, A. (2013) 'Building career PATHS (Postschool Achievement Through Higher Skills) for young women with disabilities'. *Career Development Quarterly*, 61, 330–338.

Lindstrom, L., Hirano, K. A., Ingram, A., DeGarmo, D. S. and Post, C. (2018) '"Learning to be myself": Paths 2 – the future career development curriculum for young women with disabilities'. *Journal of Career Development*, in press (doi: doi:10.1177/0894845318776795).

May, D. (2000) *Transition and Change in the Lives of People with Intellectual Disabilities*. London: Jessica Kingsley Publishers.

Migliore, A., Timmons, J., Butterworth, J., Lugas, J. (2012) 'Predictors of employment and post-secondary education of youth with autism'. *Rehabilitation Counselling Bulletin*, 55(3), 176–184.

National Autistic Society (2016) *The Autism Employment Gap: Too Much Information in the Workplace*. London: National Autistic Society.

National Autistic Society (2017) *Consultation on Improving Lives: Response from the National Autistic Society – February 2017*. London: National Autistic Society.

Neustatter, A. (2015) 'Autism is seen as a male thing – but girls just implode emotionally'. *The Guardian*, 14 July. Retrieved from www.theguardian.com/education/2015/jul/14/autism-girls-emotion-self-harm-school (accessed 1 September 2018).

Parkin, E., Bate, A., Long, R., Gheera, M., Powell, A., Bellis, A. and Beard, J. (2016) *Autism: Overview of UK Policy and Services*. Briefing paper CBP07172, 21 April. London: House of Commons.

Powell, A. (2018) *People with Disabilities in Employment*. Briefing paper CBP07540, 16 August. London: House of Commons.

Powers, K., Hogansen, J., Geenen, S., Powers, L. E. and Gil-Kashiwabara, E. (2008) 'Gender matters in transition to adulthood: a survey study of adolescents with disabilities and their families'. *Psychology in the Schools*, 45(4), 349–364.

Reine, I., Palmer, E. and Sonnander, K. (2016) 'Are there gender differences in wellbeing related to work status among persons with severe impairments?'. *Scandinavian Journal of Public Health*, 44, 772–783.

Roux, A. M., Shattuck, P. T., Rast, J. E., Rava, J. A. and Anderson, K. A. (2015) *National Autism Indicators Report: Transition into young adulthood*. Philadelphia, PA: Life Course Outcomes Research Program, A.J. Drexel Autism Institute, Drexel University.

Sainsbury, C., (2000) *Martian in the Playground: Understanding the school child with Asperger's syndrome*. London: The Book Factory.

Students of Limpsfield Grange School and Martin, V. (2015) *M is for Autism*. London: Jessica Kingsley Publishers.

Sung, C., Sánchez, J., Kuo, H.-J., Wang, C.-C. and Leahy, M. J. (2015) 'Gender differences in vocational rehabilitation service predictors of successful competitive employment for transition-aged individuals with autism'. *Journal of Autism and Developmental Disorders*, 45, 3204–3218.

Williams, D. (1996) *Autism: An Inside-Out Approach*. London: Jessica Kingsley.

Wing, L. and Gould, J. (1979) 'Severe impairment of social interaction and associated abnormalities in children: epidemiology and classification'. *Journal of Autism and Developmental Disorders*, 9(1), 911–929.

# Chapter 17

# Supported teachers supporting girls

## A whole-school model of support for the education of young people with autism

*Sarah-Jane Critchley*

## Introduction

We have moved a long way from the days when having autism meant that education was not an option. Under the Equality Act 2010, children with disabilities are entitled to an education every bit as much as children without disabilities and 'reasonable adjustments' have to be made to allow young people to participate without being disadvantaged by their disability. With the advent of the Children and Families Act 2014, this principle was furthered, and specific guidance written into the *SEND Code of Practice* (Department for Education/Department of Health 2015) to help implement a 'graduated model of provision' for children with special educational needs and disabilities (SEND) including autism.

What this means in practice is that it is the responsibility of schools and the teachers within them to educate children on the autism spectrum and to make reasonable adjustments for their disabilities. There is a much more compelling argument, though, which is that *all* children deserve the opportunity to excel and to develop their potential.

According to Department for Education (DfE) statistics for 2015/2016, there are over 100,000 autistic pupils in DfE-funded school provision (mainstream and special schools). A *minimum* of one in five of pupils identified as autistic are girls, which means it is likely that 20,000 autistic girls are in government-funded schools. With just one such school in the UK specifically for girls with communication and interaction difficulties including autism, many autistic girls will be largely unsupported. In addition, the number of children with SEND who are home-educated is rising, largely due to the absence of appropriate provision. Most parents only turn to home education when the options they are being offered are unsuitable, or their child has become unable to attend school through anxiety or illness. This can be the situation that parents of unsupported girls find themselves in after a prolonged period of struggling with the school environment, friendship issues and bullying.

Each autistic girl is different to the next, but the experience of schooling is common to the vast majority of them. There will be autistic girls with additional learning disabilities who may need a huge amount of help and support in a special school environment, and others who are able to function within a mainstream environment most of the time with far less support. What unites all of these young women is their vulnerability.

# What is the problem for girls in school?

## Social demand

School is by its very nature a social experience, with pupils educated in classes and a clear drive for co-operative working in groups. For girls who may struggle to understand the subtle social cues which make working together both effective and satisfying, they can so often find that peers are getting illogically cross with them for reasons they cannot see or understand. Without any visible cues that there may be an underlying neurological difference, it is difficult for peers to see and value the different ways of autistic thinking. Peers get frustrated and end up taking it out on the autistic pupil. Wasting time on social chit chat can bewilder and irritate the autistic pupil who gets equally frustrated and upset with no clue how to navigate the complex unwritten social rules needed to participate successfully. When both parties are wired so completely differently, it leads to a mutual lack of understanding referred to by Milton (2012) as the 'double empathy problem'.

## Sensory issues

We all experience the world through the prism of our sensory experiences which affects how we see and interact with the world at every level. Each person has their own sensory landscape, but so many autistic people experience the world in ways which are very different to most people that it was included in the diagnostic criteria when the American Psychiatric Association changed the definition of autism in their DSM-5 diagnostic manual (American Psychiatric Association 2013).

There are two types of outward reaction caused by sensory sensitivities, sensory-seeking, or sensory-avoiding behaviours. A girl who cannot bear to be touched might be hypervigilant if people get too close; for example, she may hate team contact sports and pair work in PE if it involves touching because it feels like a slap or a punch to her. Another girl may always be seen touching her friends or may get in trouble for invading the space of other pupils when she is simply unaware of where her body is in space and needs to be in contact with things to feel safe. Anyone entering a large secondary school for the first time since they were at school is far more likely to notice how loud and overwhelming the experience can be, simply because of the number of people crowded together within a small area, especially during lesson changeovers and other times when pupils move around the school. The environment itself can cause overload in autistic girls.

Each person is different, so reasonable adjustments made under the Equality Act 2010 should meet the sensory needs of the individual. This might be different to the adjustment that was made for the last autistic pupil the school supported. If a school has to fall back on adjustments that they have made in the past, it may well not help the pupil at all and might make their position even worse. Many girls are uncomfortable in asking for what they need, and will, in any case, only be able to use adjustments which the school can accommodate. As a result, unless you remember to ask her explicitly and offer a limited number of choices at a time, she may well suffer hugely rather than mention it to you. Whenever you see an unusual or undesirable behaviour, you should always explore what the reason for that behaviour is before deciding how to proceed. If it is not hurting anyone, it might be the pupil's way of coping with overwhelming anxiety, and may be best tolerated. The consequences of repeatedly telling girls that they are not allowed to do the things they do to cope (without working with them to find an alternative which works for them) can be severe.

Ideally, you should complete a sensory audit[1] of the school or setting first to find what issues might be problematic for your pupils. Some adjustments are comparatively easy to make and rely on your use of a simple strategy such as the agreement that a pupil could take their lunch in a different location in order to avoid being overwhelmed by cooking smells, for example. Other adjustments will take longer and may need changes to the fabric of the building or adjustments to the use of rooms.

Once you have made your setting as autism-friendly as possible by avoiding as many of the pupil's stress triggers as you can, then you should look at the specific profile of the young person. This is likely to be a process of exploration which should involve the girl, her parents or carers and the teaching or support staff who know her best. If you are particularly fortunate, you might also have a report from an occupational therapist (OT) identifying where the areas of sensitivity are and what you can do to avoid, or reduce the challenge, or work with that sensitivity.

### Wanting to fit in

Peer relationships can be especially problematic for autistic girls. While all teenagers struggle with friendships from time to time, the interactions between girls tend to be more emotionally finessed and reliant on rules that are not explained or discussed. It is very common for autistic girls who want to fit in to end up with a 'frenemy' (e.g. someone who she would say was a friend but can be intentionally mean and manipulative) while the girl herself has no idea why this is, what is going on, or how to deal with it. Some girls are so desperate to fit in that they will do exactly what they are told by their 'friend' whether it is a good idea or not. These girls are even more vulnerable because they will look and behave just like any other member of the group, having practised their mimicking and camouflage skills for years.

The inability to understand other people's motivations and frustrations with their lack of straightforward honesty drives some girls to isolate themselves on the grounds that it is safer than being out there. However, unfortunately, isolation makes them especially vulnerable to bullying. Most autistic girls (if they have any friends at all) will only have one or two very intense friendships which leaves them much more vulnerable if the friendships are not positive or supportive, or if it goes wrong, as they often do. Others will prefer to stand on the outside of a large group, preferring to avoid the intensity of closer relationships.

### What happens if we do not support girls?

The outcomes for unsupported autistic girls and women are very poor indeed. Recent research from Cassidy and Rogers (2017) at the University of Coventry has highlighted the long-term impact on the mental health of autistic people and discovered shockingly high rates of attempted (over 66%) and completed suicide (over 33%) especially in late diagnosed women. Autistic women without learning disabilities were most at risk of dying by suicide. We can no longer continue to ignore the vulnerable position of women and girls. While a lack of support can have catastrophic effects on undiagnosed autistic girls, the first line of defence in supporting them must be a good understanding of autism and a focus on developing and enhancing good autism practice within schools.

Some autistic girls with additional learning difficulties present in a way that is easily identifiable by diagnostic professionals; some will demonstrate the sorts of interests, profiles and approaches usually seen in autistic boys and so will be comparatively easy to identify and will meet diagnostic criteria. Other autistic girls (and some autistic boys) are so adept at camouflaging their difficulties, using cognitive strengths to compensate for their social and emotional uncertainty that they go unnoticed for years.

It should also be recognized that the number of autistic young people presenting to clinics with gender dysphoria is much higher than the general population. There will be people born as boys who identify as girls, people born as girls who identify as boys and everything in between. Having issues of gender and sexuality in addition layered on top of the identity uncertainty which affects many undiagnosed people make it especially difficult for unsupported girls. This is very sensitive work indeed which requires trained staff to support them effectively.

## Why are schools a key audience for training?

Good practice for girls on the autism spectrum must be grounded in good autism practice. With so many autistic girls in school, it is essential for schools to understand what training supports really good autism practice. The Autism Education Trust[2] has trained over 180,000 education-based staff in their training programme across England and reaches staff working across early years, schools and post-16 settings. As such, it represents the largest face-to-face training programme in Europe and possibly beyond.

The 2017 report of investigation into education by the All Party Parliamentary Group for Autism (APPGA) rightly identified the crucial role of trained staff in supporting autistic pupils. It found that fewer than 5 in 10 staff felt confident in supporting autistic children, and that 70% of parents said that support was not put in place quickly enough for their child. The APPGA report identified the following areas within its recommendations:

1    Training for school staff.
2    Reasonable adjustments for pupils on the autism spectrum in schools.
3    Provision of a specialist curriculum for all pupils who need one.
4    Measures to reduce bullying and promote inclusion.
5    And guidance for local authorities in commissioning the full range of educational provision and support.

Autism understanding should be embedded in the education system, with autism training for all teachers, including head teachers, with ongoing funding for the Autism Education Trust.

(APPGA 2017: 5)

## Talking about exclusions

Autistic pupils are excluded far more often than non-autistic pupils, and autistic boys more than autistic girls. When things go wrong in schools for autistic pupils, the results will be exclusion, illness or school refusal. Evaluation of the National Autistic Society's exclusions service by CEDAR at the University of Warwick in 2017[3] found that parent/carer interviewees had faced the following issues in relation to exclusions:

- Lack of understanding of autism on the part of schools and school staff.
- Unwillingness of schools to make 'reasonable adjustments' for pupils with autism.
- Poor communications between school and home.
- The use of informal exclusions by schools.
- School refusal as a form of exclusion.

In the case of girls who are 'flying under the radar', unidentified and unsupported, this lack of understanding leads to increased anxiety, additional mental health problems, self-harm and can result in suicide. Staff who are unaware that a girl is autistic will struggle to make the reasonable adjustments that she needs to function and are far more likely to mis-interpret behaviour that they see as 'naughty' or 'defiant' and not see it for the panic it is.

Exclusions lead to poor mental health and poor mental health increases the risk of exclu-sion according to research by Professor Tamsin Ford and colleagues (Ford et al. 2018).

Although an exclusion from school may only last for a day or two, the impact and repercussions for the child and parents are much wider. Exclusion often marks a turning point during an ongoing difficult time for the child, parent and those trying to support the child in school.

## Why do teachers need support?

For a teacher to be able to support an autistic girl in class effectively, they need to have a very solid understanding of autism and an empathetic appreciation of how her different brain will affect every aspect of a girl's school life. Time and again, research has high-lighted how young autistic people and their families want to be understood and for their school journey to look at the whole young person in front of them.

As a teacher, you want to get the best from your pupil, whatever their strengths and weaknesses and want them to perform at their very best, so that they are able to learn, you are able to teach them effectively and your school can get the results that it deserves. To do that you need to work to the strengths of young people, especially those whose neu-rology is different. Autistic girls have a 'spikey profile' and may be some of your best performers in one area or subject but need significant support in others to make it through.

It may sound like a big ask, to adapt your approach and teaching to meet the needs of a small number of pupils, but much of what is recognized as good practice in teaching autistic girls is really good practice and highly beneficial for *all* pupils.

Managing transitions effectively, for example makes the world of difference to autistic pupils, but works really well for all pupils as well. One secondary school I know developed a really effective transition booklet for example, which included details of the school day, the uniform and behaviour code, the names and faces of Year 7 staff, a map of the school which they handed out on Secondary School Transfer Day (which is a day in the summer term of Year 6 when all pupils across the county go to their new school for the day to meet their new form, teachers and to get to know the school before they start in September).

Expecting teachers to know what to do to support autistic girls with no understanding of autism is unrealistic and is likely to cause situations which would have been com-pletely avoidable if the staff had a clearer understanding.

Increasing numbers of pupils are being identified as autistic and, although still unrealistically low, the proportion of girls now getting a diagnosis is increasing. This does not mean that they should be in special schools, in fact the vast majority of autistic pupils are educated in mainstream provision. What it does mean is that getting good quality training enables a teacher to be confident that they are able to meet the needs of the pupils they support.

## What training is available?

### Conferences

As awareness of autism in women and girls grows, the training and services available to support them is slowly increasing. The National Autistic Society have held conferences on autism in women and girls for a number of years, sharing not only the issues around identification and diagnosis of women and girls, but also increasingly sessions led by autistic women sharing the impact of masking, managing relationships, pregnancy and aging in autistic women. The authenticity and importance of sharing these first person perspectives cannot be underestimated. As these conferences become better recognized, they also attract a greater proportion of autistic delegates as well as speakers.

### Face-to-face training

There are a number of professional speakers specializing in the issues facing autistic girls and women to parents and professionals including members of the Autism in Girls Forum who have contributed to this book and the NAHT conference[4] which spawned it, (many of whom are raising autistic girls as well as working with autistic girls and women, including myself[5]).

A number of autistic women deliver training. Sarah Hendrickx,[6] Robyn Steward[7] and Alis Rowe (The Curly Haired Girl Project) among others run training sessions (usually up to half a day) on autism in girls and women. The Curly Haired Girl Project[8] runs online hour long online webinars, easily accessible for many people. While Mental Health Training programmes for organizations have been developed by Katie Buckingham trading as Altruist Enterprises.[9]

### Online training module on identification of autistic girls and women

The National Autistic Society have been successful in securing funding from the Pears Foundation to develop an online module for diagnosticians and other interested people in recognizing and identifying autism in girls and women. It uses extensive filming of autistic girls and women and is a detailed description of the difficulties which they may face. Please go to the NAS website (www.autism.org.uk) for details.

### Additional resources

Although not specifically training, Professionals can also use the interviews and references included on Network Autism to gain a range of perspectives. There is a Women and Girls Group,[10] which contains a good range of useful articles and resources.

The best support works in partnership with families, and yet parents struggle to navigate the education system, feeling isolated and lacking in the resources available to professionals, which has an impact on the mental health of the whole family including the siblings of their autistic children. To meet this need, as a parent myself, I wrote *A Different Joy: The Parents' Guide to Living Better with Autism, Dyslexia, ADHD and More* ... (Critchley 2016), which refers to the differences between girls and boys and incorporates not just autism, but also other conditions which often complicate the needs of autistic young people. Only by supporting the whole person that we can help them to achieve their potential.

## Notes

1  For example, www.aettraininghubs.org.uk/wp-content/uploads/2012/05/37.1-Sensory-audit-tool-for-environments.pdf
2  See www.autismeducationtrust.org.uk
3  See https://warwick.ac.uk/fac/soc/cedar/research/aet16-17/evaluation-autism-education-trust-cullen-2017.pdf
4  See www.naht.org.uk/news-and-opinion/thought-leadership/the-big-shout-was-heard
5  See https://differentjoy.com/speakingevents
6  See www.asperger-training.com
7  See www.robynsteward.com
8  See https://thegirlwiththecurlyhair.co.uk
9  See https://altruistuk.com
10  See http://network.autism.org.uk/discussion/articles-women-and-girls

## References

American Psychiatric Association (2013) *Diagnostic and Statistical Manual of Mental Disorders* (5th edn). Washington, DC: American Psychiatric Association.
APPGA ( 2017) *Autism and Education in England 2017: A Report by the All Party Parliamentary Group on Autism on How the Education System in England Works for Children and Young People on the Autism Spectrum.* London:The National Autistic Society.
Cassidy, S. and Rodgers, J. (2017) 'Understanding and preventing suicide in autism'. *The Lancet Psychiatry*, 24 May. Retrieved from www.thelancet.com/journals/lanpsy/article/PIIS2215-0366 (17)30162-1/fulltext?code=lancet-site (accessed 13 September 2018).
Critchley, S.-J. (2016) *A Different Joy: The Parents' Guide to Living Better with Autism, Dyslexia, ADHD and More* ...London: WritingScorpInk.
Department for Education/Department of Health (2015) *Special Educational Needs and Disability Code of Practice: 0–25 Years.* London: Department for Education/Department of Health.
Ford, T., Parker, C., Salim, J., Goodman, R., Logan, S. and Henley, W. (2018) 'The relationship between exclusion from school and mental health: a secondary analysis of the British Child and Adolescent Mental Health Surveys 2004 and 2007'. *Psychological Medicine*, 48(4), 629–641.
MiltonD. E. M. (2012) 'On the ontological status of autism: the "double empathy" problem'. *Journal of Disability and Society*, 27(6), 883–887.

# Chapter 18

# Run the world, girls

## Success as an adult autistic female

*Rachel Townson and Carol Povey*

## What does success mean to an autistic female?

Success is a word that hovers around us, often used in terms of 'having it all' in areas such as finance, academia, family life and employment. However, if we look at success in this rigid manner are any of us truly successful in all areas and at all times? Can success not be finding happiness within yourself, knowing who you are and understanding your human coding? Or being able to see the beauty in the golden buttercup petal with all its integrate pigmentations that glisten in the rays of the sun?

Success is one of those terms that is hugely variable, therefore it is surely best to let the person themselves define and strive towards their own attainable version of success. As beautifully detailed by autistic speaker and academic Catriona Stewart, success should be defined by the person themselves:

> Success is being the best 'yourself' possible; included in society; accepted in the community; valued and supported in all your flawed, quirky, talented, individual, loving, human self. And most of all, finding self-knowledge and self-acceptance. That would be my definition of success.
>
> (Hendrickx et al. 2016)

This chapter is one that can never be fully complete, never describe everyone, or all life's successes, or how to achieve success. It captures, nevertheless, our thoughts as one neurotypical woman and one autistic woman, on the things we think are important for young autistic women to know to enable them to have the best opportunity of defining and achieving their own version of success.

Both authors believe that diversity should be valued and celebrated. We believe the human experience benefits from diversity. Our similarities help us to find group identities, and our differences allow us to celebrate individualism and be ourselves. Autism is a relatively new diagnosis and there is a growing understanding, well-rehearsed in other chapters of this book, that the female presentation of autism has been poorly understood in the past (Gould 2017). Sadly, our history of recognizing and valuing women who do not conform to traditional stereotypes is shameful, and in the case of autistic women, we can only speculate as to how these women have survived in times past. In the recent past many have been dismissed, their autism not recognized at all, or else they have been misdiagnosed. At best they have been considered an odd individual who does not quite fit our expectations of the societally constructed version of female; at worst they have been bullied, mocked and abused.

Within a world that promotes a strong drive for success, it is easy to understand why so many autistic individuals, especially those who fit the female presentation, are left feeling like a shell of their true self. Autistic females are trying to adhere to social expectations placed upon them, and masking and blending to fit those expectations, often without fully understanding their own self and neurological make-up. With diagnosis being so poor in this group of people it is no surprise to see high rates of burn out, and secondary mental health issues.

---

### Personal reflections I – Rachel Townson

I often say I do not feel disabled, and why should I? The only thing disabling to me is other people and their expectations. When I remove social pressure I am able to be the real me, free and successful. I am successful at being myself, being a true version of me, no masks, no burn out and no stress. As an autistic who is happily married, lives independently with her husband, is expecting our first child, has a small group of friends, has an MSc in autism, and works full-time in a job that she loves, I would appear by societal standards to be quite successful. However, I feel a crippling fear around the stability of my life on a daily basis: what if I get made redundant, what if I need to work in an office again, what if I am forced into a social world for more hours that I can handle, what if I run out of things to say when speaking one to one with someone? There are constant 'what ifs' spiralling. I am constantly on edge, constantly retracing my conversations for social blunders or subtle nuances that I have missed. It is exhausting and leaves me feeling that I am constantly failing. However, I do feel at my most successful with my small remote work team, at home, and with my husband, and with some very close friends. Extend that out a little or add in a new face, new activity or changes in demands and all that security vanishes and the seemingly continuous demolition and rebuild begin. I see success in those women who are comfortable to be their true selves at any time, place or event. This is something I try to do, but then there is the huge question – who is the real me? How do you unmask when you have spent a lifetime learning to disguise yourself? How can you show the real you when you do not know who the real you is? How does the real me behave? Who am I? And then another cycle of uncertainty begins.

---

## Masking and being successful

This aforementioned identity crisis seems to be an issue that many newly diagnosed or self-identifying autistic women face. Without truly knowing who they are it is no wonder autistic girls view the majority's behaviour as the behaviour that must be learned, copied and perfected, but as we know from history the majority is not always correct.

Autistic females often describe themselves as actresses, for many will mask, blend and fit in (intentionally and unintentionally) with others around them and this is often flawless to the unknowing eye. However, inside they may be balancing on a very narrow tight rope, and with every social event, every depletion of their social energy reserve, that rope frays little by little. As young girls, struggling to make sense of an alien world, some autistic girls look to the peer who seems to be doing everything right – having it all – and feel the best way to survive is to emulate her (Gould and Ashton-Smith 2011). Through into adulthood, there is a perception of perfectionism, which can lead to high level and chronic stress, additional mental and physical health concerns, and again the reduction of knowing one's self while striving to be 'perfect' according to socially dictated norms.

Striving to fit and masking (also known as camouflaging) is often discussed by autistic individuals, particularly women, as something that allows them to get by in the social world. For some it is used as a tool for dipping into a world not designed for them, to partake in whatever elements are required and then retract again. It can be used successfully to allow them to feel comfortable, and is not something that should be belittled, though some may argue that there should be no need for someone to conform. Where it can become destructive is when someone is masking because they do not know who else to be. They may not have built up a sense of self, from years of not knowing themselves, seeing themselves as flawed and 'broken'. This survival instinct is strong but leads to low self-identity and persona confusion. It can result in the person getting into situations they would rather not be in. Many autistic women report that they are and have been easy prey for toxic and predatory partners and friendships Without understanding themselves they cannot recognize their strengths and weaknesses and use this knowledge to protect themselves. Building up a sense of self, a knowledge of who they are, not only keeps women safe, but leads to better outcomes. Empowerment to know one's self, accept one's self, and be one's self will reduce the need for masking, and the resulting burn out and secondary mental health conditions. This can all begin with improved pre- and post-diagnostic services, and work towards a world that truly accepts neuro-diversity.

Autistic speaker Maja Toudal discusses 'energy accounting' as a successful tool for understanding your energy abilities and needs. If you imagine every event that you partake in and assign a numerical value to it depending on how much energy it withdraws from you; these items are your withdrawals. Then assign a numerical value to the items that help you relax, unwind, and build up energy; these items are your deposits. The system operates much like a bank account: you need to 'pay in' healthy deposits to offset your energy expenditure, and keep yourself from getting into debt. If you understand yourself, and therefore what your withdrawals and deposits are, you are much more likely to be able to avoid crashing into debt and therefore, in energy accounting terms, avoid burn out.

Toudal (2017) explains that for autistic individuals the things that cause withdrawals may be masking, socializing and sensory bombardment, and a deposit may be spending time researching a topic for a project. For someone not on the spectrum, this may be reversed. Difficulties in accessing timely and accurate diagnosis may result in girls who have yet to learn who they are, what their needs are, what their withdrawals and deposits are and who are their peers (sometimes referred to as their 'tribe'). Understanding yourself as early as you possibly can would help reduce the risk of being trapped in a cycle of social misunderstandings, being preyed on, and mental health breakdowns. Having that understanding enables autistic women to make connections with each other and enables them to understand and navigate a world that they feel is not built for them.

## Diagnosis

Presently, many girls are missed or misdiagnosed due to lack of understanding and misguided information (Gould 2017). Not only does this result in women not being able to access appropriate services and support, but it means that these women will struggle to fully understand themselves. They may be confused further when the wrong label is attached to them, feel they do not fully fit, and mask further to form their new identity based on an incorrect diagnosis. For many girls and women, the right diagnosis is the starting point to understanding themselves, undoing years of an abused and damaged sense of self and unpicking the potential consequent mental health conditions that have come with that.

Diagnosticians need to listen to and learn from autistic women directly to understand their differences, similarities, and how autism presents within this group of people; this is the most efficient way of understanding and making fair and better judgements during diagnosis. There is also a need for training on how to utilize clinical experience while using the current diagnostic assessment tools. The early assessment tools developed to use in diagnosis were primarily developed and validated with boys, and while some tools such as the Diagnostic Interview for Social and Communication Disorders (DISCO; Wing et al. 2002) have been developed for use with girls and women, assessment and diagnosis still relies largely on the skills and expertise of the clinical team to recognize the complex presentations that many women have developed after years of trying to fit in. Experienced, confident clinicians, who have developed the vital skill of really listening to people, are then able to make reasonable adjustments to the diagnostic tools and interview questions to identify the information required to make an informed diagnostic judgement.

There are various stories such as autistic women being asked questions like, 'Do you have friends?', and answering the direct question honestly, 'Yes, I have friends'. But what need to be explored are the types and durations of relationships, and the understanding of the definition of friendship, to find out what this means to the person. This is where clinicians will get the information to see their understanding of relationships, and their literal understanding of the world. There are countless stories from women on the spectrum about misunderstandings in their past, such as inadvertently going on a date while not realizing that was what was meant by going out for dinner, or getting into trouble with sexual advances when someone asks you back for coffee, when it does not mean coffee! If clinicians do not ask the right questions, then they are not going to get the information needed to make an informed decision and an accurate diagnosis.

Improving the diagnosis of autistic women and girls could combat a lot of the issues women and girls face; however we cannot hide from the limited post-diagnostic services available. If women and girls do not have access to the right support to understand what the diagnosis means for them, what their strengths and challenges are, relevant strategies and support from their peers and others, then are we ticking them off one waiting list for diagnosis, but adding their name to the list of those seeking support. Future post-diagnosis support needs to be multifaceted, flexible and, most importantly, available. For younger girls, it is important that families do not shy away from discussions about autism, and do access the many resources (books, the autism.org.uk website, videos, blogs and online forums) that are now available to explain the diagnosis.

From sourcing opinions in autistic online forums and hearing speakers at conferences it is clear that funding and support to set up autistic-led groups and counselling is one step in the right direction. Hearing from your own peers and knowing where you fit, is one way of starting to improve your understanding of self and self-acceptance. Meeting with like-minded individuals and sharing experiences seems to be the way for many post-diagnosis, but should there not be more than expecting autistic people just to find each other? What about those girls who have never heard the term autism before?

Changing your understanding of yourself is a time-consuming and gruelling task; without being offered the support to do this, there are real concerns about where these girls seek support and whom they go to. We need to see diagnostic improvements throughout the trajectory of diagnosis, from initially supporting those seeking a diagnosis, who may be left defenceless against a spiralling identity crisis, to more efficient and timely assessments, followed by person-centred, post-diagnostic support. By making these adjustments we can build a world where autistic females are being given better opportunities to be successful, in whatever definition of success they choose. As autistic writer and speaker Sarah Hendrickx states:

> A successful autistic woman understands that she may need to define her own model for success, which may not fit the expectations of society, and lives according to that in order to find her own fulfilment and peace of mind.
>
> (Hendrickx et al. 2016)

## Media representation

Having the understanding of who you are, what your strengths and struggles are, and who your peer supports are, are all assets in building up self-worth, sense of place in the world, and reducing burnout and secondary health concerns. The media portrayal of autism is slowly moving towards being more inclusive of the wider spectrum. More celebrities, actresses and others in the media light are disclosing their diagnosis, which is a huge step in seeing the diversity of autism, and that success in terms of career can be achieved.

The singer Susan Boyle speaks out about her success, yet also about her difficulties with her career journey and after she became famous. She was misdiagnosed with brain damage as a child and, although she knew the label did not fit her, she was teased and bullied throughout her life, and it was only when she went to a specialist that she got the correct diagnosis of autism and instantly felt more secure in her identity (Deveney 2013). Susan's success and high media profile led to many recognizing autism in a wider light. However, television sitcoms and films still tend to portray a much narrower understanding of autism.

Many autism charities in the UK have campaigned to raise awareness of autism, and worked with the media to widen the public knowledge of the range of autism presentations, yet globally we still have a long way to go. There are constant discussions within autistic women's forums about not being considered autistic due to good eye-contact, not demonstrating stereotypical behaviours such as hand flapping, or holding down a career or maintaining a relationship. So it appears that, despite some advances in the media to include autistic girls, and the disclosures of autistic celebrities, understanding is still not filtering through to all. For future generations we hope this reaches greater numbers so that everyone may start to truly see the full spectrum and everyone's abilities, worth and differences.

## Maternity, menopause and other bodily changes

As with all female journeys into adulthood, there are significant changes through puberty and adolescence, and then again in womanhood, when your hormones change for various reasons such as pregnancy and menopause. Historically autism research has focused on autistic boys and men due to the diagnostic bias, and to date there remains limited research focusing on life transitions for women on the autistic spectrum. Women are left overlooked and many consider themselves invisible to researchers and the academic world. Despite the limited research into the experiences of women during these phases we do know from life stories that hormones do seem to have an impact on the autistic characteristics of the person. Research is needed as a first step towards providing appropriate support and resources.

During pregnancy some autistic women report being less able to tolerate the non-autistic world – for example, due to sensory fluctuations outside their normal experiences – and many report feeling more stereotypically autistic in their thinking(e.g. more linear and direct). This of course needs to be explored further to gather a reliable sample, but it is something in future that we should be focusing on. As discussed by Lana Grant (2015), the autistic female may have differences in experiences and intensities during pregnancy and motherhood compared to those the non-autistic mother. We have very limited support for our autistic mothers; midwives have an extremely limited knowledge of autism and, unless they have a personal interest, they are likely to have no knowledge of autism other than the deficit model (that some non-autistic mothers might be concerned about having an autistic child).

---

### Personal reflections II – Rachel Townson

Anecdotally, when trying to conceive I really struggled with my need for control, order and planning. Not being able to plan when I would fall pregnant and when I would have the child and life plan to such detail left me frustrated, scared and developing some mental health problems such as panic attacks and depression. I luckily reached out and made contact with Lana Grant, and she was able to support me through my frustrations, and I took up a non-connected hobby to distract myself. However, I am one of the fortunate few to have contact with people such as Lana. On a quick internet search the hits returned were catastrophic. When searching 'autistic and trying to conceive' the results focused on how to avoid conceiving an autistic child, what to do if you want to avoid passing on genes, and how to 'deal' with an autistic family if you are a medical professional; soul-destroying messages as a female trying to start her family. I have since then read Lana's book *From Here to Maternity* (Grant 2015), and joined various online platforms for autistic mothers, and the support is incredibly positive. By contrast, when mentioning autism to my midwife there was no interest in adaptions, questions of what I would like to experience in our journey together, or seemingly any recognition that I was disclosing something to get access to support. However, mention the words depressed and anxious and support is flagged up, albeit still minimal. I hope in years to come autistic women document their experiences and more professionals take lessons from our experiences and adapt their practice to be fitting to all mothers.

---

## What about older autistic women?

The main body of this book is looking at autism in girls, but of course, autistic girls grow up to be autistic women, and they grow into middle and old age. Middle age can be a time of growing confidence for many women, but there may be greater barriers and challenges on the journey into self-knowledge and confidence for autistic women. Our understanding of autism in older age is poor (Charlton 2017), and the first generation of autistic people who were diagnosed in childhood is only just reaching old age. In those early days there was thought to be a male-to-female ratio of at least 4:1 (Ehlers and Gillberg 1993), with Hans Asperger reporting no females at all in his subject group. These figures resulted in very few women being diagnosed in childhood in the 1960s and 1970s. We therefore have very limited understanding of their needs and how best to ensure they live healthy, happy and long lives. Older women who have been diagnosed in later life often have very complex histories, and their needs in older age may include support to make sense of some of the issues, and perhaps injustices, that have affected their lives.

In 2015, Cos Michael, an autistic consultant, posed a number of questions in an article written for Network Autism (Michael 2015; see also Michael 2016). She recognized that while there are some issues of ageing that affect men and women alike, the impact and outcomes may differ according to gender, and she called for research into the lives and needs of older autistic women.

We remain in the dark, for example, about the impact of menopause on autistic women, with questions pending around changes in processing speed, anxiety, the effects of hormone replacement therapy (HRT), and sensory experiences of women pre-, during and post-menopause.

On a far more positive note, there are some inspiring examples of autistic women who have achieved great things in older age. In 2017, Dr Dinah Murray was recognized by being awarded the National Autistic Society's lifetime achievement award for her campaigning work, Dr Temple Grandin achieved her PhD in later years, and there are many examples of vibrant and nurturing community support provided by older women who are determined that young autistic women will have the support to enable them to thrive.

## Conclusion

In order to provide a world where autistic females can thrive in whatever definition of success they choose, we need to improve our understanding, research, and recognition of the widely varying characteristics of the autism spectrum across gender, age and culture. There remains a long way to go, but understanding is slowly increasing, led by autistic women themselves, and there is a real determination that those young girls moving into adulthood should be able to lead safe, happy lives where they know themselves and can determine their own version of success.

## References

Charlton, R. (2017) 'Researching autism and ageing'. London: Network Autism' [Online at: http://network.autism.org.uk/good-practice/evidence-base/researching-autism-and-ageing; 29. 1. 18].

Deveney, C. (2013) 'Susan Boyle: my relief at discovering that I have Asperger's'. *The Observer*, 8 December. Retrieved from www.theguardian.com/music/2013/dec/08/susan-boyle-autism (accessed 29 January 2018).

Ehlers, S. and Gillberg, C. (1993) 'The epidemiology of Asperger syndrome'. *Journal of Child Psychology and Psychiatry*, 34, 1327–1350.

Gould, J. (2017) 'Towards understanding the under-recognition of girls and women on the autism spectrum'. *Autism*, 21(6), 703–705.

Gould, J. and Ashton-Smith, J. (2011) 'Missed diagnosis or misdiagnosis?: girls and women on the autism spectrum'. *Good Autism Practice*, 12(1), 34–41.

Grant, L. (2015) *From Here to Maternity: Pregnancy and Motherhood on the Autism Spectrum.* London: Jessica Kingsley.

Hendrickx, S., Stewart, C., Honeybourne, V., Steward, R. and Cathy (2016) 'What does success mean for an autistic woman?'. Retrieved from http://network.autism.org.uk/knowledge/insight-opinion/what-does-success-mean-autistic-women (accessed 29 January 2018).

Michael, C. (2015) 'Autism, ageing and women: not invisible, just ignored'. Retrieved from http://network.autism.org.uk/knowledge/insight-opinion/autism-ageing-and-women-not-invisible-just-ignored (accessed 29 January 2018).

Michael, C. (2016) 'Interview with Cos Michael: autism and older women'. Retrieved from http://network.autism.org.uk/knowledge/insight-opinion/interview-cos-michael-autism-and-older-women (accessed 29 January 2018).

Toudal, M. (2017) 'Energy accounting: an interview with Maja Toudal'. Retrieved from http://network.autism.org.uk/knowledge/insight-opinion/energy-accounting-interview-maja-toudal (accessed 29 January 2018).

Wing, L., Leekham, S. R., Libby, S. J., Gould, J. and Larcombe, M. (2002) 'The Diagnostic Interview for Social and Communication Disorders: background, inter-rater reliability and clinical use'. *Journal of Child Psychology and Psychiatry*, 43(3), 307–325.

# Chapter 19

# Epilogue
## A call for action

*Wenn Lawson*

An epilogue implies the bit that comes after the main event … or an after-thought. But this epilogue is more a continuation of what has been said already, as well as a call for action. Females differ hugely in their expression of gender, not just with how different they are from males, but in how different they are from each other too. There are girly, frilly, ultra-feminine girls, while others show less dominant female attributes and sit at the further end of the female spectrum where females resent almost any hint of being female and live as tomboys, even if they have XX chromosomes. Gender identity is not so much about chromosomes as it is about gender identity in the brain. Therefore, being female and having different chromosomes to males and different neurobiology than males will mean the profile of autism in females presents differently to that seen in males.

As we know, until recently the idea of females and autism received very little attention (McPartland and Volkmar 2013), and, according to Lai et al. (2011), 'girls who appear to be cognitively able or appear to have better communication skills may have been under-diagnosed' (cited in Moyse and Porter 2015: 187). As well as being under-diagnosed or misdiagnosed with some other ailment (e.g. social phobia, depression, challenging behaviours and so on) the needs of females in general have been overlooked and their contributions undermined (Moyse and Porter 2015). Yet, despite this, there is an increasing bulk of literature that discusses the differences in girls compared to boys (e.g. Attwood 2007; Cridland et al. 2014; Dean et al. 2014; Dworzynski et al. 2012; Harrop et al. 2015; Head et al. 2014; Moyse et al. 2015; Nichols et al. 2009; van Wijngaarden-Cremers et al. 2014). This knowledge must be translated into practice. It might be that changing the long-held attitudes of practitioners takes time. There are many misconceptions about how autism 'shows', and this is getting in the way of seeing autism and how it impacts in different individual genders.

In the past, Wing et al. (2011) described in detail the triad of impairments that affect those with autism. The triad was listed in the fourth (text revised) edition of the *Diagnostic and Statistical Manual of Mental Disorders* (DSM-IV-TR) (American Psychiatric Association 2000) as impairment of social interaction, impairment of social communication and impairment of social imagination; however the current edition (DSM-5; American Psychiatric Association 2013) has now combined the three domains into two: issues with the social interaction and communication domains. DSM-5 has also combined previously separate diagnostic areas and categories together as autism spectrum disorder, whereas earlier versions identified separate conditions; for example, 'Asperger's disorder', 'pervasive developmental disorder–not otherwise specified' (PDD–NOS) and others. These changes to the DSM may not have been helpful. We are encouraged to view autism as a spectrum of difficulty, but when so much is merged, the danger is that individual experiences of autism can be overlooked.

The other issue that might be muddying the waters is the theory that autism is influenced prenatally by testosterone leading to an extreme male brain (EMB). However, this has predisposed many clinicians to think of autism as a predominantly male disposition, which has meant they have 'missed' the signs of autism in females and given, due to their bias in thinking of autism as the result of EMB, a mental health diagnosis instead. Research has shown that although there is some evidence that EMB may impact autism in females, there is not evidence that it impacts the brain in male autism (Lai et al. 2013); how it impacts on the female brain is still being debated. For example, research by Carter et al. (2007) shows female toddlers with autism being less socially competent than boys. They were also better at non-verbal problem-solving than the boys:

> The findings revealed a statistically significant interaction between child sex and cognitive domain (verbal versus nonverbal) and child sex and the 5 Mullen Scales of Early Learning (Visual Reception, Fine Motor, Expressive Language, Receptive Language, and Gross Motor), indicating that girls and boys with ASD show different cognitive and developmental profiles. Consistent with the expectation that boys would show more advanced development, boys evidenced stronger verbal and motor skills, particularly once differences in visual reception were covaried. Controlling for language level, girls evidenced significantly stronger skills in visual reception, or the nonverbal problem solving domain. In addition, boys were described as having more advanced social functioning than girls …
>
> (Carter et al. 2007: 94)

As Zücker Björne has pointed out:

> This all runs contrary to Baron-Cohen's idea of the male brain. Or, if you wish, the girls are more male than the boys. Given the fact that there are so very few studies addressing the cognitive profiles of autism from a gender perspective, it is important that the popular accounts are modified somewhat by more rigorous studies.
>
> (Zücker Björne, personal communication, 2007)

It seems that, whatever one's gender, if the individual is 'somewhere' on the spectrum of autism our thinking and problem-solving abilities differ from that of the neurotypical world. However, just because one is different or arrives at an understanding by taking a different route, this does not mean there is not value in our processing or problem-solving attributes. It makes no sense to say that just because we did not do it typically, the way we did something was wrong.

If we look at the profile for many females, it appears (seemingly) they may not have a problem with communication. Autism is known to be a communication disorder, and many females appear to be communicating well with good eye contact and so on. Any discrepancy is likely to be put down to bad manners, lack of discipline or to the individual being strong willed or extremely shy. However, the very names we give to these behaviours should give us a hint that all is not well. We need to look beyond the behaviour and ask certain questions. For example, is this behaviour being used out of frustration due to not comprehending social norms, social expectations or processing social 'instincts'?

In cognitively challenged female individuals with a low IQ, autism operates at the severe end of the spectrum and is rarely questioned, but, in high functioning female individuals the double X chromosome often gives them the feminine ability to mask their difficulties. They copy behaviour in social settings; this suggests they have social understanding and the true nature of the effort this takes is not seen. So, when they appear not to understand or exhibit 'challenging behaviour', they are thought of as being naughty, difficult or attention seeking. How do these females whom society expects to be socially competent, cope in a world that expects them to be able to read body language when by the very nature of their diagnosis they struggle to do so? How can they be friendly, sociable and happy in a group and understand the hidden curriculum (the unspoken rules of human interaction)? How can they perform in society at the expected level as well as manage their daily lives? We need to address this and enable females by reducing demand, working with their strengths and accommodating any sensory dispositions they live with.

According to Marshall (2014) the cultural expectations for females to participate in social communication, such as chit-chat, small talk and gossip, is exhausting for those with high functioning autism. There is also a lack of social understanding which leads to confusion around things such as teasing, bullying and bitchiness often displayed by typically developing teens. Many high functioning female autistic teens become anxious in large group situations, and prefer to have their one friend or a select small group of friends.

Females on the spectrum often suffer with alexithymia. Alexithymia is an inability to describe emotions in the self, so describing how they feel in social situations is hard. Instead the level of avoidance behaviour increases via complaints of headaches, stomach aches or incidents of school refusal. Facial expressions for many may not match their moods; often an individual will say they are fine, and look happy on the outside, but actually they are withdrawing internally. Females also tend to be more passive-aggressive in their behaviour and use avoidance as a way of coping with the social demands placed upon them.

Much of this emotional disconnection for females is due to poor interoception skills. Emma Goodall writes:

> Interoceptive awareness … can be broadly defined as the conscious perception of internal bodily cues such as heartbeat and breathing and is related to emotional experiences. Awareness of both biological and emotional internal body cues are affected in individuals on the autism spectrum.
>
> (Goodall undated, citing Schauder et al. 2015; Mahler 2016)

Poor interoception is easily remedied with appropriate exercises (ways to connect to one's breathing, heart rate, sense of thirst or hunger, pain, temperature and so on). These are not difficult though and can be practised in all schools and would help all children. We just need this built into our curriculums.

Girls can sometimes blame others, internalise their feelings or develop co-morbid conditions such as anxiety, depression, eating disorders or hyperactivity. As well as not being able to communicate with their peers, this group also struggles to understand the hierarchies within a societal structure and can get into trouble with adults due to the way they speak with them.

According to Nichols et al. (2009), girls on the spectrum present subtle differences in their behaviour that are often missed. For example, they are often able to answer questions about social situations, social communication and friendships but are slower to process the information. This would present great difficulty in understanding the conversations that go on between teenage girls within a group situation. Their answers to these questions also reflect only a basic understanding, not a deeper social understanding. This understanding is lacking in the social comprehension, cognition and awareness seen in their peers of typical developmental age. The courage it must take autistic girls to simply have a go!

Girls with autism often struggle at school in unstructured social playtime. Girls with autism want to have friends but lack the 'innate' knowledge and skills to make and keep them (Attwood 2007). Girls with autism are often excluded from play and the social play that happens at school, meaning they then miss out on the needed skills to help shape their identity (Moyse et al. 2015).

I was listening recently to a mum speak about the 'group' her daughter attends. The small group of autistic girls meet together in a safe space, which is fully inclusive and where autism is celebrated. The girls, because they have found their tribe and know they are accepted as and for whom they are, naturally learn the social understanding to accompany the social skills they are learning. These are not being taught through a 'social skills' program but through affirmed friendships, shared interest and having any support needs met.

If having difficulty navigating the teenage years is hard for typical developing children how much more so is it for girls with high-functioning autism? According to Attwood (2007) girls fly under the radar as they learn to develop coping mechanisms. They have the ability to mask their social inadequacies through copying or mimicking those around them. They also learn and adhere to the social rules, learning acceptable behaviours for certain situations. This works for a lot of girls, but affects the mental health of many other girls with an increase in anxiety due to the fear of rejection.

> Girls on the autism spectrum are more likely to come to the attention of health professionals due to difficulties with anxiety, depression, eating disorders, behavioural problems and/or social skills challenges. The presenting problem then becomes the 'diagnosis', with the larger picture and explanation for feeling 'different' being missed.
>
> (Marshall 2014: 37)

According to Yaull-Smith, girls with autism have a desire to please and fit in which makes them:

> hypersensitive to the environment, vulnerable and easily manipulated, so they are conditioned to conform to the social norm but, as a result risk losing a sense of identify – not least because social etiquette and mores change and develop over time and because a large part of conformity for girls in particular, is to please others.
>
> (Yaull-Smith 2007: 23)

As a result of being a girl on the spectrum and also having to contend with the societal pressures placed upon girls throughout the teenage years, their physical, mental and emotional health suffers. This road is often fraught with difficulty, misunderstanding and anxiety for the girl involved. It is important that as parents of girls on the spectrum we provide space, a place of safety within the home for the young person to feel they can truly be themselves and to always show respect and love towards them.

## Girls become women

Girls become women and the expectations on women only grow bigger. Women are expected to marry, have a family, run a household and often some form of employment too. The DSM-5, for the first time, includes sensory issues in the criteria denoting autism. Women must face many challenging changes to their bodies, including menstruation, growing through puberty into the curves and shapely form of womanhood. The expectation is that 'She will cope. It's natural, it has happened to all women since time began,' and so on. But, if you cannot cope with these changes, with their different smells, feelings and expectations, you may decide they will not happen to you. You may decide not to grow up, to act like a child, not to eat and employ any other behaviour you believe will keep you from such a fate.

Then there is the issue of sexuality and keeping safe. For some females this is a major issue. Some have little understanding of sexual etiquette, even if they have a normal IQ. The literal, black and white thinking processes in autism might mean if someone says, 'Can you have sex with me?' the person may reply 'Yes' because they perceive the question to mean 'Is it possible for you to have sex with me?'. This literal thinking fails to negotiate the bigger picture.

---

### Myths and truths to consider for some girls when wondering about the autism spectrum

1   She is too social to be autistic. She has friends or wants to have friends so she cannot be autistic. **MYTH**
2   She looks at me when I speak to her, so she cannot be autistic. **MYTH**
3   Girls follow the rules – they are less likely to act out due to a need to please others. **TRUE**
4   Girls will mimic others so they blend in – and their true difficulties are often overlooked because of this. **TRUE**
5   Girls may find communicating their feelings unavailable to them and may become mute within the classroom, despite talking at home. **TRUE**
6   Some girls may not want to be the centre of attention or have the spotlight on them. **TRUE**. Others LOVE the spotlight! **Also TRUE**
7   Girls may have a love of technology, horses, animals, reading and/or friends. **TRUE**
8   Girls may live their lives through others and find personal autonomy elusive. **TRUE**
9   Some girls live with severe anxiety. **TRUE**
10  Many girls have performance issues and will not settle for less than perfect. **TRUE**
11  Girls may be unable to stop certain behaviours – having to twirl or spin, pick at their fingers, scrunch up their toes or face, have a need to twitch. **TRUE**
12  Girls need to tune into their cues and follow them strictly to know what comes next. **TRUE**

13   Girls find it difficult to process lots of information at once. They need to do one thing at a time. **TRUE**

14   Girls need consistency, structure and continuity. **TRUE**

15   Girls exhibit rigid behaviour's and resist change. **TRUE**. Also **TRUE** though, some girls do not have an issue with change.

16   Routine is very important to girls and if it changes they need to have this visually presented or written down. **TRUE**

17   Girls find body language and facial expressions difficult to read. **TRUE**

18   Girls often have an inability to understand jokes or make jokes that others do not understand. **TRUE**

19   Girls need to have others explain in many different ways what is happening and how things work. It is important to try many different ways to answer the questions or explain, but when all else fails a good YouTube video or asking Google works a treat! **TRUE**

20   LOTS and LOTS of questions about life are often repeated and answers fail to make sense. **TRUE**

21   Girls show an inability to move on and let negatives go; they fixate on stuff and do not know how to process this or let it go. **TRUE**

22   In school, girls are often missed as they appear to be conforming. The teachers and professionals do not see the issues that are going on at home – the lack of sleep, the outbursts, the lack of understanding. Professionals have to listen to the parents, and parents have to take notes and document what is happening. **TRUE**

(Lawson and Reid 2017)

Utilizing interests and strengths is the best way forward in autism. Finding ways to explore the hidden curriculum of any social society is made so much easier and available when individuals can access it via their interests. When individuals on the spectrum are not interested, motivation is switched off. Working together within individual interests is the remedy for this.

Professionals cannot afford to stay ignorant any longer. We have no excuses for not acting on our given knowledge. At least 50% of the population is female, and there must be a response from us to this very urgent call to action.

This book has provided its readers with all the necessary information to notice, explore and support autistic females in the various ways they need. Do not let them down!

## Helpful websites

https://taniaannmarshall.wordpress.com/2013/03/26/moving-towards-a-female-profile-the-uni
    que-characteristics-abilities-and-talents-of-asperwomen-adult-women-with-asperger-syndrome/
www.amazon.com/Am-Aspiengirl-Characteristics-Females-Spectrum/dp/0992360900
www.scientificamerican.com/article/autism-it-s-different-in-girls/
https://iancommunity.org/ssc/girls-autism-hiding-plain-sight
www.youtube.com/watch?v=oZhZ0k1lyF8
www.youtube.com/watch?v=i4zMeIZfU-s
www.youtube.com/watch?v=IvhiW7ilTDk

# References and further reading

American Psychiatric Association (2000) *Diagnostic and Statistical Manual of Mental Disorders* (4th edn). Washington, DC: American Psychiatric Association.

American Psychiatric Association (2013) *Diagnostic and Statistical Manual of Mental Disorders (5th edn).* Washington, DC: American Psychiatric Association.

Asperger, H. (1944) 'Autistic psychopathy in childhood'. In U. Frith (ed.), *Autism and Asperger Syndrome* (pp. 37–92). Cambridge: Cambridge University Press.

Attwood, T. (2007) *The Complete Guide to Asperger's Syndrome.* London: Jessica Kingsley Publishers.

Carter, A. S., Black, D. O., Tewani, S., Connolly, C. E., Kadlec, M. B. and Tager-Flusberg, H. (2007) 'Sex differences in toddlers with autism spectrum disorders'. *Journal of Autism and Developmental Disorders, 37(1),* 86–97.

Constantino, J. N. and Charman, T. (2012) 'Gender bias, female resilience, and the sex ratio in autism'. *Journal of the American Academy of Child and Adolescent Psychiatry, 51(8),* 756–758.

Cornish, M. T. C. and Rinehart, N. (2014) 'Does gender matter? a one year follow-up of autistic, attention and anxiety symptoms in high-functioning children with autism spectrum disorder'. *Journal of Autism and Developmental Disorders, 44(5),* 1077–1086.

Cridland, E. K., Jones, S. C., Caputi, P. and Magee, C. (2014) 'Being a girl in a boys' world: investigating the experiences of girls with autism spectrum disorders during adolescence'. *Journal of Autism and Developmental Disorders, 44(6),* 1261–1274.

Dean, M. C., Kasari, W., Shih, F., Frankel, R., Whitney, R., Landa, C. *et al.* (2014) 'The peer relationships of girls with ASD at school: comparison to boys and girls with and without ASD'. *Journal of Child Psychiatry and Psychology, 55(11),* 1218–1225.

Dworzynski, K. I., Ronald, A., Bolton, P. and Happé, F. (2012) 'How different are girls and boys above and below the diagnostic threshold for autism spectrum disorders?' *J Am Acad Child Adolesc Psychiatry, 51(8),* 788–797.

Goodall, E. (undated) 'Interoception as a building block for wellbeing: both physical and mental health require self-connectedness'. Retrieved from www.academia.edu/30595958/Interoception_as_a_building_block_for_wellbeing_both_physical_and_mental_health_require_self-connectedness (accessed 14 September 2018).

Halladay, A. K., Bishop, S., Constantino, J. N., Daniels, A. M., Koenig, K., Palmer, K., Messinger, D., Pelphrey, K., Sanders, S.J.' Singer, T. A., Lounds Taylor, J. and Szatmari, P. (2015) 'Sex and gender differences in autism spectrum disorder: summarizing evidence gaps and identifying emerging areas of priority'. *Mol Autism, 6,* 36.

Harrop, C., Shire, S., Gulsrud, A., Chang, Y. C., Ishijima, E., Lawton, K. and Kasari, C. (2015) 'Does gender influence core deficits in ASD? An investigation into social-communication and play of girls and boys with ASD'. *Journal of Developmental Disorders, 45(3):* 766–777

Head, A. M., McGillivray, J. M. and Stokes, M. A. (2014) 'Gender differences in emotionality and sociability in children with autism spectrum disorders'. *Mol Autism, 5,* 19.

Kanner, L. (1943). 'Autistic disturbances of affective contact'. *Nervous Child, 2,* 217–250.

Lai, M.-C., Lombardo, M. V., Pasco, G., Ruigrok, A. N. V., Wheelwright, S. J. *et al.* (2011) 'A behavioral comparison of male and female adults with high functioning autism spectrum conditions'. *PLoS ONE, 6(6):*e20835 (doi:10.1371/journal.pone.0020835).

Lai, M.-C., Lombardo, M. V., Suckling, J., Ruigrok, A. N. V., Chakrabarti, B., Ecker, C., Deoni, S. C. L., Craig, M. C., Murphy, D. G. M., Bullmore, E. T. and Baron-Cohen, S. (2013) 'Biological sex affects the neurobiology of autism'. *Brain, 136,* 2799–2815 (doi: 10.1093/brain/awt216).

Lawson, W. (1988) *Understanding and Working with the Spectrum of Autism.* London: Jessica Kingsley Publishers.

Lawson, W. (2011) *The Passionate Mind: How Individuals with Autism Learn.* London: Jessica Kingsley Publishers.

Lawson W. (2013) 'Autism spectrum conditions: the pathophysiological basis for inattention and the new Diagnostic and Statistical Manual of Mental Disorders'. *OA Autism, 1(1)*, 1–5.

Lawson, W. and Reid, K. (2017) 'A summary of some issues for girls on the autism spectrum'. *Autism Network (Delhi), 12(1)*, 5–6.

Mahler, K. (2016) *Practical Solutions for Improving Self-Regulation, Self-Awareness and Social Understanding of Individuals with Autism Spectrum and Related Disorders.* Shawnee, KS: AAPC Publishing.

Marshall, T. A. (2014) *I Am Aspiengirl: The Unique Characteristics, Traits and Gifts of Girls on the Autism Spectrum.* Peregian Beach, Queensland: Aspiengirl.

McPartland, J. C. and Volkmar, F. R. (2013) 'Asperger syndrome and its relationships to autism'. In J. D. Buxbaum and P. R. Hof (eds), The Neuroscience of Autism Spectrum Disorders (pp. 55–68). Oxford: Elsevier Press.

Moyse, R. and Porter, J. (2015) 'The experience of the hidden curriculum for autistic girls at mainstream primary schools'. *European Journal of Special Needs Education, 30(2)*, 187–201.

Myles, B. S. (2005) 'The cycle of tantrums, rage, and meltdowns in children and youth with Asperger syndrome, high-functioning autism, and related disabilities'. Retrieved from www.isec2005.org.uk/isec/abstracts/papers_m/myles_b.shtml.

Nichols, S., Moravcik, G. M. and Tetenbaum, S. P. (2009) *Girls Growing Up on the Autism Spectrum: What Parents and Professionals Should Know about the Pre-teen and Teenage Years.* London: Jessica Kingsley Publishers.

Schauder, K. B., Mash, L. E., Bryant, L. K. and Cascio, C. J. (2015) 'Interoceptiveability and body awareness in autism spectrum disorder'. *Journal of Experimental Child Psychology, 131*, 193–200.

Van Wijngaarden-Cremers, P. J., van Eeten, E., Groen, W. B., Van Deurzen, P. A., Oosterling, I. J. and Van der Gaag, R. J. (2014) 'Gender and age differences in the core triad of impairments in autism spectrum disorders: a systematic review and meta-analysis'. *Journal of Developmental Disorders, 44(3)*, 627–635.

Wing, L. (1981) 'Sex ratios in early childhood autism and related conditions'. *Psychiatry Res, 5(2)*, 129–137.

Wing, L., Gould, J. and Gillberg, C. (2011) 'Autism spectrum disorders in the DSM-V: *Better or worse than the DSM-IV?'* Research in Developmental Disabilities, 32, 768–773.

Yaull-Smith, D. (2007) 'Girls on the spectrum'. *Communication* (National Autistic Society UK), Spring, 20–31.

Zücker Björne, P. (2007) *A Possible World: Autism from Practice to Theory.* Thesis. Lund: Lund University Cognitive Science.

# Index